Sea Kayaking
Virginia

Sea Kayaking Virginia

A Paddler's Guide to Day Trips from Georgetown to Chincoteague

Andrea J. Nolan

THE COUNTRYMAN PRESS
WOODSTOCK, VERMONT

Library of Congress Cataloging-in-Publication Data

Nolan, Andrea J.
    Sea kayaking Virginia : a paddler's guide to day trips from
  Georgetown to Chincoteague/Andrea J. Nolan.— 1st ed.
      p. cm.
  Includes bibliographical references and index.
  ISBN 0-88150-628-1
    1. Sea kayaking—Virginia—Guidebooks. 2. Virginia—Guidebooks.
  I. Title.

GV776.V8N65   2005
  796.122'4'09755—dc22

                                     2004063473

Book design and composition by Faith Hague Book Design
Maps by Paul Woodward, © The Countryman Press
Cover photo © Paul A. Sonders/Corbis
Interior photography by the author unless otherwise specified

Published by The Countryman Press, P.O. Box 748, Woodstock, VT 05091
www.countrymanpress.com

Distributed by W. W. Norton & Company, Inc., 500 Fifth Ave., New York, NY 10110

Printed in the United States of America

10 9 8 7 6 5 4 3 2

To my mom
For her encouragement of my dreams

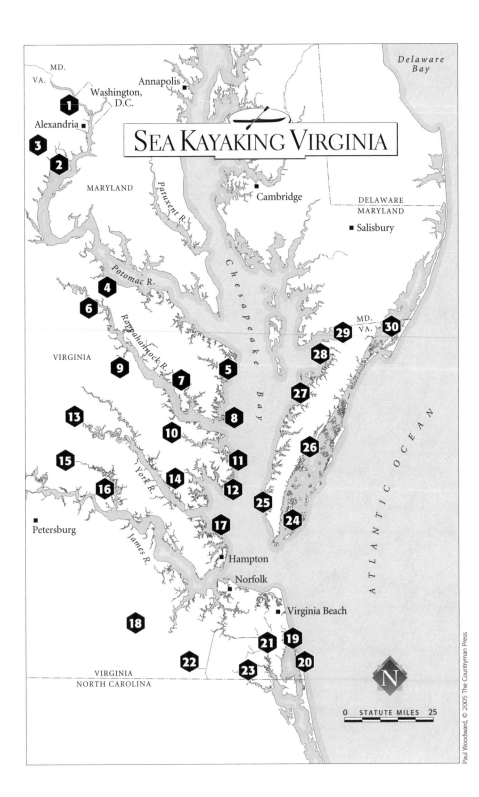

Contents

Acknowledgments

MANY PEOPLE were instrumental in helping me write this book. Thanks to the various Virginia guide companies that contributed their knowledge and insight about their home waters, particularly Judy Lathrop of Atlantic Kayak, Randy Gore of Tidewater Expeditions, Lillie Gilbert of Wild River Outfitters, and Dave Burden of Southeast Kayaks. Also, thanks to the Chesapeake Bay Foundation, the Virginia Department of Conservation, and the Nature Conservancy. Keep on doing everything that you are doing. Thanks to the guys at Springriver, my home kayak store, for all the support through the years. Thanks to Kermit Hummel, Jennifer Thompson, Clare Innes, Nicole Blouin, and everyone at Countryman Press for all your assistance throughout the writing process. Thank you Jan, Jim, Cindy, Scott, and Christine for housing me; thank you Lee, Kate, Priscilla, Darla, Mary, Andrew, and all my friends for the paddling companionship and mental support; and thank you Nolan for being my inspiration and making me laugh. A special thanks to Sarah, Brad, and Jodie, who supported me in every way possible, and read and edited countless pages with only my gratitude as their reward. Thank you, thank you, thank you.

Introduction

VIRGINIA IS A STATE of intimate natural diversity. The coastal plain flows east from the fall line, and hundreds of rivers, creeks, and bays sprawl over the rolling flatland. From the freshwater marshes of the upper tidal Potomac and Rappahannock, to the Chesapeake saltwater marshes of Mathews County, to the dark cypress swamps of southeastern Virginia, to the salty coastal bays of the barrier islands, all of these environments are united in one state—Virginia.

These trips, this book, represent one year of paddling. I kayaked Virginia from winter to autumn and saw the state in all its shades of beauty. I was repeatedly amazed by its diversity and within a weeklong trip would paddle in coastal Atlantic bays, in cypress swamps, on the salty Chesapeake, and along miles of freshwater marshes, without traveling more than 60 miles. I fell in love while writing this book. I fell in love with Virginia's slow rivers, its thick accents, its hardworking people, its friendly fishermen, its fragrant forests, its dense marshes, its clear blue bay waters, and its ancient swamps. I left each waterway with reluctance, never believing that I would find anything that would match it in beauty. But then, after I departed the delicate beauty of a freshwater marsh, I would be stunned by the majestic strangeness of a cypress wilderness, and my perspectives and notions about what is beautiful were transformed.

These 30 trips represent hundreds of waterways. Some I selected for their wilderness; and others, like Georgetown, for their civilization. Some are small, winding waterways engulfed in marsh, while others are open bay paddles along miles of beach. The rivers of the Old Dominion are steeped in human history, whether it is the twelve-thousand-year-old civilization that still lives along the banks of the Pamunkey, or the

Sea kayakers will find miles of wild Chesapeake and Atlantic beaches

more recent Colonial history that is memorialized on Popes Creek, at the birthplace of President George Washington. Some places, like Lake Drummond, I selected for their uniqueness; while others, like Urbanna, because they represent dozens of similar waterways. These 30 trips are a sampling. They present beautiful places and demonstrate a way to see them. My aim is to present a departure point for exploration, not only of these creeks and bays, but of all of Virginia.

The book is arranged by geography, with descriptions beginning in the north and roughly moving southward along the western shore of the Chesapeake. The descriptions then move across the Bay and up the Eastern Shore of Virginia. All of the trips in this book are either there-and-back journeys or circumnavigations, which allows paddlers the flexibility to travel in one car or to travel alone. There-and-back paddling allows you to see the world twice and enables you to peer more deeply into the trees and into the grass. Kayakers need not travel far or be in a terrible hurry. Sailboats are for traveling widely; powerboats are for moving fast; kayaks are for traveling deeply.

Each trip follows the same format. It begins with a brief listing of trip features and length, which will allow you to thumb through the book to find an island circumnavigation or a paddle with primitive camping. The trip description that follows provides both specific information about the boat landing, beach, bathrooms, fees, and hours, and a broader introduction to the launch site, which can include some notes about accommodations and outfitters. (Refer also to appendix B for this type of information.) Driving directions are given from the nearest major roadway, and a map of the waterway is included with every description. You should supplement the driving directions with a current state map because roads can be rerouted and place names can change. Also, supplement the book's maps of the waterways with your own navigational charts and topographic maps.

The route descriptions are meant not as the definitive guide to these waterways but rather as an introduction. As a professional kayak guide, my primary job, beyond instructing and keeping my clients safe, is to present a way to see the world, and I bring that ethic into the trip narratives. Information about the natural and social history of these waterways is interwoven with more practical advice like where to find a good beach to stop for lunch. Tips on how to spot a bald eagle are combined with advice about where to find the channel in a shallow, deep-mud tidal river.

There are countless ways to kayak the same trip. Many kayakers paddle to see wildlife and will gladly spend an hour paddling 1 mile, pausing often to watch and study the world around them. For others, kayaking is primarily a sport, and while nature is a benefit, it is secondary to exercise and athleticism. I have taught and guided both types of people, and while these routes are mostly skewed toward nature watching, you can adapt the trips in this book to serve any purpose— from marathon paddling to fishing expeditions. Paddle longer or shorter routes, explore side passages, and venture off the map and out of the scope of the descriptions. Make these trips your own.

Following that spirit of exploration, there is a section about alternative trips at the end of every trip description. These list the locations and routes in the same general area. As every description includes at least one and at most five alternative trips, there are over a hundred trip ideas in this book. Additionally, while natural history information is interwoven through all the descriptions, certain subjects like osprey or horseshoe crabs deserved their own section and are interspersed throughout the text in sidebars.

All of the routes are day trips and will take most paddlers between four to eight hours to paddle. Some are a little shorter, some a little longer, and they all can be adapted into a multi-day paddling vacation. Almost every trip is within a 30-minute drive of another trip, and there is information about camping and hotels in appendix B. Some rivers and bays even have primitive camping along the route.

I worked for the Chesapeake Bay Foundation, and every summer we would run special trips for schoolteachers, following one river for a week, starting near its headwaters and ending on a Bay island, providing a vivid and real look at the concept of a watershed. It is easy to do a similar type of trip using this book. Pick a river, like the Potomac, and follow it downriver. Begin in Georgetown, then paddle Popes Creek, then Reedville, and camp in Westmoreland or stay in a bed & breakfast in Reedville. Then, board a ferry and head over to Tangier for a few days of kayaking in a uniquely Chesapeake waterman community. This is a rich and wonderful way to see and understand an area.

During the Georgetown trip, on Roosevelt Island, you will find a marble slab engraved with President Theodore Roosevelt's thoughts about nature. The second quote on the plaque reads, "There are no words that can tell the hidden spirit of the wilderness that can match its mystery, its melancholy, and its charm." This is my love letter to Virginia, and I cannot hope to match its beauty with my words. But hopefully I can inspire you to find its beauty for yourself—to paddle deeply and widely all across this diverse, watery state.

General Geography of Virginia

The coastal plain is the domain of the sea kayaker. This is the relatively flat land that lies east of the fall line. The fall line is a dramatic land change, marked by waterfalls and rapids, and the area to the west is the piedmont, which is characterized by rolling hills, nontidal water, and rapid currents. The fall line is roughly marked by I-95, and all of the trips in this book fall to the east of the interstate, with the exception of Fountainhead. All of the Eastern Shore of Virginia is within the coastal plain, and like much of the plain, it has been repeatedly been submerged throughout the geologic history of North America.

The region's dominating landmark is the Chesapeake Bay, which has 12,000 miles of total tidal shoreline, including its rivers and creeks. Twenty-one of the day trips in this book are along these shores. The 64,000-square-mile watershed begins with the headwaters of the Susquehanna, outside Cooperstown, New York, and drains six states: New York, Pennsylvania, West Virginia, Virginia, Delaware, and Maryland. The Bay is between five-thousand to fifteen-thousand years old and was formed when the ice melted from the last ice age and the ocean rose, drowning the Susquehanna River Valley. The Susquehanna flows 444 miles from New York to Havre de Grace, Maryland, where it widens and transforms into the Chesapeake Bay. From there, the Bay flows for about 190 miles to the Atlantic Ocean, through Maryland and ending in Virginia. As an estuary, the Bay is a mixture of salt and fresh water, with the salt levels increasing the closer you get to the Atlantic Ocean. Thus, for a long river like the Rappahannock, you will paddle in fresh water by Wilmot Wharf, along brackish marshes at Belle Isle, and see salt marshes at Fleets Island.

The six trips below the James River, in southeastern Virginia, drain into the Albemarle Sound, in North Carolina. The sound does not reach the Atlantic Ocean until the Oregon Inlet, thus all of these waterways are fresh and nontidal, including the vast coastal waters of Back Bay, which are only separated from the Atlantic by 100 yards of dune. Most of these rivers and bays do not have any current of their own, and while their general flow is southward, their currents and tides are determined by the wind. The Blackwater River is the exception, but its southward flowing current generally is not too strong. This is the beginning of the Deep South. Open marshlands are replaced by warm-water cypress swamps that are filled with water stained amber black by the tannic acid released by decaying cypress trees. Animals such as black bear, fox, bobcats, cottonmouths, and white-tailed deer all thrive in this dark wilderness.

There are three coastal bay trips, in the salty waters that lay behind the barrier islands of Virginia. The 18 islands in this archipelago are like giant sandbars and were established by a variety of forces. Coastal rivers, such as the Machipongo, deposit their sediment as they flow toward the Atlantic, helping to create the interior islands; while the exterior islands are constantly losing and gaining sand as their sediments roll southward with the natural current of the coast. With this dynamic land shifting, the islands absorb hurricanes, waves, and winds, thus protecting the mainland of the Eastern Shore Peninsula. The entire peninsula is a major part of the eastern migratory flyway, and while it is filled with birds year-round, it is particularly populated during the spring and autumn migrations.

Seasons

The waterways described in this book change weekly, evolving with the rolling of the seasons, so the clear-water, springtime Piscataway in no way resembles the warm-water, grass-filled creek that flows between lush green shores during the summer. Until you have paddled a creek every week for a year, you will not even begin to see the full shape of water. Just as every season has its own allure, each also has its opposing detriments.

Summer

This is the most popular season for boating, for everyone from kayakers to sailors to powerboaters. The temperature is in the mid-80s, and the water is warm. The world is green and in bloom with colorful flowers. You can swim and soak up the sun on remote, wild beaches, and you can paddle well into the night during the long days of the summer. Blue crabs are plentiful, and osprey, terns, and pelicans feast on the abundant fish.

Just as birds and animals abound, bugs are also plentiful in the summertime. Most biting insects lay low in the heat of the day, so you are generally safe while out on the water. However, bugs can wreak havoc on a riverside picnic, particularly in coastal salt marshes or in shaded and wind-sheltered areas. The insects are even worse after the sun sets, so this is not the optimum season for marsh-side camping trips. It is possible to get serious illnesses from insects, such as the West Nile virus from mosquitoes and Lyme disease from ticks, so use insect repellent and wear long sleeves and a hat.

Heat is both the major allure and danger of summer in Virginia. The average temperature between June and August is in the mid-80s, but all of these months can have sustained stretches of 90- and 100-degree weather, combined with T-shirt–wringing high humidity. The hot days are a great time to paddle the wooded, freshwater locations found on the smaller tidal tributaries like Morris Creek and the Blackwater River. Dehydration is common, and if you feel thirsty, then you are already dehydrated. Headaches are a common side effect, as your body is put under intense strain by lack of fluids. If you do not take care of yourself, you can end up with heat exhaustion (the result of severe dehydration) or even heat stroke, (a dangerous elevation of your body's core temperature). The hotter it gets, the slower you should paddle. Drink a lot of water, get wet often, and wear a hat that you can keep soaked with water. If you start to get a headache or feel queasy or weak, stop paddling and get cool and hydrated. Dunk yourself in the water, seek shade, and drink water. Also, wear sunblock. Not only is sunburn uncomfortable and can cause skin cancer, it also increases dehydration.

During the summer's hot weather and diminished rain, the Chesapeake's stinging jellyfish and sea nettle dominate the calm salty waters of the Bay and lower reaches of the tidal rivers. Most saltwater areas develop nettles by late June, making it difficult to cool off without being stung. The sea nettle sting is not dangerous for most people; however you will develop a red stinging rash that lasts for about 30 minutes. Some relief can be found by scraping the affected area clear of the microscopic stinging nematocysts that are suspended in the slime and by rinsing the wound with vinegar (or urine).

Autumn

Early autumn is the most forgiving of Virginia's seasons. The insects begin to die, the jellyfish disappear, and the air cools to a pleasant 70 degrees for September and October, and remains in the low 60s for much of November. This is one of Virginia's driest seasons, and the water remains reasonably warm until late October. While hordes of tourists clog the Blue Ridge Parkway in search of fall foliage, you can enjoy a solitary paddle down rivers rich in autumn color, like Popes Creek, Fountainhead, and the Rappahannock. The autumn also transforms the saltwater marshes into golden seas of grass. The waters and sky fill with migrating waterfowl, which presents a real problem for kayakers because many of the trips described in this book pass by hunting areas, and it is vital to respect hunters' rights. Never paddle near hunting grounds around sunrise and sunset and avoid popular hunting areas, like Saxis, during duck season. In autumn, the still, summer air is replaced by the winds of changing seasons, so while the autumn is great sailing weather, it can be a challenging season for open-water paddling, and the air temperature can change dramatically from day to day.

Winter

In the winter, you have the water to yourself. Generally the only other people on the open Bay are commercial watermen; and on the smaller tidal tributaries, you will often never see another human. Virginia's creeks and rivers can occasionally coat over with ice, but the area's temperate climate usually keeps the waterways clear and navigable. Winter waterfowl like sea ducks and loons fill the back bays, and not a single insect remains to bite you as you explore the marshes. All underwater grasses also die, allowing free navigation in small guts, canals, and creeks that were impassable during the summer.

The average daily air temperature from December through March ranges from the mid-40s to mid-50s; the water cools to a similar temperature. The very real danger of winter paddling is hypothermia, which is when your core body temperature falls below 95 degrees (mild) or 90 degrees (severe). Most kayaking fatalities are from immersion hypothermia, which can occur when someone capsizes in cold water. Without proper clothing, submersion in 40-degree water can lead to loss of the ability to function within 8 minutes, and severe hypothermia and unconsciousness in 30 minutes. You can lose . Severe hypothermia can be fatal, which is why victims require immediate advanced medical attention.

Boat graveyards are a common sight near watermen villages

In order to prevent hypothermia, you need to wear a wetsuit or drysuit when the water is below 60 degrees. Wetsuits insulate you by trapping a warm layer of water against your skin. Drysuits are more expensive but keep you entirely dry, and thus can keep you warmer longer. They are non-insulating, so you need to wear layers of synthetic long underwear and clothing underneath the drysuit. Test your clothes before you paddle. Perform several rescues in a row with friends and gauge your comfort level to see if you are adequately dressed. You need to increase your protection if you are shivering or experiencing any diminished capacity after this exercise. No matter how excellent you are as a kayaker, the stakes are raised when the water and air are both below 40 degrees, where there is very little margin for error. All winter paddling must be done with a paddling partner.

Spring

This is a time of rapid change and beauty. Trees begin to bud and spring peepers fill the night air with their songs. Flowers bloom and the honking of northward migrating geese once again fills the air. It is mating season; osprey and eagles are nesting, and horseshoe crabs by the thousands fill May beaches with their annual spawn. Terns, pelicans, and shorebirds are also breeding, laying their eggs on the upper sections of beaches. This is a time when the prime real estate should be reserved for the birds, and kayakers need to stay well away from any nesting areas. The bugs are largely still dormant through March and April, making it one of the best times for paddling salt marshes like Chincoteague.

While spring is uniquely beautiful, it can also be the most dangerous time for kayakers, as they are lured onto the water by the warm air. However, while the air temperatures of April are often in the mid-70s, the water takes much longer to warm up and will still be hovering in the mid-50s. You must dress for the water temperature and always err on the side of overdressing, because if you begin to overheat, you can always cool off in the cold water that surrounds you.

Spring can be a windy and rainy season, so be sure to monitor the forecasts carefully. Hypothermia can also come from the constant exposure to low temperatures and damp weather. A steady drizzle during a 50-degree day can easily cause the ill-prepared paddler to progress from the shivering and irritable lethargy of mild hypothermia to severe hypothermia. This is a danger from spring to autumn. Mild hypothermia often exhibits as the *umbles,* which is when the hypothermic person fumbles, mumbles, tumbles, grumbles, and stumbles. Hypothermic people also display a loss of judgment and personality change, often becoming either quiet and withdrawn or aggressive and irritable. Mild hypothermia can be treated by getting into dry, warm clothes, getting out of the cold/wet elements, and eating sugary, warm food—fuel for your body's energy fires. If the condition is not treated, it can progress to severe hypothermia.

Weather

While the weather forecasts provided on the morning news are entertaining, we kayakers need a bit more information when preparing to head out onto the open Chesapeake. Cable television's all-weather stations give better information, as do the various Internet weather resources, some of which are included in appendix C. However, the best information for the boater comes from the marine weather radio. These radios tune into exclusive all-weather frequencies, and they provide up-to-date weather reports, including wind predictions and small-craft advisories, giving specific forecasts for each area of water. The radios are available at most electronics and boating stores.

Many weather radios are portable, so you can take them with you and check on the weather while you are out on the water. However, you should also become familiar with reading the weather yourself, using clouds, winds, and air temperature fluctuations as your guide. Developing a *weather eye* is particularly important for summer paddling because almost every afternoon, somewhere in Virginia, there is an intense, brief squall with high winds, lightning, and downpours of rain and even hail. Buy a weather book and teach yourself some cloud reading. Be alert if the wind increases, or dramatically shifts direction, or if the air temperature radically changes or seems to be more oppressive with humidity than usual.

Try to reach land if you notice a squall approaching—unmistakable bands of dark clouds that tower high in the sky. On the open Bay you can see a squall while it is 30 minutes to an hour away, depending on its speed. However, if you are in a densely forested swamp, your first clue of an approaching storm might be thunder. Count the time between a flash of lightning and the boom of thunder; it takes 5 seconds for the sound of thunder to travel 1 mile, so if you count 30 seconds between the flash and boom, the storm is 6 miles away. You should be off the water by the time the lightning is 3 miles away, and once you are on land, look for shelter within a grove of trees. However, if you are in an open marsh, do not stand under the one lone group of trees; instead, sit on your life preserver on the marsh grass. Sitting makes you small and non-attractive to lightning, and your life jacket helps buffer you from any ground currents of electricity. People have been struck in groups as they gather together for safety, so do the opposite and stagger your group away from one another so that if the worst happens, only one person is hit. Once you are situated, put on your rain gear and enjoy the show. Most squalls do not last for more than 45 minutes, and usually are even shorter.

Wind

Wind is a major factor while planning any trip. The difference between 15 and 25 knots of wind is significant and can turn a fun paddle into a day spent at camp reading a good book. Wind is the product of air moving from a high- to a low-pressure area. This often occurs as high-pressure and low-pressure fronts collide, which can be predicted on a morning weather forecast. Wind is also locally generated; as the land warms, hot air rises from it, thus lowering the air pressure near the ground. Air pours in to fill the void, and wind results. Locally generated winds generally end with sunset, while winds associated with weather fronts can last all day and night. A strong sustained wind can completely overpower a weak tidal current, making a high tide rise to several feet above normal or creating a low tide so low that there is no water left in a creek. The currents of southeastern Virginia's rivers, creeks, lakes, and bays are determined solely by the wind, and so an accurate wind prediction is very useful in deciding your paddling direction and knowing whether there will be any water left in shallow areas like Back Bay.

Plan your paddle based on the predicted wind, and try to arrange to have the wind at your back at the end of your paddle. A straight line is not always the most efficient way to travel between two points, and when it is windy you may want to avoid paddling across coves. Instead, duck into the lee of the wind alongside the shore. During extremely windy conditions, you might want to rethink your destination entirely. Most trip locations in this book generally have another location within a half- to 1-hour drive, and so you can easily shift your paddle from an open bay exposure like Saxis to a more protected location like Pitts Creek. Most important, work on your kayaking skills, so that paddling with wind need be only a minor challenge rather than a reason for calling off a trip.

The best predictions can be wrong and wind can be local, so you must learn how to read the wind speed and direction once you reach your paddling site. To find the direction of the wind, turn your head until you hear the wind the same in both ears—you are facing the direction the wind is coming from. A helpful guide for gauging the wind speed is the Beaufort Wind Scale (see appendix D), which provides practical ways to measure the wind speed based on the movement of the water and trees. The scale uses knots, which is nautical miles per hour, or the equivalent of 1.15 standard miles per hour.

Waves and Wakes

A side effect of wind is waves, the character of which is determined by the combination of fetch, velocity, and duration of the wind. Fetch is the distance that wind travels, so if a wind is blowing across the wide-open waters of the Chesapeake Bay toward Old Plantation Creek, its fetch is greater, thus generating larger waves, than when blowing across the headwaters of Morris Creek. The waves will be larger several hours into a windstorm than they were at the beginning. As swells reach land, they begin to stack up on themselves due to the drag created by the shallow bottom. The crest begins to move faster than the bottom, then ultimately falls, creating a breaking wave. This usually happens gradually over the gently sloping bottom of the Chesapeake Bay. However, areas that have a steep drop, like dredged channels, can result in quicker forming and more powerful waves. Breaking waves often happen away from land, on the sandy shoals and deltas that are common around river mouths or across stretches of shallow coves.

The other common type of wave is the boat wake. These wakes are predictable when there is very little boat traffic or you are on large open water. However, in more congested areas, like Mason Neck, multiple waves can slosh back and forth, bouncing off one another and off the surrounding cliffs and seawalls. This creates confused seas that last well after any one boat has passed you. The rebounding of waves from bulkheads is called clapitus, and it can be dynamic, as the rebounding wake and incoming wake create a super wave that can leap straight into the air with explosive power. For this reason, you should stay away from seawalls whenever there is a lot of boat traffic. You also need to develop your paddling skills so that you are comfortable in both types of waves, and paddle a boat that is appropriate for the conditions—a flat-bottomed recreational kayak is simply disastrous in 2-foot waves.

Tides

While the trips in southeastern Virginia and on the two reservoirs are nontidal, the remainder of the Chesapeake and coastal bay trips are governed by the gravitational pull of the moon. The tides are generally gentle, with a tidal range from 1 to 3 feet. This range increases during the new and full moon (when the sun and moon are in line) and are called spring tides. Conversely, neap tides are the weak tides that occur during the midway point of the moon's cycle, when the sun and moon are at right angles. Most rivers on the Bay have four tides a day, two highs and two lows, each flow lasting 6 hours and then separated by a ½-hour-long slack tide.

Most of our tidal currents are weak, and you need not arrange your trip around their flow. The exception to this rule is the Pamunkey River (and the Mattaponi River, which is mentioned as an alternative trip). The particular tides of these rivers are discussed in the Pamunkey River (trip #13) description. You can use various weather internet sites to find out the projected tides, and most marinas carry local tide charts. Tidal currents also increase when water is compressed from a wide to narrow passageway, such as under a narrow bridge or from a large waterway to a small channel.

While mild, the currents can assist you in your journey, and it is nice to use the power of the water's flow for even a portion of your trip, particularly at the end of a paddle. The tide charts will tell you when you will have water to paddle in; a rise or fall of only 1 to 3 feet can make a significant difference in areas where the slope of the Bay takes ¼ mile to change 1 foot. Guts that are impassable at mid-tide are full of water at high tide, and the water can rise high enough to wash away your kayak during an hour of beachcombing.

Tools and Skills

This book is not an instruction manual, and it will not teach you how to kayak. There are many fine books and schools that can help you build your skills and buy the right gear. However, here are a few general notes about the gear and skills that are necessary for the waters of Virginia.

Kayaks

The waterways in this book vary from winding guts that are barely wider than a kayak to open rivers and bays that are 1 to 35 miles wide, and you will often paddle both types of water during the same trip. This variation requires an adaptable boat.

One popular choice is the short recreational kayak, which is similar to a canoe and very stable in flat water. These boats are inexpensive and come in either an open cockpit design or as a sit-on-top boat. Tandem sit-on-tops can be adapted for a solo paddler or as a triple kayak that can hold two adults and a child. Traditional canoes can also be included in this category, with the additional benefit of plenty of room for gear and extra passengers. All of these boats are excellent crafts for exploring the twisting waterways of small creeks and rivers like the Blackwater. They are generally easy and comfortable to paddle. The open cockpit also makes portaging over snags easier, allowing the paddler to stand up in the boat, step onto a log, pull the boat over, and then step back into the boat. However, these craft are a liability on open water whenever there is wind or waves. The wind bullies around the high-sided recreational boats, and something that is wide-bottomed and stable in flat water can be easily pitched over by strong waves. If you do capsize, while you can climb back onto a self-bailing sit-on-top boat, the open cockpit of other recreational boats can become swamped and extremely difficult to rescue or bail in open water. Additionally, even in the best of circumstances, the wider and shorter a boat is, the harder it is to move through the water, making paddling distances more work in a recreational kayak.

The opposite of a recreational kayak is the expedition kayak, which follows the same lines and designs of the original arctic kayaks. It is generally a closed-deck boat, 15 to 18 feet long and 22 to 24 inches wide, with internal walls, both forward and aft that serve as bulkheads to separate the cockpit from the bow and stern sections, thus ensuring that the boat will not sink when capsized and swamped. These dimensions make the kayak feel less stable initially—a sometimes overwhelming or frightening experience for a novice paddler. However, this very instability is actually what allows the expedition boat to handle smoothly in rough seas, as waves roll easily beneath them. It can take longer to feel comfortable in these boats, and you need to develop skills for turning and maneuvering them in the small spaces of guts and creeks. However, most people will pick up the basics of kayaking in a half-day class. Professional instruction is useful when learning rescues and strokes. Expedition kayaks are more expensive than recreational kayaks, but the expense (and extra effort) pays off with a boat that is fast, versatile, and adaptable. You can paddle your expedition kayak absolutely anywhere.

The hybrid kayak is a middle ground for those who do not like the confinement of an expedition kayak but want to be able to paddle all the trips in this book. These kayaks combine the comfortable wideness of recreational kayaks with the enclosed cockpit and narrower hull design of the expedition kayak. This is a compromise, so you will never be able to do everything in a hybrid that you could do in an expedition boat, but you can come awfully close, and the design and quality of these boats is constantly improving. There are also several great models of sit-on-top kayaks that mimic the dimensions and speed of expedition boats. These are great summer boats, but you do get wet in them, so they are less than ideal for year-round paddling. Talk with your local boat outfitter when you are buying a boat, and consider taking a couple of classes before making your kayak purchase so you get the boat that matches your needs.

Gear

The following are the top 15 items that you should never leave without for a day trip:

- *Paddle.* Spend a little extra money here because you will be holding it all day and every ounce makes a difference. Make sure the paddle is visible—buy one with white blades or add reflective tape to the blades and shaft ends.
- *Spare paddle.* You should have at least one spare paddle per group. Stow a break-down paddle under your bungees. You will

not need it often, but you will be happy to have it when somebody snaps a blade or loses a paddle—kayak long enough and this will happen, guaranteed.

- *Personal Flotation Device (PFD).* The coast guard requires that you have a whistle attached to your PFD, but they do not require you to wear the PFD. Of course, a PFD only works when you are wearing it, and no one plans to have an emergency capsize, so wear the PFD. That said, I will admit to gauging the risks of the day and paddling without my PFD while with competent friends on a hot calm day in shallow water. However, this safety judgment is the exception and not the rule, and it is always safest to wear your PFD, so buy one that is comfortable and get used to wearing it.

- *Spray skirt.* This is just for hybrid and expedition kayaks. It is not necessary to wear this during many of the trips in this book, but it will help keep you warm and dry in cool weather and is essential in rough weather. I use more breathable nylon in the summer and warmer, more water-repellent neoprene in the winter.

- *Paddle float.* This rescue device is useless if you do not learn and practice the skills for using it. You slip this inflatable bag over the end of your paddle, which will then serve as an outrigger to allow you to more easily re-enter your boat after capsizing.

- *Bilge pump.* For bailing the boat. The portable versions of this device also make excellent squirt guns.

- *Sponge.* For bailing the water that the bilge pump does not remove from the boat.

- *Water.* Have a water bottle accessible, and bring at least a half-gallon of spare water per person for a day trip.

- *Food.* Kayaking and fasting are not a good combination. Pack a lunch and snack items, bringing more than you usually eat because you will be exerting yourself.

- *Map or chart.* Keep a map/chart of the area in a clear plastic bag on your front deck, along with any paddling notes.

- *Flashlight.* I keep a waterproof light (with a flashlight and strobe) secured to my PFD so that way I never leave home without it. You never know when your paddle might run a little late, either because you spent an hour watching osprey build their nest or you got a little lost.

- *Thin, strong rope.* Bring along about 25 feet. This can be used for tying up to trees or docks and as an emergency tow rope.
- *First-aid kit.* Bring at least a minimum kit of Band-Aids and aspirin, along with duct tape, which can secure bandages and repair boats. More complete kits are available at outdoor and boating stores. Most important have the skills to handle a medical emergency in the wilderness: Take a first-aid/CPR course or, even better, a wilderness medicine course. Kayaking is much different from working out on the rowing machine at your gym—you need to be able to take care of yourself in the wilderness.
- *Flares.* These are required for any open water more than 1 mile wide. You will likely never need them, but you never plan on having an emergency. I triple-Ziploc mine and then use duct tape or bungee them into my boat, leaving them there for the season. That way I never forget to pack them.
- *Warm clothes and rain gear.* Pack these in a dry bag. I have treated people for mild exposure hypothermia as late as June and as early as September, so bring a synthetic fleece sweatshirt and a rain jacket and you will be covered. Bring more layers of clothes as the weather cools.

There are several other items that are also useful to bring along:

- *Sunblock and bug spray.* The sunblock is a summertime must. You are out in the elements, so protect yourself.
- *Hat.* For sun and bug protection in the summer and for warmth in the winter.
- *Cell phone and/or VHF marine radio.* These are nice backups to bring along, although you will often be out of range during many of these trips.
- *Tow belt.* A 25-foot cord can be used as a tow rope, but the belt is an excellent investment if you are ever a leader of a group or the best paddler among your friends.

- *Compass.* You can buy a compass to attach to your boat or use a small handheld backpacker's compass. Most routes in this book can be navigated by sight using charts and landmarks; however, a compass is useful for the more open-water trips and while exploring the many guts of the barrier islands.
- *Field guides.* It is cool to see beautiful plants and wildlife; it is even cooler to know what you are seeing.

The one thing that you need to leave behind is a copy of your paddling itinerary. This need not be a formal report but it can be as simple as telling a reliable friend where you are going and making plans to call them when you are done. Tell them what time to start worrying, and make sure they know what color your boat is and who you are kayaking with. You can take this safety routine a step further and give them the emergency contact names and telephone numbers of your paddling companions. You can also leave them with the emergency numbers for the state police or coast guard. But, regardless of how thorough your itinerary, make sure somebody knows where you are and when to expect you back home.

Skills

To put it simply, you must know how to kayak in order to use this guidebook. If you do not know how to paddle, then you should kayak with knowledgeable friends, a paddling club, or commercial guide companies until you become a competent kayaker. You need to be able to steer your boat and have a comfortable and efficient forward stroke. You need to know how to be rescued and how to rescue others in the event of capsize. You need to be comfortable in choppy seas, rolling swells, and wind, and able to perform low and high braces for any trips with open water and/or powerboat traffic.

It is always safest to paddle with two or more people because, not only are there more people to take care of a rescue or an emergency, but you are more visible to other boaters. However, paddling solo can be a wonderful experience as long as you are aware of the extra risks. You must be able to rescue yourself with a paddle float, and your strokes and bracing skills should be solid. Ideally, all solo paddlers should also be able to roll their kayaks. If you cannot roll or comfortably rescue yourself but still want to paddle solo, you should restrict your paddling to the many smaller waterways in this book where the shoreline can serve as your safety reserve. The waters of Virginia can be deceptively calm, and conditions can change in an instant with summer squalls, afternoon wind, or a passing squadron of powerboaters. Do not take a recreation boat out on an improper waterway or paddle in a location that is beyond your skill level, no matter how pretty the day starts out to be.

There are several avenues for learning how to kayak. If you already have your own kayak, you can learn from friends and supplement that instruction with a book about kayaking strokes and rescues. Or, you can join a club like the Chesapeake Paddlers Association. They have informal instructional paddles at least once a week and also run organized classes. You can seek out instruction from one of the several excellent commercial outfitters in Virginia. Their professional instructors are well trained and certified by the American Canoe Association and/or British Canoe Union, thus ensuring that your instruction will be thorough. You are responsible for your skill level, so seek out the knowledge and then practice, practice, practice.

Navigation

As is said about God, navigation is in the details. If you are crossing the open ocean, a minor detail like 1 minute of latitude over thousands of miles can mean the difference between arriving in Nova Scotia or Florida. For a kayaker, the details have more to do with which gut will lead to the other side of a marsh. For that degree of detail, you need a large-scale chart or map. Maps focus on the detail of the land, while charts focus on the detail of the water, showing water depth, channel markers, and fish traps. At a minimum, a good kayaking chart will have 1:40,000 scale. The smaller the second number, the larger the scale, so a 1:100,000-scale chart covers a much greater area (with much less detail) than a 1:40,000-scale chart. Most charts are made with large boats in mind, and thus smaller scale charts are the norm. Even if you find a large-scale nautical chart, it is not uncommon to kayak right off the map, into the headwaters of a creek that was not navigable for a sailboat but has another few miles of water left for a kayak. Nautical charts are carried at most marine stores and marinas.

Topographic maps are a good alternative to nautical charts. They come in large-scale, 1:24,000 grids, with excellent detail of the land patterns like cliffs, marshes, side creeks, and bridges. Individual grids of topographic maps can be purchased directly from the USGS (see appendix C), or at some outdoor stores. You can also use topographic map software, which will let you print out any area you want on your home printer. County road maps are also good resources. They lack the topographic detail of elevation change but can show creeks in even greater detail than a topographic map. Also, many marinas and bait shops will carry detailed maps for their local river. These maps are sometimes homemade sketches and sometimes glossy GMCO or DeLorme productions. Once you have gathered the right maps and charts for an area, you should keep them and the paddling notes on your deck where you can easily access and refer to them. A cheap Ziploc bag can work, or you can buy a thicker plastic chart cover that you can use again and again.

All of these routes can be paddled by comparing your location on the water to your chart, without any need to use dead reckoning or compasses. Useful aids to navigation include channel markers and lighthouses, and landmarks like major bends and bridges. A watch can be your best navigation tool in the tidal marshes where markers and landmarks are lacking. If you know your paddling pace, you can time yourself to know your approximate location and can use that to pinpoint where you are on the chart. Your paddling pace can vary according to wind, your companions, and whether your trip is focused on bird-watching or speed. I paddle 1 to 2 miles an hour with friends or leading a group. Solo, I rarely drop below 3 miles an hour. Test your pace by timing yourself as you paddle a well-marked distance. Do this often and you will begin to gauge your own speed intuitively.

While not generally necessary, a compass can also be a useful tool, particularly in restricted visibility situations, such as during a heavy rain/fog or at night. A compass is also useful for finding and keeping your bearings while paddling in salt-marsh labyrinths as found in the Virginia Coastal Reserve. Be sure you are comfortable with using your compass and navigation skills before you really need them. Community colleges and the coast guard auxiliary often teach excellent coastal navigation courses, and there are several good books specifically written for sea kayak navigation (see appendix C).

Rules of the Road

We are little boats in a big world. Channels into marinas and populated rivers are clearly marked, with red channel markers on the right side and green channel markers on the left side, as viewed when when traveling upstream from a larger body of water to a smaller body of water. The saying *red, right, returning* is a helpful way to remember this. Most often, these channel markers are day markers on wooden pilings that are driven deep into the river bottom. The red markers are triangular, even-numbered signs; the green signs, square and odd-numbered. The numbers increase as you head upstream. There are also floating buoys in deeper water. The round, green cylinder buoys (called cans) and the red cone-shaped buoys (called nuns) are numbered and arranged the same as the day markers. The reason kayakers need to know how channels are marked is so that we can stay out of them. They are for deep draft boats, and these vehicles depend on having a clear passage on the channels. Large boats like tugboat/barge combinations are not very maneuverable and can not stop or turn quickly. Big cargo ships can take over 1 mile to stop, and a ship captain once told me that the nickname for kayakers are *click-clicks*, because that is the sound the boat makes when they run us over. I think to say that we would make any noise at all is a gross exaggeration. When you have to cross a channel, cross at a right angle, and do as your mother taught you, and look both ways.

There is another set of rules governing the water away from channels: the rules of right-of-way, which have numerous details dealing with boats being towed, two powerboats approaching one another, etc. The rule that applies to kayakers is that powerboats must give way to boats under sail or human power, unless a channel restricts them. That means if a powerboat does not see you in deep open water and runs you over, they are in the wrong—they were supposed to give you, the little kayaker, the right-of-way. My personal rule is the one of mass tonnage, which holds that any boat that weighs more than mine has the right-of-way, and it is my job to stay out of its way.

Also, for common courtesy, here are a few more guidelines. Stay out of the way of fishermen's lines, whether they are fishing from land or from a boat. Never pull up a crab pot or disturb any sort of trap, for doing so is to meddle with someone's livelihood. When you are launching from a boat landing, do not hold up boat traffic. Drop off your boat to the side of the landing and have all of your gear arranged and stowed before you move onto the landing. Just be a good neighbor, and you will do fine.

Minimum-Impact Kayaking

Kayaking is an intrinsically minimum-impact activity. Kayakers do not consume or discharge any fuel, and we need not leave any trace that we have visited a place. Beyond making no impact on the land and water around us, we should leave the marshes and beaches better than when we found them. Carry out all of your trash, from paper bags to orange peels, and scoop up other trash that you may see. Plastic bottles will not take up much space in your hatch, and the water will be a little bit cleaner for your effort. Obey NO TRESPASSING signs, and if you need to rest alongside private property, like a farm, stay below mean high tide, which is public domain. Also, be careful when watching wildlife so as not to harass the animals by paddling too close to their homes or nests. It takes very little effort to be a low-impact paddler. Just treat the water with care, respect private and public property, and do not try to pet the wildlife.

In Closing

While I spent one year exploring Virginia for this book, I will spend a lifetime getting to know this enchanted state. It is a graceful land, with subtle beauty and grandeur. Paddle one river over and over, or explore 30 in a year. Paddle fast and paddle slow. Bounce through October waves and skate over slick, calm August water. Just kayak often.

Happy paddling!

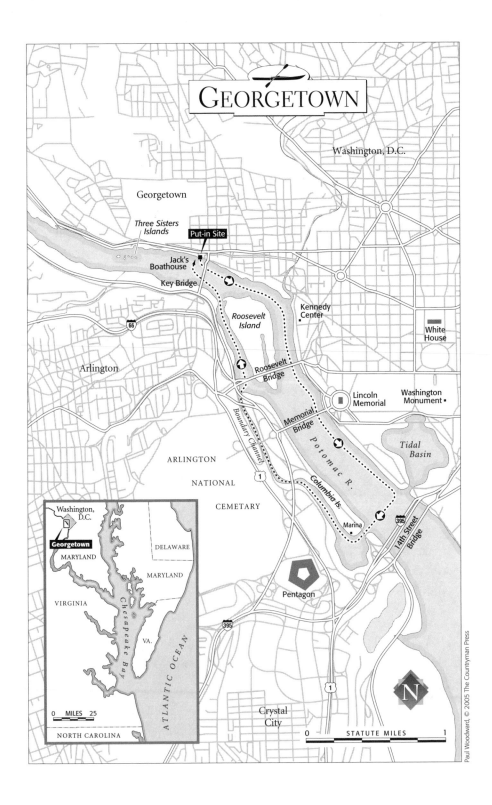

GEORGETOWN

Washington, D.C.

Georgetown

Three Sisters Islands

Put-in Site

Jack's Boathouse

Key Bridge

Roosevelt Island

Kennedy Center

White House

66

Arlington

Roosevelt Bridge

Lincoln Memorial

Washington Monument

Boundary Channel

Memorial Bridge

Potomac R.

Tidal Basin

ARLINGTON

NATIONAL

CEMETARY

1

Columbia Is.

Marina

14th Street Bridge

395

Washington, D.C.

N

Georgetown

MARYLAND

DELAWARE

MARYLAND

VIRGINIA

VA.

Chesapeake Bay

ATLANTIC OCEAN

0   MILES   25

NORTH CAROLINA

Pentagon

395

1

Crystal City

N

0   STATUTE MILES   1

Paul Woodward, © 2005 The Countryman Press

Part I — Northern Virginia/Northern Neck

1.

Georgetown

Features: D.C. monuments, cherry blossoms in the spring, George-town University, the Pentagon, and hidden city wilderness.

Length: 8 to 10 miles.

Put-in site: Jack's Boathouse, 3500 K Street Northwest, Washington, DC 20007, 202-337-9642, www.jacksboathouse.com. Jack's is the launch location and offers a large assortment of kayak and canoe rentals in the heart of Georgetown, which is nestled in the shadow of the Key Bridge. Jack Baxter established the boathouse in 1945, and Jack's son Frank now manages the shop. Both he and his little boathouse seem like they would be more likely found in a bayou town or a small mountain resort, not in the heart of D.C. But here they sit, ready to help all willing and able kayakers onto the water.

This is primarily a rental location; however, private boats are welcome to use the facility for a $5 launching fee per carload. This nominal fee is waived if even one person in your party is renting a kayak. There is a port-a-john on-site and a couple of picnic tables, and the launching is done from a long, low wooden dock.

The Chesapeake Paddlers Association uses Jack's Boathouse as their home base in D.C., kayaking from its docks every Thursday night from spring through fall. Atlantic Kayak leads trips similar to this paddle, but they leave from Alexandria. Their guides are well versed in the history of D.C. and can regale you with a much fuller version of the legend of the Three Sisters.

Directions: From Northern Virginia, take US 50 to I-66. After crossing the Theodore Roosevelt Memorial Bridge, take the E Street (I-66 East) ramp toward the Kennedy Center/Whitehurst Freeway. Merge onto the Potomac River Freeway North. Take the US 29 South exit toward the Whitehurst Freeway. Continue on US 29/K Street by going down under the Whitehurst Freeway to the left. Follow K Street to the end, and you will see the sign for Jack's Boathouse on the left. (Directions are also available at www.jacksboathouse.com.) There is limited parking in the small parking lot but plenty of metered street parking in the area.

THE POTOMAC ORIGINATES deep within the Blue Ridge Mountains as a rushing white-water river that widens and strengthens as branches and tributaries come together, culminating just north of the nation's capital in the final cascading rapids of Great Falls and Little Falls. Then, alongside the shores of D.C., the river slowly settles into the coastal plain, becoming the tidal waterway that will finally end its journey at the Chesapeake Bay. Along this transition from moving to tidal waters, nestled underneath the Key Bridge is weathered, little Jack's Boathouse. A motley assortment of worn floating docks and a sea of canoes and kayaks wait to transport the patron to a slower time and sleepier city than the modern D.C. that lies up Georgetown's steep hills. From this quiet start, the kayaker can take in a view of the nation's capital that few visitors ever see, but which affords one of the best views around of the city's most famous monuments. As paddlers float by important buildings and bridges, collegiate rowing teams sprint past in their pursuit of perfect synchronicity, and hidden worlds of wilderness are discovered within the limits of this powerful city. More so than any other in this book, this trip is absolutely unique.

Trip Description

To begin your journey, swing your bow to the left to head downstream, and let the current take you underneath the stone arches of the Key

Bridge, named for Francis Scott Key, the author of the "Star Spangled Banner" and once a resident of Georgetown. While the river is tidal here, the current is still governed by the force of the upstream rapids, resulting in a constant downstream flow of water in all but the driest of droughts. Unless there has been upstream flooding, the current is generally mild, allowing for easy there-and-back travel from Jack's. There is a 6-knot speed limit in this area, so powerboats are not a major presence or concern.

Once you are under the bridge, paddle across and downriver from Jack's to travel alongside the wooded eastern shoreline to an 88-acre island. This small speck of land has gone by many names over the years. Originally called Analostan by the Native Americans, the island was named My Lord's Island by Lord Baltimore when he gave it as a gift to Captain Randolph Brant, who then named it Barbados. After going through several more name changes, it was purchased by the Roosevelt Memorial Association in 1931, and it was officially designated as Theodore Roosevelt Memorial Island in recognition of the former president's great contributions to the conservation and stewardship of the country's natural resources. There are hiking trails on the island, one of which leads to a memorial that includes a 17-foot statue of Roosevelt surrounded by reflecting pools and fountains. The sandy beach at the island's northern tip is one of the best spots on the river to land for a hike or for a leisurely lunch break later in the day.

Across the water from Roosevelt, on the eastern shore of the river, is a long, 10-foot-high concrete flood wall. As the mural of team names on this wall indicates, this stretch of water is the domain of collegiate and club rowing teams, and you will likely share the early part of the paddle with at least one rowing team. There are three rowing club boathouses nearby. Just above Jack's is the Potomac Rowing Club, and above that is the Washington Canoe Club (which branches beyond rowing teams to racing canoes and kayaks). Farther downstream is Thompson Boat Center which is home to many rowing teams (including Georgetown University) and also offers canoe and kayak rentals, providing a launch alternative to Jack's if you are looking for a shorter paddle. The rowing teams travel along straight lines at relatively high speeds and their boats are remarkably non-maneuverable. Make sure that you do not stray into their way or you may be run over by them or by one of the motorized chase boats that accompany them during their training.

The multicolumned Washington Harbor office and restaurant complex dominates the south end of the wall and is a popular docking spot for pleasure boaters seeking an afternoon or evening on the town. The columns are more than merely decorative; floodgates can be raised between them during periods of high water. After you pass Tompkins's Boathouse, you will paddle alongside the Kennedy Center for the Performing Arts, an expansive white building with various quotes from President Kennedy carved into the stone sides. You will likely want to paddle back across the river at this point so that you can appreciate these finer details of the cityscape. South of the Kennedy Center is a grouping of three small high-rises, which are unremarkable and barely warrant mentioning, except that they make up the infamous Watergate Complex, where the fall of Richard Nixon's presidency began.

After passing underneath the Roosevelt Bridge, which is distinctive with its gold statues of horses and riders, continue alongside a stone retaining wall. Look to the right (west) and you will see a long, sloping green lawn with a white manor house at the top. The lawn is part of Arlington National Cemetery, and the house belonged to Robert E. Lee. It was built by George Washington Parke Custis, the grandson of Martha Washington, and was named the Arlington House after the family's home on the Eastern Shore. General Lee lived here with his wife, Mary Custis, for 30 years until he resigned from the federal army to head the army of the Confederacy, consequently losing his house and land to the federal government during the Civil War. After the war, the family won a lawsuit to get the land back, but it had already been converted for use as a military cemetery.

The stone wall ends, and the ceremonial stairway entrance to D.C. from the water begins, revealing the squared, Greek form of the Lincoln Memorial. The Washington Monument, which at 555 feet is visible during much of the paddle, comes into fuller view, allowing for the beautiful vista of both monuments together. After paddling underneath the Arlington Memorial Bridge, a mix of weeping willows and cherry

The author in front of the Lincoln Memorial   LEE GARDNER

trees line the shore. The trees were a gift from Japan in 1912, and their blooming is celebrated every year during the end of March and beginning of April with the National Cherry Blossom Festival. The sight of these trees in their full pink glory is worth the entire paddle. The web site at www.nationalcherryblossomfestival.com offers a good prediction of peak bloom, along with all the festival information. The 6-knot speed restriction ends below the Arlington Memorial Bridge, so you need to be cautious in your monument- and cherry-tree viewing, making sure to stay near shore. The shoreline is part of West Potomac Park, and is managed by the National Park Service. South of the park, the shore bends in toward the gated entrance to the Tidal Basin, and the Jefferson Memorial rotunda becomes visible. The Tidal Basin used to be a popular whites-only swimming beach for a few years in the early 1920s but was closed in 1925 due to health concerns and because there was no comparable beach access available for African Americans in the city.

It is about 2 miles from Jack's to here, about a 1- to 1½-hour trip, with plenty of time allowed for sightseeing. Upon reaching the Tidal Basin, and before passing underneath the bridges for I-395, you need to make the ½-mile crossing of the Potomac in order to finish the trip. Do this by paddling back northward on the western side of Columbia and Roosevelt Islands. Experienced kayakers can usually cross the river here, but beware of high-speed boat traffic in the summer, with resulting high wakes. If this crossing looks too dicey because of wind or powerboats, then simply paddle back upstream and cross over after the Memorial Bridge, where the speed limit is restricted to 6 knots. As you cross, look upriver and you can see the landmark spire of Georgetown University's church, which towers over Jack's Boathouse.

When you reach the southern tip of Columbia Island, make sure you turn around to get another view of the monuments before paddling underneath the stone arch of the Georgetown Parkway Bridge. On your right is the Navy and Marine Memorial. This sculpture commemorates all Americans who have been lost at sea, and is viewable from the water. The Columbia Island Powerboat Marina occupies the southern inland tip of land, and all boat speed is once again restricted to 6 knots. Their boat ramp is tucked among their numerous piers, just above the marina office and café. Kayakers are welcome to both land and launch from here at no cost, in accordance with the marina's fair and simple rule that if they do not have to lift the ramp to accommodate your boat, then you do not have to pay. They have rest rooms, and their cold sodas and hot lunches are a nice indulgence. As you paddle past the marina, the low-slung Pentagon will come into view straight ahead, its imposing architecture standing in stark contrast to the monuments that we just left behind and serving as a solemn reminder that D.C. is home to much more than monuments and parks.

The Boundary Channel makes up the back side of Columbia Island. It is small and nicely protected from wind, providing a serene paddle alongside this 1-mile-long island. About midway up the island, you will pass underneath a bridge with an echoing stone archway. The next ½ mile of water is a waterfowl nesting area, and all powerboats are prohibited. This is the realm of the sea kayaker, and among all this quiet nature, it is easy to forget that just minutes ago you were paddling alongside the monuments of D.C.

Turtles dot the shoreline on warm days, lining up head-to-tail along every protruding log, feet spread-eagled to soak in every available drop of sunshine. Green herons, ducks, and kingfishers can also be found along this quiet stretch. You will pass underneath the Arlington Memorial Bridge, with a bull-head frieze at its center, and then, after a footbridge and two more road bridges, you will reach the top of Columbia Island. This area is only passable at high tide, but if you cannot float over it, the bottom is firm enough to permit dragging your craft over the shallow area. Once you round the top of the island, a gorgeous view of the Lincoln Memorial and the Washington Monument is revealed—creating the best and most dramatic vantage point of the trip.

There is a small inlet between Roosevelt and Columbia where you could head out to the Potomac; however, stay on the inside (western side) of Roosevelt Island in order to complete the full loop. Paddle underneath the large, multi-span Theodore Roosevelt Memorial Bridge, and then underneath a wooden footbridge. Roosevelt is about half the length of Columbia Island, and once you pass underneath the footbridge, you can see Jack's and the spires of Georgetown University. Launching kayaks is permitted from the mainland side, where there is a parking area with a low seawall and gravel shoreline. The only good landing spot on the western side of the island is just upstream of the footbridge. However, the best way to visit the island on foot is by rounding the tip and ducking back along the other side to land on the small beach that you passed at the beginning of the paddle. While this is a good staging point for a hike around the island, make sure to lock up your kayak—if you would not leave your bicycle unlocked, then you should not leave your kayak unsecured.

A good view of Georgetown is provided as you paddle back toward Jack's Boathouse. You may notice that the topography of Georgetown is different from the rest of D.C., and that is because Georgetown sits on the final foothills of the fall line, unlike the low-lying swampland of the rest of the capital. It is a unique neighborhood, with a distinctly old-world harbor feel to its steep streets and alleys. Towering above this landscape is Georgetown University, a Jesuit-run institution since 1789.

If you still have the wind and energy, paddle upstream past Jack's to extend your trip into the wilderness. You will pass a small waterfall overflow from the C&O Canal, which parallels the river. Above the waterfall, you will pass the Three Sisters, which is a grouping of three rock islands that are a favorite perch for cormorants. Many legends accompany these rocks, the most popular of which concerns three Indian sisters who were going to marry three Indian braves, until the men where killed by warriors while on a simple fishing trip. The sisters vowed revenge and made rafts to cross the river to kill the guilty warriors, but their rafts capsized on the way across. The sisters were killed, and the three rock islands rose up at the site of the capsize. The river is said to be cursed at this point and many people still drown in the strong current, curse or no curse, so be sure not to flip. Besides the exposed Three Sisters, there are many more rocks submerged just below the water's surface, so do not be startled if you find yourself unexpectedly perched on the tip of a hidden boulder. The current becomes increasingly strong as you head upstream toward Little Falls. If you persevere, you will reach Fletcher's Boathouse in about 2¼ miles from Jack's, and you will reach the end of navigation at the base of Little Falls in another mile.

President Kennedy once said, "I look forward to an America that will not be afraid of grace and beauty." This quote was memorialized on the side of the Kennedy Center, and its truth stayed with me throughout the day that I scouted this paddle. It is a wonderfully reassuring thing to me that our nation's capital is situated in a place of grace and beauty because one would hope that such a spot might gentle the souls and up-lift the minds of all the legislators who work along its shores.

Alternative Trips

Either by extending the above trip, or by leaving from the Columbia Marina, head downstream from the Tidal Basin for 1½ miles to the Washington Channel. Another area option is to launch from Gravelly Point Marina, which is off the George Washington Memorial Parkway, just north of Reagan National Airport, and paddle south to Dangerfield Island and then to the Alexandria waterfront. Or, you can launch from Belle Haven Marina, off the George Washington Memorial Parkway, south of Alexandria, just below the Belle Haven Country Club. You can paddle south into Dyke Marsh, or paddle north, alongside Alexandria to Dangerfield Island. Atlantic Kayak offers versions of these routes, which are especially popular as moonlight paddles.

2.

Mason Neck

Features: Bald eagles, cliffs, freshwater marsh, and forested land.

Length: 8 miles.

Put-in site: Mason Neck State Park, 7301 High Point Road, Lorton, VA 22079, 703-550-0960. The park is open from dawn to dusk, and there is a $4 entrance fee for weekends and holidays, and a $3 entrance fee for weekdays. The landing is a strip of beach for car-top boats only. There are several temporary parking spaces for loading and unloading, with permanent spaces up the hill. There are bathrooms near the playground, which you pass just before the landing. This is a day-use-only park, but there is camping on the other side of the peninsula at Pohick Bay Regional Park. For out-of-town visitors this can be a great, cheap base camp for touring nearby Washington, D.C. There are kayak and canoe rentals at Pohick, along with guided tours. The Atlantic Kayak Company also runs excellent tours out of Pohick and Mason Neck.

Directions: *From the north,* on I-95 South, take exit 163, County Route 642 (CR 642) toward Lorton. Turn left at the bottom of the ramp onto Lorton Road/CR 642. This area seems to be constantly under construction, which can change some road exits and road names. When in doubt, follow the road signs for Mason Neck State Park. Take a right on Armistead Road, and then a right on US 1 South. Go about 0.1 mile to the traffic light on top of the hill and take a left onto Gunston Road. There is a sign for Pohick Bay, Gunston Hall, and Mason Neck State Park. Follow for about 4.4 miles and then take a slight right onto High Point Road. Follow for 2.3 miles and then take

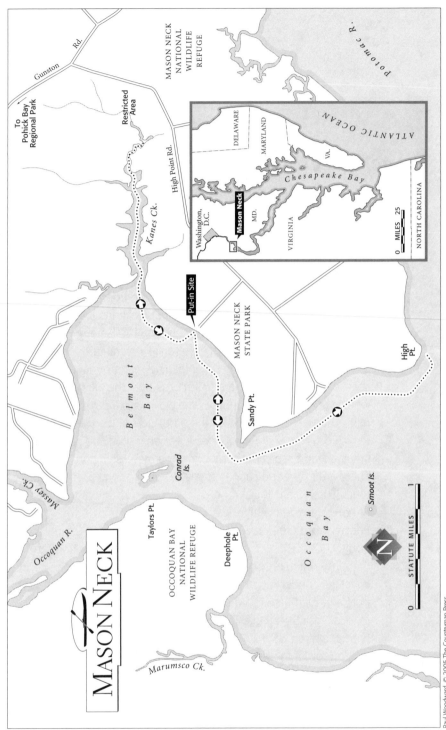

MASON NECK

To
Pohick Bay
Regional Park

Gunston Rd.

MASON NECK
NATIONAL
WILDLIFE REFUGE

Potomac R.

Restricted
Area

High Point Rd.

Kanes Ck.

Put-in Site

ATLANTIC OCEAN

DELAWARE

MARYLAND

MD.

Chesapeake Bay

VA.

Washington,
D.C.

Mason Neck

VIRGINIA

NORTH CAROLINA

0   MILES   25

MASON NECK
STATE PARK

High
Pt.

Belmont
Bay

Sandy Pt.

Conrad
Is.

Massey Ck.

Taylors Pt.

Occoquan R.

OCCOQUAN BAY
NATIONAL
WILDLIFE REFUGE

Deephole
Pt.

Occoquan
Bay

Smoot Is.

Marumsco Ck.

N

0   STATUTE MILES   1

Paul Woodward, © 2005 The Countryman Press

a right to stay on High Point Road. Go through the park gate
and follow the signs to the visitors center. Just before the visitors center, take a left at the car-top boat ramp, down a gravel
road to the water. *From the south,* on I-95 North, take exit 161
for US 1/Fort Belvoir. Go north on US 1, then take a right on
Gunston Road, and follow the directions above.

THIS IS A POPULAR TRIP among Northern Virginia kayakers, and for
good reason. With high cliffs, meandering creeks, expansive marshland,
and skies full of bald eagles, Mason Neck would be worth paddling even
if it was miles from civilization, let alone being conveniently located in
the heart of the D.C. suburban sprawl of Fairfax County. There are numerous routes to choose from, with plenty of options to satisfy both
the sport paddler looking for distance and the bird-watcher looking for
nature. The Chesapeake Paddlers Association (CPA) was sponsoring a
paddle in the area when I arrived at the park on Labor Day Sunday with
two novice kayakers in tow. While there were about 20 people in the
CPA group, our routes crossed only once during the day. The route we
paddled leans heavily on the bird-watcher side and was fitting in distance and pace to get novice paddlers to fall in love with the water
without being too stiff the next day from the unfamiliar exercise.

Trip Description

From the landing, paddle to the right, up Belmont Bay into the quiet
waters of Kanes Creek. You can see the mouth of the Occoquan River
to the left/northwest, with the span of the US 1 bridge barely visible
where it crosses the river. The shoreline has a thin strip of brown sandy
beach, with one-story-high wooded banks above them. In about ½ mile,
bear right into the wide opening of Kanes Creek. There is a well-kept
duck blind on the northern tip of the creek, and an osprey nest at the
top of a tree behind that. The right side of the creek is a continuation
of the cliffs of the river, and the left/north side is a beautiful, green, wild
freshwater marsh with three-square rush, spatterdock, and cattails. My
friends and I zigzagged our way into the creek, chasing one piece of

Paddling among the spatterdock of Kanes Creek

beauty after another. Then, in about ¼ mile upstream on the right/east side, we pushed our way through a sea of spatterdock and into a small side creek.

Our detour off the main flow of the creek was immediately rewarded with the sight of some bald eagles. Not just one or two, but five eagles all in flight at one time. They crisscrossed the sky, flying from tree to tree, swooping low over the marsh, and rising high into the air, hovering aloft on thermals. These eagles are why we have the park today. In 1965, two eagles' nests were found in the area. This was at the height of the bald eagle's demise, and a committee was immediately formed to save the land from impending development. With the help of the Nature Conservancy, Virginia slowly began to purchase the land that would later make up the park. The 1,800-acre state park was opened to the public in 1985, and abuts the 2,000-acre federally protected Mason Neck Wildlife Refuge, which was formed for the same reason of protecting eagle habitat, and was the first refuge in the United States formed for that express purpose.

We eventually continued up Kanes Creek, but the long time spent eagle watching made a rest break necessary because I very rarely paddle over an hour at a time without stretching my legs. While there is a small sandbar beach just below the eagle-filled detour, above the creek all easy break spots disappear. However, we found a spot with a firm, sandy bottom at the base of a steep sloping hill, on the outside of a bend to the left. Always look to the outside of bends for rest spots because it is here that the coarser sediment is dropped, creating shallow, gently sloping edges. Conversely, the inside corner will be deep, with a bottom made of finer, more silty mud. The water felt good on our feet, and the only inconvenience of this rest spot was the constant plunking of acorns in the water. We were lucky, and although a few nuts cracked hard upon our kayak decks, no one caught an acorn on the head.

With each looping bend upriver, Kanes Creek becomes increasingly beautiful, with an enveloping wetland of wild rice and cattail, and sycamore, birch, and oak filling in the deep forest beyond the lowlands. There is a gut on the left/west side of the creek that you should explore either on the way up or down the creek. Paddling ends about 1 mile up Kanes Creek. It is stopped not by fallen trees or overgrown vegetation, but by the true purpose of the park. Because the park's objective is the conservation of wildlife and eagle habitat, the inner sanctum of the park is off-limits to humans, providing a large area where eagles can nest without human disturbance. This restriction is enforced by NO TRESPASSING signs in the upper creek and has been a beneficial policy for great blue herons as well, which have established the largest rookery in the mid-Atlantic region here, with over 1,400 active nests.

We watched a few more eagles soar as we made our way downstream and took a side detour into the creek's other gut before stopping on the sand beach below the eagle-filled detour. Although we paddled only 2 miles there and back, by the time we reemerged onto Belmont Bay, almost three hours had passed. The change in the river was dramatic. Not only had the wind picked up to a stiff 10 to 15 knots but where in the morning we saw nothing but open water, at least 50 powerboats were now anchored just above Sandy Point. People were swimming, drinking, listening to music, and generally celebrating the last weekend of summer. One of the strange things about the Chesapeake boater is that most people believe that the boating season ends with Labor Day. Thus, when the air cools a bit, and the wind picks up enough to allow good sailing, the creeks, rivers, and bays empty of boats. While I find this phenomenon strange, I also embrace it because that leaves more undisturbed water for me to kayak.

Bald Eagles

The national symbol of the United States is the largest bird of prey in Virginia and is distinctive and easy to identify with its white head and tail. Bald eagles like to sit three-quarters of the way up in a tree along the water's edge, so you should develop the habit of scanning this section of the tree line on all of Virginia's rivers. Despite their bold markings, it takes a keen and practiced eye to spot them, for they are much more cautious than other birds and will usually fly away well before you reach their perch. Even if you cannot see their white heads and tails against a pale sky, they are easily identified in flight by their broad 6- to 8-foot flat wingspan and graceful flight. This grace distinguishes eagles from vultures, which, while of a similar size, have a V-shaped upward tilt to their wings and are rocky in their flight.

The bald eagle is an adaptable eater and will as readily eat dead fish and carrion as it will hunt for live fish, birds, and mammals. They breed in the late winter months and build nests throughout Virginia, high in mature trees like loblolly pines, at least 80 feet off the ground. They add to these nests every year, building them to dimensions of up to 8 feet wide and to weights of 1 ton. Eagles live in breeding pairs, sharing the duties of nest building and child rearing. The young eaglets are able to fly in three months and are on their own after four months. Immature eagles are dark brown for their first three to four

The Mason Neck Peninsula was once known as Doggs Island and Doegs Neck, after the Dogue tribe of the Powhatan Confederacy. They called the Occoquan River Valley home, and the river's name comes from the surrounding land, which they called *"at the end of the water."* While the river kept its name, the peninsula was renamed after its most famous resident, George Mason IV. His Gunston Hall Plantation made him one of the wealthiest, and thus most influential men of Colonial Virginia. He was the primary framer of Virginia's Declaration of Rights in 1776, which served as the inspiration for part of the Declaration of Independence, and for the Constitution's Bill of Rights. He was a key member of Philadelphia's Constitutional Convention, although he ultimately refused to sign the constitution, partly because it lacked the Bill of Rights.

years of life, but they grow increasingly mottled with white, until they finally grow the distinctive white head and tail feathers that mark them as mature bald eagles. Even while immature, eagles are full-sized and are thus still easy to identify with their wide, flat wingspan.

I spent my childhood outdoors, lived along the water as a college student, and worked on the water during and after college, but I did not see my first bald eagle until I was in my early 20s. Conversely, while scouting this book, I saw eagles on almost every trip, often several at a time. The difference between now and then is the banning of DDT, a pesticide that was once widely used on mosquitoes. This spraying unintentionally harmed eagles, osprey, and other species, which caused their eggs to have shells so thin that they broke when their mother sat on them. Eagles began to rebound when DDT was banned in 1972, and there were close to eight-hundred eagles counted in the Chesapeake Bay in 2000, with almost three-hundred of these in breeding pairs. Despite this fantastic rebound, their recovery has been a bit slower than that of the osprey, partially because eagles are much less tolerant of humans and like to build their nests well away from boat or human traffic. Thus, as development continues to boom in Virginia, preserved and protected riparian lands are more and more essential for the eagle's continued survival.

The paddle up Kanes Creek and back can be the perfect distance for beginners, or for a half-day paddle. However, to extend the 4-mile round trip, paddle around Sandy Point toward the open waters of the Occoquan Bay and the Potomac River. The water around the point can be choppy and confused with the combination of wind, waves, and powerboat wakes, but if the wind is westerly, the water will settle out once you make it around the point and into the lee of the shore. As the water grows wider, the impact of boat wakes also diminishes. The perfume of honeysuckle filled the air here, and the shoreline was filled with low-lying woodlands, rimmed with a thin strip of beach. This can make for a much more secluded and relaxing break spot than the beach along the north shore of Belmont Bay. If you continue around the growing bluffs of the shoreline, you will reach the riprap-protected shore of

High Point, which is where the Occoquan Bay officially joins with the Potomac River. If you continue to paddle north from here, you will soon reach the Great Marsh, which is the largest freshwater marsh in Northern Virginia and home to many herons and eagles. However, I was content with my day and headed back home. I am certain that sport kayakers will cover at least twice the distance that we took half a day to paddle. However, we saw eagles, we saw forests, we saw beauty— you do not have to paddle far to see a lot.

Alternative Trips

There are many routes to follow when kayaking from Mason Neck. A popular one-way route is to kayak from Mason Neck to Pohick Bay (Pohick Bay Regional Park, 6501 Pohick Bay Drive, Lorton, VA, 703-339-6104). This approximately 10-mile paddle is on open water, so be sure your skill level is up to the long exposure, and pick a calm day over a windy one. For other there-and-back trips, you can paddle from Mason Neck, out across Belmont Bay, to small Conrad Island. From there, paddle south around Deephole Point, and then west into Marumsco Creek. Some people head up the Occoquan River, even paddling as far as the historic town of Occoquan; however, this route is heavily traveled by powerboats that are heading to and from the river's many marinas.

The car-top launch at Leesylvania State Park provides access to the southern shore of the Occoquan Bay, and you can also explore Nebasco, Farm, and Powells Creeks from the park, which is off CR 610 south of US 1. Leesylvania State Park, 2001 Daniel K. Ludwig Drive, Woodbridge, VA 22191, 703-670-0372.

3.

Fountainhead

Features: Nontidal reservoir, with wooded shoreline, migratory
waterfowl, and plentiful white-tailed deer.

Length: 12 miles.

Put-in site: Fountainhead Regional Park, 10875 Hampton Road,
Fairfax Station, VA 22039, 703-250-9124. The park is part of
the Northern Virginia Regional Park Authority (NVRPA), which
provides wilderness escapes to the urban populations of Washington, D.C. and the suburban counties of Northern Virginia.

There is a $2 launch fee for carried boats, payable at the
small bait and snack shop, which is up the walkway from the
landing. They also sell a good map of the reservoir for $3. Ca-
noes are available for $6/hour or $28/day for Northern Virginia
residents, with the fees slightly higher for nonresidents. The annual fee ranges from $30 to $50, depending on your residency.
Powerboats launch from here as well but are restricted to 10-
horsepower motors, so the boats are small and do not move
terribly fast.

The park is open from March 20 through November 7,
making this the only trip description in the book that is closed to
winter paddling. There is car camping upstream at Bull Run Regional Park. This campground is less than 30 miles from down-
town Washington, D.C., making it a cheap and convenient place
for out-of-state visitors to stay while visiting the nation's capital.

Directions: From I-95, take exit 160 onto VA 123 North toward Occoquan. Follow for 4.5 miles, and then take a left onto Hampton
Road. Follow this for about 3 miles, and then take a left into the
park. Both turns are well marked with brown park signs.

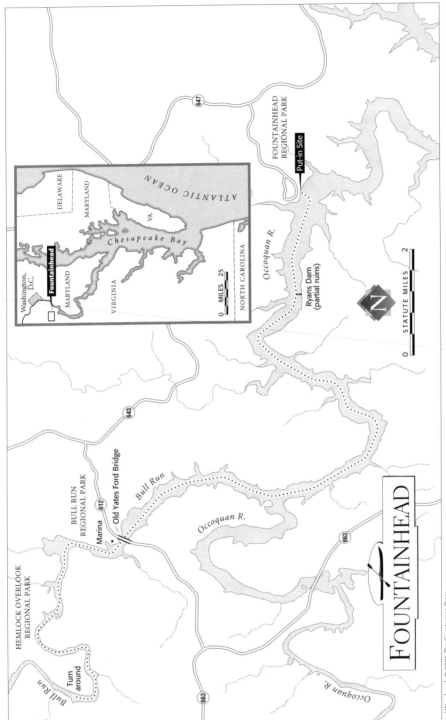

THE OCCOQUAN RESERVOIR is a 2,100-acre expanse that provides water to the city of Alexandria and to Fairfax County. It is a well-managed fishery, with largemouth bass, crappie, catfish, and perch. The lake has also been stocked with northern pike since 2001. It is a pocket of woods and water in the midst of Northern Virginia, and was recommended to me by Woody Woodward. He is a kayak enthusiast who began paddling in 1999 and subsequently chronicled all of his kayaking trips on his web site at www.kayaktrips.net. Woody's site offers a wealth of kayaking ideas. It also includes reviews of gear, books, and videos and provides useful links to other sites. This is his favorite trip in Northern Virginia.

Trip Description

From the landing, paddle right to head west, upriver. You can see the remaining structure of the old Ryans Dam upriver about 1 mile, on the southern bank. The right/north side is all park land, and is thus entirely forested. The left/south side has occasional large homes, which are mostly hidden behind the trees. This should be a gorgeous paddle during the foliage change of late October, because the forest is a rich deciduous mixture of oak, beech, river birch, sweet gum, elm, cottonwood, and maple, with the occasional cedar and pine tree mingled in to the composition. Blue herons and geese were my constant avian companions.

Once you reach Ryans Dam, you can see a large red house on the right that belongs to the park. There is a sign with the number 13 in black on a yellow background directly across from the dam. Signs such as this are place markers so that if someone breaks down or runs into trouble on the lake, they can radio or phone in their location to the park staff. The color scheme changes to blue/white as you get farther away from the park headquarters. They were not precisely placed, but they are about ½ mile apart, sometimes a little less. The only power-boaters on the reservoir are fishermen, and on their way to their fishing spots they will move as fast as their 10-horsepower motors will take them. However, once you reach their destination, they move slower than the slowest kayaker. On most days, it can be quite safe to crisscross the reservoir, chasing whatever beauty you see. Or you can take the more staid approach, paddling up one side of the lake and coming back down the other. I did a little bit of both, zigzagging more in the beginning of the paddle when my arms were fresh and the surrounding world was new, and then following the shoreline more in the afternoon when the number of fishermen began to increase.

Despite the fact that this reservoir is man-made, there is an abundance of wildlife along the shore. Great blue herons stalked the edges, and blue-white kingfishers dashed ahead of me throughout the paddle, scolding my presence with their rattling cry. Little green herons perched on fallen tree limbs, fishing for minnows and frogs in the shallow water. White-tailed deer quietly came to the shoreline throughout the day, descending the steep hills to the water's edge, grazing on the succulent marsh vegetation and drinking from the clear water. I saw a doe and two fawns, groups of two or three adults, and a few lone bucks. The groups sometimes allowed me to drift within 30 feet, while the lone deer often slipped away while I was just crossing over from the opposite shoreline.

There are numerous side coves to explore. The first is almost directly across from Ryans Dam; the second, in another mile on the north shore, and the third, in another ½ mile on the southern shore. Much of the wildlife that I saw was along the shores of these coves. About ½ mile past Ryans Dam, the waterway curved to the southeast with a 90-degree bend. Then, in about 1½ miles, the water bends to the right, for a northwestern flow. The left bank is high here, but there are plenty of great break spots along the right bank. There are small, brown sand beaches to be found all along the length of this paddle, and the reservoir bottom is firm. As refreshing as the water looks on a summer day, there is absolutely no swimming here, so resist the urge to capsize in the summertime. (Although I found that the rotary cooling of an Eskimo roll is a legal and handy way to beat the heat of the summer.)

After the number 15 sign, all the remaining signage is in white letters on a blue background. About 4 miles from the boat landing, the two rivers that form the reservoir split ways. The Occoquan River branches to the left/south, and Bull Run heads off to the right/

northwest. There is a swamp of drowned trees on the opposite bank of this T-junction, and numerous fishermen were working the countless holes and snags of the area.

Bear right to head up Bull Run. The reservoir has created flat navigable water above the fall line, allowing sea kayakers to paddle in an area that would have been more suited to a whitewater boat. Thus, the piedmont scenery of rolling hills and rocky shores is not similar to any of the other trips in this book, all of which are well within the relatively flat coastal plain. The piedmont and the coastal plain are roughly delineated by I-95. The rocky makeup of the land is even more accentuated in Bull Run, with diagonal slashes of shale spilling into the water.

You will reach the Old Yates Ford Bridge about 2 miles from

A still morning on the Occoquan Reservoir

the split of the two rivers. The boat landing for Bull Run Marina is on the upriver (northern) side of the bridge. This landing is also operated by the NVRPA. Here, canoes can be rented, and the Hemlock Overlook Outdoor Center runs moonlight paddles at least twice a month during the summer. There is a picnic table on the point by the boat slip, and you will find a snack bar, vending machines, and restrooms up the hill from the landing. You can land on the boat slip, on the low floating docks that frame the slip, or on the small gravel beach that is just above the slip.

There is a little marsh island above the ramp, which is barely passable on the right side. I had to pole through the mud to get back onto clear water—so you should bear to the outside of this little island unless you want to get your boat dirty. The wildlife increases considerably upriver of the marina, and the backed up water of the reservoir gives way to the more natural shores of the river. Egrets, cormorants, herons, and osprey were visible on every turn, and a bald eagle flew high above the river's flow. The river bends to the left/west about ½ mile above Bull Run Marina, and you can clearly see the soccer fields of Kincheloe Playing Fields at the top of this bend.

After this bend the waterway becomes even smaller, with a lot of dead trees along the edges. In about ½ mile, the river doglegs slightly south, which brings you to a wooded island that is passable on both sides. Egrets, herons, geese, and red-bellied turtles all call this island home. This is a convenient place to turn around, creating a round trip of 12 miles. Or, if you have the energy, you can continue upstream from here for a little ways more, alongside the wooded shoreline of Hemlock Overlook Regional Park. This occupies the northern/ right shore above the small tree island and is home to George Mason University's team-building and experiential education center. However, the fact that this waterway is called a "run" signifies that it has a one-way flow, thus it is running downstream. Therefore, as you leave behind the influence of the dam, the current will begin and then increase to the point that you can not paddle against its force.

You might want to save some time at the end of your day to visit a nearby historical site. When you kayak at Fountainhead, you are paddling on water that is just 20 miles or so downstream from the first major battle of the Civil War, fought on July 21, 1861. The hills around the battlefields were lined with spectators from D.C. who did not want to miss the first skirmish of what all thought would be a short-lived war. Ten hours later nine-hundred men lay dead, and all hope that the war would be short and bloodless was dashed. This was known as the Battle of First Manassas; the second battle at Bull Run (the Battle of Second Manassas) would prove even bloodier. Fought by seasoned veterans, that battle raged from August 28 to August 30, 1862, and resulted in an important Confederate victory and over 3,300 men dead. Manassas National Battlefield Park now preserves the battlefields, and it is well worth the short drive from Fountainhead.

Alternative Trips

For more area paddling, you could also paddle downstream toward the dam. This stretch is slightly more populated, but you could cheer on the crew teams from area high schools. Or, for an alternative to kayaking, there is an 18-mile mountain bike trail that runs from Fountainhead to Bull Run Regional Park: so if you camp at that park, you can do some cross-training, seeing the valley by water on one day and by bike on the other day. South of the nearby town of Onancock is Quantico. There is canoe and kayak access to Quantico Creek from the town park, and the military base keeps much of the shoreline in a wooded, albeit off-limits, state. For more information about the Occoquan Water Trail, you can contact the NVRPA at 703-352-5900 or visit www.nvrpa.org. The water trail begins in Bull Run and ends at Pohick Bay.

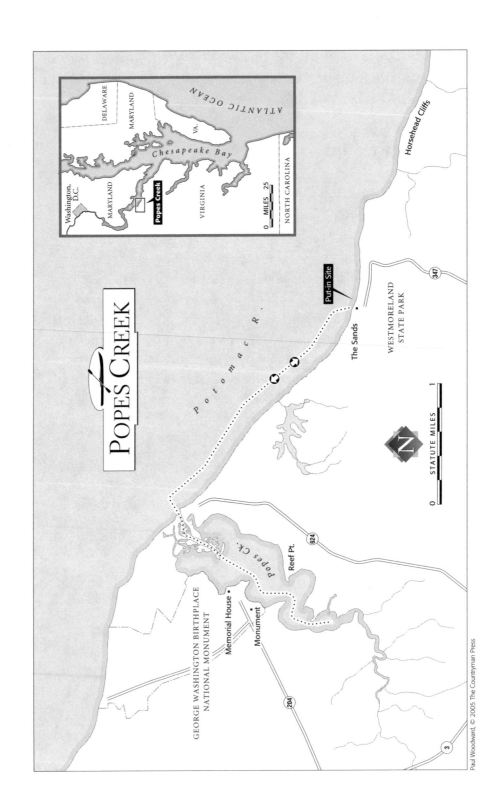

POPES CREEK

DELAWARE
MARYLAND
VA.
ATLANTIC OCEAN
Chesapeake Bay
Washington, D.C.
MARYLAND
Popes Creek
VIRGINIA
NORTH CAROLINA

0 MILES 25

Horsehead Cliffs

Put-in Site

The Sands

WESTMORELAND
STATE PARK

347

Potomac R.

GEORGE WASHINGTON BIRTHPLACE
NATIONAL MONUMENT

Memorial House

Monument

Popes Ck.

Reef Pt.

624

204

3

N

0   STATUTE MILES   1

4.

Popes Creek

Features: George Washington's birthplace, combination of open water and brackish creek, bald eagles, cliffs, beaches, fossils.

Length: 8+ miles.

Put-in site: Westmoreland State Park, 1659 State Park Road, Montross, VA 22520, 804-493-8821. This state park is the launch site for the day's paddle. There is a $3 day-use fee for weekdays and a $4 day-use fee for weekends from April 1 through October 31, plus a $3 boat launch fee.

The park offers kayak rentals and tours from the beach near the swimming pool (the previous park boathouse was destroyed by Hurricane Isabel). The park also has excellent hiking trails, beaches, a swimming pool, a fishing pier, rustic and furnished cabins, campgrounds, and a conference center. Bathrooms are available near the campground store and the visitors center. While the metal-grated boat launch is acceptable for launching kayaks, I would recommend launching instead from the small sand beach to the left of the landing.

Call the main state park number (1-800-933-PARK) for camping or kayak reservations. Part of the paddle is by the edges of the George Washington Birthplace National Monument, Route 1, Box 717, Washington's Birthplace, VA 22443, 804-224-1732.

Directions: From Frederick (I-95), take VA 3 East for about 40 miles to the park's entrance, and then turn left onto VA 347 (about 17 miles after crossing US 301), which is the entrance to Westmoreland State Park. From Tappahannock, follow US 360 East to Warsaw. Turn left on VA 3 at the second stoplight. Stay on this road for about 6 miles, past Montross. Take a right into the park's entrance on VA 347. Follow the park signs to the boat landing.

AFTER LEAVING BEHIND the high sand cliffs of Westmoreland State Park, this route travels over almost 2 miles on the open Potomac River before entering Popes Creek through a shallow entrance that prevents all but the smallest and most intrepid powerboaters from entering. Popes is a beautiful brackish creek, with a forested, marsh-lined shore, which is enough to make this route worthy of inclusion in this book. However, what really makes this paddle stand out from all others is the land that surrounds the creek. It is here that George Washington was born on February 11, 1732, and spent his first three years of childhood before his family relocated to the larger house in the more remote Little Hunting Creek Plantation (later renamed Mount Vernon). Popes Creek Plantation remained in their family and he visited it often, even returning as a young surveyor to create a detailed map of the area, whereupon he reportedly deemed the plantation the finest of his family's lands. If the creek was good enough for George, it certainly is good enough for me.

Trip Description

The first 2 miles of this trip are on open water, so wind can cause trouble, especially for the less experienced paddler. Pay special attention to what the weather is predicted to do in the afternoon before setting out on your journey. While the northwest wind that is common in the spring and summer can be of good aid for your return home, a strengthening southern wind can spell trouble for your return trip in the afternoon. If a strong southern wind is predicted, then you may want to paddle the alternative trip description and save this route for a calmer day.

Swing your boat to the left to head northwest, upriver and toward Popes Creek. Modest houses populate the shoreline, most with new docks built in 2004, courtesy of the destruction of Hurricane Isabel. While this is wide-open water, and home to many powerboats, they are generally farther out in the center of the Potomac, which is about 4 miles across here. Thus you are much more likely to encounter the boats' wakes than you are to run into trouble with the boats themselves.

It can actually be a little safer and calmer to paddle at least 50 yards from shore to avoid being caught in any breaking wake waves. After a little over 1¼ miles of paddling, you will begin passing alongside a short cliff with a beach at its base and a farm field above. You will see a few more houses at the end of this long beach, and then a blue two-story building bristling with antennas, cameras, and satellite dishes. I was not able to confirm the purpose of this building, but it appears to be a weather station.

On the other side of this building is the entrance to Popes Creek, with a long strand of bleached-white beach north of the opening. Due to the shallow and narrow passage, the current at the mouth can be fast and strong, particularly at a peak ebb flow. When this is paired with a northern wind, the waves can churn a bit in the open water outside the mouth, even stacking up some nice surfable waves in the right conditions. While the ebbing current is tough to paddle against, it is possible to make headway into the creek, and the current's power lessens considerably once you are inside the mouth. At the lowest of tides, you may have to drag your boat across the shallow sandbar opening.

Inside the mouth, the creek broadens into a wide shallow delta, splattered with small marsh islands. While we did not find any true channel through the middle of the delta, it would most likely be found by edging along the sides of the creek. However, even at mid- to low tide we were able to float across the sand flats, with the water becoming quite shallow to about a foot in depth before getting deeper nearer the farthest and highest island. Most of the islands are pure marsh, with some low marsh elder shrubs, but this last island contains some trees, along with a gravelly beach for landing a couple of boats.

Directly across from the creek's mouth, a Colonial-style house is nicely situated on top of the creek's highest bluff. This was built in 1932 to mark George Washington's 200th birthday and is the most visible landmark of George Washington Birthplace National Monument, which is managed by the National Park Service. The 550-acre park is a living monument that functions as both a reconstruction of a Colonial plantation and as a site for archeological, biological, and historical research. When my friend Lee Gardner and I scouted this trip, the park ranger on duty welcomed us to beach our kayaks in the wooded picnic area to the right of the main park lands. This allowed us to spend a leisurely hour exploring the monument's grounds and listening to interpretative talks. However, the park's official policy prohibits boats from landing on park property, so to fully explore the park's shoreline, kayakers would have to join the landlubbers, entering the park by car and paying the $3 entrance fee. Despite this inconvenience, it is well worth seeing the plantation by both water and land.

The reconstructed house is far larger than Washington's original birthplace, which was destroyed by a fire in 1779, but it is an example of Colonial architecture worth viewing, even if only from the water. If you do walk around the park, you will also see the U-shaped footprint of the original house about 100 feet from the 1932 building, along with a kitchen garden, animal pastures, and a good vista of the river from within a grove of cedar trees. A 1-mile nature trail, burial grounds, and a modern visitors center are also on the site.

To the right of the house, the creek's edge is densely forested with a rich assortment of coniferous and deciduous trees—loblolly pine and willow oak as the dominant species, including Virginia's largest loblolly. This is a second-growth forest, since the original forest of Colonial times was logged entirely over the years. One of the logging practices of the time was for the British Navy to use the King's Stamp to mark the straightest and longest trees for cutting. Thus the best genetic stock was removed first from this forest, leaving the legacy of smaller and more crooked trees that dominate the forest today. However, it is still a healthy and mature forest, and many of the oldest trees would have been saplings when George Washington was a boy. In the midst of these woods is the picnic area of George Washington Birthplace National Monument.

After coasting along the wooded shorelines and small cliffs of the plantation, round a point, on which stands a towering grove of cedar, and head your kayak upstream for more exploration. If possible, plan your upcreek navigation for high tide because the creek's broad and wide meanders make the main channel elusive for even the most river-savvy paddler. Try to follow the natural flow of the river as you head upstream. Meanders are nature's way of reducing resistance, so follow the water's bend, keeping in mind that the deepest water is on the outside of the turns and sediment is dumped on the inside. In between bends, the channel slowly diagonals across the breadth of the river so that the channel is again on the outside of the next bend. Slow down, think like a river, and you will do fine.

A few houses are spaced along the southern side of this section of the creek, numbering on average one house for each of the early bends. About ¼ mile upstream from the last house, on the southern side of the river, there is a little gravel beach that leads into a pasture. This is an excellent rest spot and is the only reliable dry land in the upper section of the creek. The upstream stretches turn to freshwater and the shoreline here is predominantly a mixture of cattail and forest land. As you paddle the wild back section of Popes Creek, it will not be hard to imagine a young George Washington exploring this land by foot and boat. The head of navigable water is about 3 miles upriver of Popes Creek Plantation. You can likely reach even farther at high tide, probably ¼ mile, and maybe even into the small farm pond. However, when we scouted this trip we failed to be prudent with our tidal observations. Not only did we mistime our upcreek explorations, but we were paddling near the end of an ebbing tide, causing us worry about whether we would have enough water to get out of the creek. This added some adrenaline and light anxiety to our trip, especially because the earlier sections of meander are over a deep, soft mud, and we both breathed a considerable sigh of relief when we reached the open waters of the mouth of the bay. Throughout the paddle the creek bed varies from a thick, rich detritus, to a sandy bottom, to a gravel bottom, to detritus again.

On your way out of the creek, you will see the park's miniature replica of the Washington Monument. Once back on the river, you can extend your day by paddling northward on the Potomac, where the shoreline continues as a beautiful combination of cliffs, forests, and beaches. Otherwise you can spend your afternoon as Lee and I did, lounging with blissful laziness on the long strip of sandy beach. There

The beautiful, brackish water of Popes Creek

is nothing quite as sweet as carefree relaxation after a morning of hard paddling. Much of this beach is owned by the National Park Service, but the area below mean high tide is common ground.

As I finished the day-long exploration of Popes Creek, my mind drifted back to when I was first introduced to Westmoreland State Park many years ago, guiding a group of schoolteachers on a weeklong summer trip. The night was thick with humidity so we stole down to the water for an evening swim. As we plunged in we set free a shower of light in the water. The Potomac was filled with a host of animals glowing with bioluminescence. From jellyfish to microscopic bacteria, every creature in the river—now including humans—sparkled with the cool light of luciferin. We swam for a long time, taking turns to climb onto the dock to watch the surreal sight of glowing human outlines swimming in the darkness. That night we hiked back to camp by the light of our clothes that still glowed with the power of the Potomac's water.

Alternative Trips

An easy extension or alternative to this day trip can be made by heading south from the boat landings, alongside the towering cliffs that make up the next 4 miles of shoreline. The cliffs are divided up into three sets, and the first group is called the Horsehead Cliffs. There is a small bay and a little beach at the base of the towering banks, and fossilized sharks' teeth can be found by carefully combing the wet sand. The next grouping is known as the Stratford Cliffs, and Robert E. Lee's birthplace lies inland of these bluffs. The final set is called the Nomini Cliffs, and these are the largest of the three groups, stretching southward on the Potomac for about 2 miles. South of Westmoreland, you can launch on the scenic waters of Nomini Creek from a landing at the end of CR 645.

You can also launch north of Popes Creek in Rosier Creek. It is a beautiful, brackish creek that provides access to the open Potomac and you can paddle downriver to the waterside town of Colonial Beach. Or, you can launch in Colonial Beach, and paddle south to Mattox Creek and Popes Creek. Both landings are accessible from VA 205.

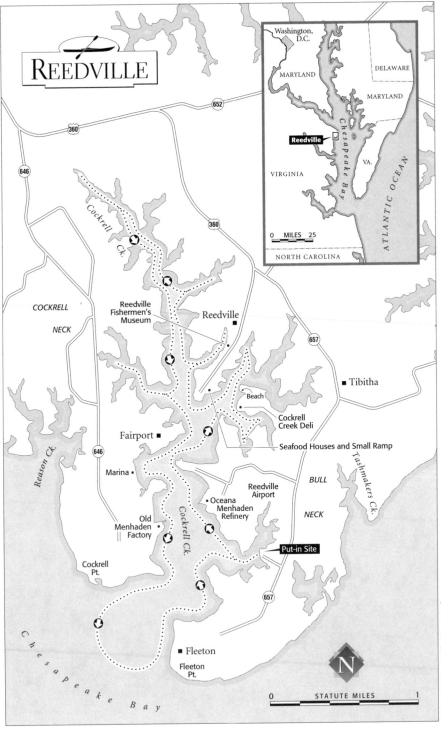

REEDVILLE

Washington, D.C.

MARYLAND

DELAWARE

MARYLAND

Chesapeake Bay

Reedville

VIRGINIA

VA.

ATLANTIC OCEAN

0 MILES 25

NORTH CAROLINA

652

360

646

Cockrell Ck.

360

657

COCKRELL

NECK

Reedville Fishermen's Museum

Reedville

Tibitha

Beach

Cockrell Creek Deli

Fairport

Seafood Houses and Small Ramp

646

Reason Ck.

Marina

BULL

Tashmakers Ck.

Reedville Airport

NECK

Oceana Menhaden Refinery

Old Menhaden Factory

Cockrell Ck.

Put-in Site

Cockrell Pt.

657

N

Fleeton

Fleeton Pt.

Chesapeake Bay

0 STATUTE MILES 1

Paul Woodward, © 2005 The Countryman Press

5.

Reedville

Features: Historic town of Reedville, home to the Atlantic's menhaden fishing fleet.

Length: 8 to 14 miles.

Put-in site: The public launch is just south of the town of Reedville and has two concrete ramps and plenty of parking. There are no bathroom facilities. Reedville has several restaurants and also contains the Reedville Fishermen's Museum, which is worth visiting before, during, or after your paddle.

Directions: Take US 360 (which is accessible from US 301 by following VA 3). Just prior to entering Reedville, bear left at the Y-junction onto County Route 657 (CR 657). Follow this for 2.2 miles and then take a right on CR 692/Shell Landing Road. There is a brown public boat landing sign at this turn. Follow the road for 0.2 mile until it ends at the water.

REEDVILLE IS THE TOWN that menhaden built. While menhaden have no value as a sport or food, a commercially lucrative fishery has grown around this small, bony and oily species of herring, which is processed into valuable fish oil and meal. In 1874, Captain Elijah Reed from Maine purchased land along Cockrell Creek and brought the menhaden industry to Virginia. Since then, Reedville's menhaden industry has gone through many evolutions, with various factories opening and closing along Cockrell Creek. Just as Nantucket was the center of America's whaling fleet, Reedville was the center of the menhaden fleet. The use of steamships, and then later of airplanes and diesel engines, changed and enhanced the fishery, and Reedville has remained one of the largest fishing ports along the Atlantic Coast. Despite the international importance of this port, Reedville is still a small town, tucked snugly between two fingers of the creek, allowing the kayaker to view many of the town's historic homes from the water.

Trip Description

The landing is on a small finger of Cockrell Creek, and you need to head left/west to paddle out toward the main creek. There was an osprey nest directly across from the landing, and these hawks will accompany you for much of the paddle. When you reach the main creek, bear right to head upriver. Small planes may fly low above you as they land and launch from the small airfield to your right. These planes are instrumental in the fishery and take off whenever a menhaden ship heads out on the Bay. By flying low over the water, the planes can spot the large, dense schools of menhaden. They then radio the school's location to the ship's captain, directing them to their quarry.

After the airport, you will pass the Oceana menhaden refinery on the right, with its distinctive spiraled smokestack. While Reedville has been host to dozens of different menhaden companies, Oceana now holds the monopoly. In 2001 Oceana was the most productive nongovernmental processing facility in the world. They own the current factory on the right/east side of the creek, along with the old factory on the left/west side of the creek. I stayed alongside the east shore on my way upcreek, and then paddled past the old factory on the west bank on my way back down the shore. It is important to pick one side or the other because the center of Cockrell Creek is relatively busy with powerboats. Weekday traffic is dominated by the large menhaden ships and by watermen in their small diesel-powered workboats. The weekend brings an increase in waterborne tourists to the area, with numerous sailboats and powerboats plowing up and down the center channel.

The menhaden fishery is active from May through October, and you will likely see boats at the piers every day during these months. Take the time to pause and watch the operation, but remember that the crew is working hard, so do not make them nervous by drifting too close to their boats. You can take a closer look at the inactive fishing ships that are across the creek at the old factory on the way back down the creek. The fish are vacuumed out of the hold and into the refinery. They are cooked and then squeezed by giant screw presses, separating the solid from the liquid. The solid fish meal is used as a high-protein animal feed and fertilizer. The fish oil is used in cosmetics and cooking. Europe has long prized fish oil as a cooking ingredient, and menhaden products account for 40 percent of the United States fish export. The FDA has only recently approved the nutritionally rich fish oil as a food product in the U.S., a policy change that has served as an additional boon to the local economy. Menhaden are also used throughout the Bay as a baitfish for crab pots and as the churned-up chum that charter boats scatter behind them to attract the sport fish for their clients.

The long brick structure and smokestack of an old refinery is on the inside corner as the creek makes a significant bend to the right/east. While you may have smelled the Oceana menhaden refinery, the odor is much less pungent now than it used to be when this brick smokestack was in use. Not only does the new factory's chimney have scrubbers to clean the oil and smell from the smoke, it is significantly taller than the old smokestack, thus releasing the smell higher in the air and away from the noses of the town's residents. The ruins of another brick smokestack stand on the northern/outside corner of the bend, along with the remnants of the pier of a long-gone refinery. As you paddle around the bend, you'll see the town's water tower straight ahead, and the main flow of the creek goes to the left. However, it is worth exploring the right side of the creek, and the right side of the town of Reedville. The Cockrell Creek Deli is situated at the top point of the first side-creek on the right. It is a full-service fuel dock, seafood market, and crab house. While their dock is too high for kayakers, there is a small beach just north of the store with a sign that says PETS ARE WELCOME. Since I place pets and kayakers in the same category, I regard this as an excellent (and easy) place to pull up your boat to visit the deli. Just make sure you pull your kayak well above a rising tide. The deli has dozens of picnic tables and Adirondack chairs on the back lawn, and they will provide you with excellent sandwiches or set you up with a traditional Chesapeake Bay crab feast. However, you may want to explore the rest of the creek before you tuck in to a long meal, taking advantage of the deli's hospitality on your way back downstream.

Reedville is directly across the finger of water from the deli. Many of the waterside homes date back to the late 1800s and early 1900s and were the homes of the menhaden captains. For three generations, the same family has operated the small marine railway that is just up the cove from the water tower. Below the water tower are the old pilings of a tomato packinghouse, an industry that used to supplement the local economy. The Steamboat Wharf Seafood Company is on the eastern side of the town's point, and was, as the name indicates, built on top of an old steamboat dock. Past that company is the Crazy Crab restaurant, and on the northwestern side of the point's corner is the Pride of Virginia Seafood Company. Both Steamboat Wharf and Pride of Virginia are active seafood packinghouses that service the local waterman community, buying their catch and selling it to the larger markets. Although I was on the water at 8 A.M., some watermen were coming in to unload the fish from their pound nets at the Pride of Virginia dock, wrapping up their morning workday, which began well before dawn. Another waterman worked his small Chesapeake dead rise boat, pulling up crab pots that he had set throughout Cockrell Creek.

This whole point of land used to be occupied by the original Reed factory, and the tall Queen Anne–style house that is just up the cove from the Steamboat Wharf Seafood Company was built by Elijah Reed's son, George. There are many more captains' homes on the other side of the cove, on the sheltered northwestern side of town. As you paddle up the cove, you will be heading toward the brick Bethany Methodist Church, which was built in 1901. Just south of the church is the Reedville Fishermen's Museum, which is housed in several historic homes. The museum is unmistakable because their dock houses some of their restored fleet of boats, including their skipjack the *Claude W. Somers* and their Chesapeake bay boat, the *Elva C.* The museum supports a large boat restoration effort, which is directed by Jay Rohmann, an avid Chesapeake kayaker. There are always numerous restorations and replicas being built in the busy warehouse, and the *Claude* and the

Menhaden fishing fleet

Elva are in excellent condition. The museum also has a gallery of exhibits about the local fisheries, especially about the menhaden industry, and gives tours of the beautifully restored William Walker House. The *Elva C.* takes out periodic early morning tours to follow the watermen as they tend their pound nets.

The entrance fee for the museum is only $3 for adults and is well worth the price of admission. The only question is how to get from your kayak to the museum. The museum staff used to welcome kayakers to land in the marsh by their dock, but their neighbors have begun to complain about this activity. So you can hail a staff member from your boat and ask permission to land there, or you can paddle back to the town's point. Tucked between the Steamboat Wharf Seafood Company and the Crazy Crab is a small gravel ramp. The ramp belongs to the restaurant, but it is generally acceptable to land here. However, be courteous, and if the restaurant is open, stop inside to ask permission to leave your boat while you stroll into town. Landing here will also give you a chance to see the town's beautiful homes from both the watermen's and landlubbers' perspectives. Be sure to take a walking guide brochure from the museum, which provides an informative history of over 20 homes in the historic district.

There is still much more paddling to be done once you have finished touring and touring the town and paddling its shoreline. As you head up the main creek, the houses on the left and right banks are fairly spread out, with numerous coves to wander in and explore. I saw herons, egrets, geese, kingfishers, and cormorants during my paddle upstream. The houses on the left/west side give way to farms for a while, with fields that are lined with a thin creekside buffer of trees. There is an E-shaped cove indentation into the farm fields with thin, brown sand beaches between the trees and water, across the creek from a point with a loblolly pine and gazebo. I found this a convenient place to land after spending a relaxed hour exploring the rest of the coves in the upstream portion of the creek.

After the cove, houses reappear on both sides of the creek; however, as the creek narrows, the homes grow smaller and more recessed, and the depth of the woods increases. For the last ¼ mile, the individual houses disappear entirely, and you'll see an occasional small pier on the left and a picturesque farm on the right. Unlike many creeks in the Bay, Cockrell ends rather abruptly at a salt marsh without the usual wandering and tapering off of navigable water. It would have been a peaceful spot for reflection, except that as I approached the end of the creek, my presence caused a black rat snake to stir. It was draped along a dead tree limb about 12 feet above the water, and as it moved the entire limb gave way, sending branch and snake crashing to the water. This crash in turn drove the farmer's dogs into a frenzy, and I quickly left that spot to the stunned snake and the barking dogs.

I paddled along the western side of the creek on my way back to the landing. The Tangier Island Ferry leaves from the marina that is across the creek from the old brick smokestack. The old menhaden factory is south of the marina, with a tall black smokestack, big warehouses, hangers, and conveyor belts, all in various states of disrepair. The refinery's docks are used to house some of the inactive and current ships of Oceana's fleets. They are large military-looking ships painted a uniform battleship gray. This military appearance is not coincidental because many menhaden boats are in fact old navy minesweepers. Although large schools of menhaden are caught in the Chesapeake, the names of these boats, such as the *Atlantic Breeze,* speak of the wider-ranging voyages these ships undertake to catch their prey. Two boats hang off either side of the active ships, and these smaller tenders are used to set the purse seine net. They are deployed after the airplane pilot radios a school's location, and then the two boats rapidly separate, each spooling out the purse seine from their sterns. They make a complete circle around the school, thus closing the net. They then cinch the net up, slowly gathering it in hand over hand until all the fish are contained in a smaller portion of the net called the bunk, hence the fish's local nickname, "bunker." The large ship then comes alongside and lowers a vacuum into the bunk and sucks out all of the fish. I once had the opportunity to board a menhaden ship as it was sucking up its catch, and the sight was absolutely stunning. Thousands upon thousands of fish filled the hold, all purely menhaden with absolutely no bycatch of other fish. A single seine can pull in a 300,000-pound catch.

If you still have energy and time to burn, you can paddle out to the Bay, which is about 1 mile south of the landing cove. The billboard on the right advertises the Reedville Buzzards Point Marina, welcoming all boaters to Cockrell Creek. Do not be fooled by what appears to be a lighthouse to the left. It is actually a creative sunroom built as a replica of a lighthouse on the end of a large home's dock. However, if you still have time for kayaking out on the bay, you likely did not eat enough crabs at Cockrell's and should seriously consider turning your boat around for another go at the picnic table.

Alternative Trips

There is some excellent wilderness paddling to be had at the northwestern reaches of the Great Wicomico River. There is a boat landing at the end of VA 707 (off VA 360). From there you should paddle upriver to the Bush Mill Stream Natural Area Preserve. The wetlands are lush and the forests are deep, and you will be well removed from most signs of civilization. Ferries leave from Reedville for both Tangier and Smith Islands. The *Chesapeake Breeze* leaves from the sailboat marina daily at 10 and returns at 3:30 (804-453-BOAT). The *Captain Evans* leaves from the Reedville KOA Kampground and heads to Smith Island (804-453-3430). See the Onancock Alternative Trip (page 244) for more information about Tangier, and see *Sea Kayaking in Maryland's Chesapeake Bay* for more information on Smith Island.

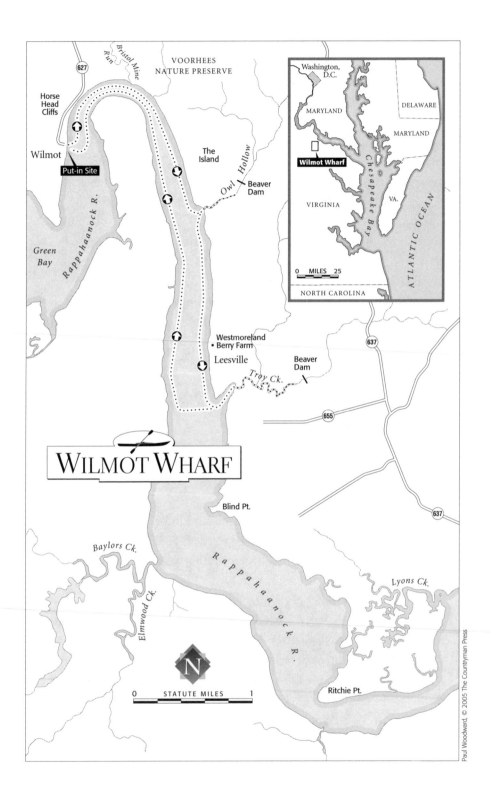

6.

Wilmot Wharf

Features: Cliffside paddling, bald eagles, autumn foliage, Westmoreland Berry Farm, and hiking at the Voorhees Nature Preserve.

Length: 10 miles.

Put-in site: The launch is a public landing at an old steamboat
wharf and brick factory. Its location does not appear on the
usual boat landing guides, save one map that shows it containing only a fishing pier and no ramp. However, it is a full-service launch with a small gravel ramp, plenty of parking, and a
port-a-john. As all maps and guides are somewhat fallible, it
never hurts to follow roads that end at the water—you might
get lucky with an excellent boat landing such as this.

Directions: If traveling from the west, follow VA 3 for 6 miles east of
US 301, and then take a right on County Route 681 (CR 681)/
Rollins Fork Road. Follow for 0.3 mile and then take a right on
CR 627/Wilmot Landing Road. Follow for 2.5 miles to the
landing, bearing left in about 1 mile in order to stay on Wilmot. If
you are traveling west on VA 3, take a left onto CR 627. In 0.3
mile take a left to stay on CR 627/Wilmot Landing Road.

IN THE AGE OF THE RAILROAD, the Chesapeake Bay was the domain of
steamboats. Owned by the railroad companies, these boats were an extension of their lines and the easiest way to travel around Virginia. Every
river had numerous steamboat wharves, and this paddle travels between
the wharves of Wilmot and Leesville. Wilmot was the site of a brick factory, and steamboats were employed to transport its product to market.
Leesville was a typical ferry wharf, used for transporting all the mail and

goods of the community, and the general store attached to the wharf was the local gathering place. Not only were the ferries a practical means of transportation, but a ferry ride was also an excursion in its own right, with people coming from as far as Baltimore and Norfolk to travel through the graceful landscape of the Rappahannock River Valley to the riverside town of Fredericksburg. While all the ferries are now gone, the river remains in all its beauty. It is a scenic place to paddle any time of the year but is particularly stunning in the autumn, when the surrounding forests make the shorelines glow with color.

Trip Description

Paddle left from the launch to head downstream. The tidal current is fairly strong. You can paddle against it, but it is nice if you can time your trip to correspond with the tides. I paddled this route with my friend Lee Gardner, and we lucked into catching the tide in both directions, resulting in a pleasurable paddle with very little effort exerted. Just downriver of the riprap of the landing you can see remnants of the wharf's past, with hundreds of bricks spilled all over the shoreline. Many of the pale red-and-yellow bricks are still in good shape, with the Wilmot stamp still legible on them.

The cliffs of the left bank echo the colors of the bricks, with tones of red and blond. The right/southwestern bank is cloaked with low-lying swamp, marsh, and forest land, with all three ecosystems merging indiscriminately. There are occasional homes high above on the cliffs, but it is mostly a wild landscape on both sides of the river. We began to see bald eagles within minutes of leaving the landing. An immature eagle took flight from directly over my head—so close that I could hear the rustle of its feathers and the creaking of the branch as the large bird took off, relieving the limb of its weight. The mature eagles were more wary, taking flight before we were within 100 feet of them. While I have seen many eagles around the Bay, I have never paddled a location where they were so prevalent or active. Eagles soared above us for the entire duration of our paddle, serving as our guides for the day.

Since this is a there-and-back trip, you can paddle alongside one shoreline in the morning and the other on the return trip, leaving the

Cliffside paddling near Owl Hollow

center of the river to the powerboaters. We chose to paddle under the shadow of the cliffs on our way downstream so we could explore any side creeks that looked interesting. About 1 mile from the landing, at the end of the river's sharp bend to the south, you will pass a long sloping lawn leading to a small private dock. Bristol Mine Run is just upstream of the dock but is impassable due to fallen trees.

About 1 mile from Bristol Mine Run, the north shore of the river doglegs slightly northeast and then back again southeast. The cliff here is mostly bare, towering at least 100 feet above the river, and the entrance to Owl Hollow is just beyond that wall. In the summer months you will need to push past the spatterdock (yellow pond lily) by the entrance but will be rewarded by clear water just beyond that. Head underneath the wooden footbridge and into a healthy freshwater marsh where spatterdock, pickerelweed, tear thumb, and wild rice grow. Frogs were hopping and croaking all around us as we paddled about ⅓ mile up the hollow until we were stopped by a nicely constructed beaver dam. Contrary to popular belief, beavers do not live in the dam, but rather build it to control and shape their living environment. They build their lodge in the pond that the dam creates; the constant water level ensures that the entrance to their house will remain safely underwater, away from the reach of predators. With this system, they can also swim beneath the ice during a cold winter, freely getting to their underwater food caches of branches (beavers primarily eat tree bark).

When we left the hollow, we saw a strange shape swimming on top of the water. Upon closer investigation, we discovered that it was a northern water snake with a fish trapped in its jaws. The snake was working at rotating the fish around so that it could swallow the still-flapping fish head first. Then a beaver surfaced a few yards later and swam along with us for a short way downstream. It is these sorts of encounters that make each paddle a new experience. You never know what you will see, but the more you get out on the rivers, the better chance you will have to see just about everything.

The dock for the Westmoreland Berry Farm is about 1 mile downstream from Owl Hollow. The dock has three long benches framing its outermost section and is built on the site of the old Leesville steamboat ferry dock. Although the wooden dock is too high for kayaks, you can land your boat on the small, brown sand beaches to the south of the structure. The farm is open to the public, and you are welcome to sit on their dock to eat your brown-bag lunch. Or, you can pack some money and walk up the little hill from the river to the shore. Be sure to pull your boat above the high-tide line, or tie it to a tree for even greater assurance that you will have a boat to return to. Once you walk up the small bluff behind the dock, you will see the farm's fields in front of you, and the farm's store is ½ mile to your left. A towering structure of long skinny ramps and platforms frames the driveway by the store, serving as home for the goats that reign high above, keeping an eye on all that goes on. Not only can you buy the farm's signature jams, syrups, fruits, and berries at the store, you can also purchase your lunch or dessert here. While the menu is limited, you cannot beat the cheap price of their barbecue, and their ice cream sundaes come topped with the farm's own berries.

A talented goat at Westmoreland Berry Farm

The owner of the farm is Alan Voorhees, who originally bought the land from the Leesville Wharf to Wilmot Wharf as a real estate investment. He subsequently hired Chuck and Anne Geyer as farm managers, who placed about 150 acres under cultivation. He left the rest of his acreage in its natural state of forest and wetlands, donating about half of it to the Nature Conservancy and giving Wilmot Wharf to the state to create the public boat launch. The wooden footbridge on Owl Hollow is part of a series of hiking trails that leave from the farm, providing up to 6 miles of hiking in wandering routes. Mr. Voorhees's good stewardship and conservation of his land created an important centerpiece in a string of protected lands along the river, called the Rappahannock River Valley National Wildlife Refuge. The protection of this lush riverside is what allows for such a safe and fertile home for the bald eagles.

We paddled downstream from here, past the white house on the point and into Troy Creek. The white house has a beautiful, small wooden deck built down the hill from it, right over the water. While it had a picnic table when we passed it, it is a registered duck blind. Only steps away from the warmth and comfort of the house, it is the most convenient duck blind that I have seen in all my years on the Chesapeake.

You will pass a farm and another duck blind on your right as you paddle into Troy Creek. There are several more blinds along this waterway; so during hunting season, be wary of paddling this creek, avoiding it during morning and evening hours. That way you will not frustrate hunters by scaring away their prey, and you will also avoid the tragedy of catching a low shotgun blast. Despite the material, Kevlar kayaks are hardly bullet-proof.

We startled numerous ducks and geese and watched a few more eagles fly as we meandered about 1 mile upstream. The upper section of the creek was surrounded by lush freshwater marsh, and the creek itself was filled with dense mats of coontail, a common type of submerged aquatic vegetation, with small killifish minnows swimming and living along the edges of the grass. The passageway steadily narrows, and then becomes choked with spatterdock until navigation ends with a beaver dam.

Although there was much more river to paddle downstream, the tide had shifted and we were saturated with beauty. There will always be more rivers to paddle, more creeks to explore, and more wildlife to see. As for Lee and I, we were content to float back to the landing on the rising tide, drifting alongside the swamplands, watching eagles fly and fish swim.

Alternative Trips

The Rappahannock has endless water to explore but few public places to get onto the river. You can launch upriver in Port Royal and investigate the area up and downriver from the US 301 bridge. Cat Point Creek, south of Wilmot, is accessible through the campground of Heritage Park Resort. Totuskey Creek is below that, accessible via a public boat launch by the VA 3 bridge. All locations are well worth paddling. For more information about current or future landings on the Rappahannock Water Trail, call 540-373-3448 or visit www.riverfriends.org.

7.
Belle Isle

Features: Brackish marsh, hawks, woodpeckers, and bald eagles. Small creeks combined with the open water of the Rappahannock.

Length: 8½ miles (with much more available).

Put-in site: Belle Isle State Park, 1632 Belle Isle Road, Lancaster, VA 22503, 804-462-5030. Belle Isle is a 700-acre state park that was established in 1992. It does not have any camping facilities, but there are two houses for rent: the Bel Air Mansion, which sleeps six, and the Bel Air Guest House, which sleeps eight. There is a $3 fee per car on weekends ($2 on weekdays). The car-top launch site is at the end of a small cul-de-sac. You can park here temporarily for unloading and loading but then must move your vehicle to the parking lot (which is only 50 yards away). The launch has a low dock and a small, brown sand beach, and most kayakers will find it easier to use the beach.

While there are no bathrooms at the car-top landing, there are some in the park, at the day-use area, and at the trailered launch site. There is a short nature walk, boardwalk, and dock by the landing. Plenty of grills and picnic tables are located throughout the park, making this an easy place to combine a day of paddling with an afternoon of barbecuing. The park rents canoes and recreational kayaks for $6/hour, $12/half day, and $22/day.

Directions: The way to the park is clearly marked by brown park signs from both directions. From points east, take VA 3 West to Lively, and then turn left onto VA 201. Turn right on VA 354 at

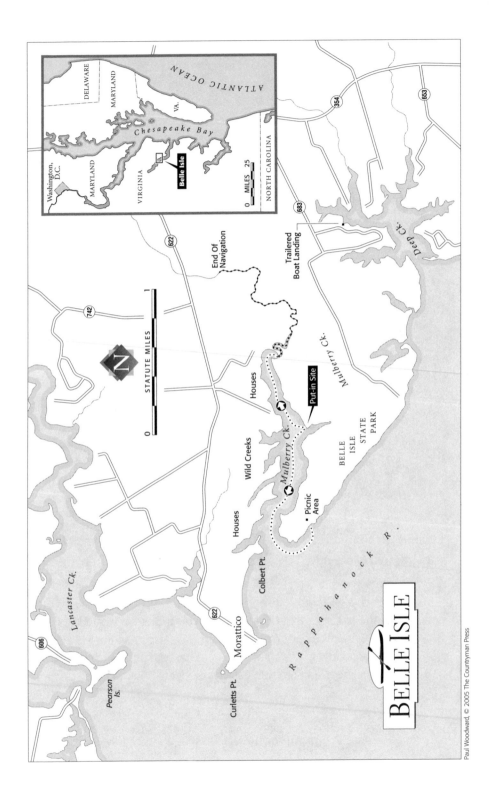

DELAWARE

MARYLAND

MARYLAND

Washington, D.C.

VIRGINIA

MARYLAND

Chesapeake Bay

VA.

ATLANTIC OCEAN

Belle Isle

NORTH CAROLINA

0   MILES   25

354

653

622

683

End Of Navigation

Trailered Boat Landing

Deep Ck.

742

N

STATUTE MILES

0   1

Houses

Mulberry Ck.

Put-in Site

Wild Creeks

Houses

Mulberry Ck.

BELLE ISLE STATE PARK

Picnic Area

Lancaster Ck.

Colbert Pt.

606

622

Morattico

Pearson Is.

Curletts Pt.

Rappahannock R.

BELLE ISLE

Paul Woodward, © 2005 The Countryman Press

St. Mary's White Chapel. At County Route 683 (CR 683), turn left and follow the road into the park. From points west, take VA 3 East. Turn right on VA 354, and then turn right on CR 683 and follow this into the park. Once you are past the park gate, follow the signs to the car-top launch, taking a right by the park office and following the road as it wraps its way down to the water.

THE BELLE ISLE PENINSULA is ideally situated on the northern shore of the tidal Rappahannock River, 10 miles upriver of the beautiful town of Urbanna. With its combination of high wooded ground, deepwater creeks, and protected coves of marshland, the peninsula has likely been populated for thousands of years. When colonists settled here in the 1600s, they supplanted the Powhatan confederacy tribe, the Moraughtacunds, and replaced their village with a plantation. Belle Isle was farmed for the next 400 years, until the state saved it from becoming a housing development by purchasing the peninsula in 1992. Much of Belle Isle continues to be farmed, but the forest buffers and marshes are left to flourish, providing a green habitat for hundreds of species of plants, birds, mammals, and reptiles.

Trip Description

The car-top launch places you on Mulberry Creek, with the open Rappahannock toward the left/west. Begin your trip by heading the opposite direction, paddling to the right/east, toward the inland wanderings of the creek's headwaters. Belle Isle State Park protects 7 miles of shoreline, including all of the southern shore of Mulberry Creek. The northern shore has a scattering of houses, and many of these homes have osprey platforms built in front of their property. There are peeler crab traps along both shores, with a fence of chicken wire leading out in the water to a wire cage. Be careful not to paddle over them at high tide, or you could end up damaging both the trap and your kayak.

In ½ mile you will reach an area where the creek appears to end in a cove, and there is a group of houses bunched along the northern shore. This is just a false end to the creek, and you actually have two passages beyond this cove. The creek's natural flow bends to the south, so bear right along the shore and paddle toward the tree line of Belle Isle. It is shallow, so be careful to stay with the main channel, which runs diagonally toward the bend. The water deepens around the hairpin bend, then the creek wraps back to the west. The water is still shallow here, and the channel once again runs diagonally along the broad meander. When you reach the houses on the northern shore, you will see the creek's other passage on your left, which is a channel that has been dug along the northern bank to bypass the long meander, bringing deep water to the houses' docks. This man-made passage has redirected most of the tidal current's power and is likely the reason that the water in the natural meander is so low.

The creek once again bends to the right/south, away from the houses, and then straightens and deepens along the wooded banks of Belle Isle. After about 100 yards of straight, southeastern flow, the creek begins to wander again and immediately diminishes to a quarter of its width. Bend after bend the creek narrows and narrows, and you leave all civilization behind. There is no human noise here, just beauty. A red-tailed hawk soared above me, and a pileated woodpecker flew onto a tall dead tree. Beside the woodpecker's perch was another dead tree that hung over the creek, creating an arched gateway to paradise. The world beyond is a wilderness of woods and marsh.

The bends increase as the creek plunges deeper into the brackish marsh valley, and fast kayakers will find trouble as they overshoot the turns and mire their bows deep in the mud and grass. Slow down and work on leaning your boat while turning. Paddle quietly. The creek narrows so much that your blades are paddling grass instead of water. But, impossibly, the creek continues onward, and so did I, cheered on by the beauty until I finally became wedged in the marsh about 2 miles from the landing.

This is the place for stillness. I propped my feet on my deck, pulled out my binoculars, and watched the world. Minutes passed, and the birds resumed their business. Rails chattered in the marsh and I watched as the red-tailed hawk reappeared above me, hunting the marsh for his lunch. I could hear the woodpecker a mile away, hammering on his tree, and sparrows and blackbirds flew all around.

The river valley is filled with a classic, healthy brackish/saltwater marsh. The subtle changes of elevation, from 2 to 6 inches above sea level, result in a change of species. The grass along the water's edge is the dominant salt-marsh cordgrass, which is also commonly known by its Latin name, *Spartina alterniflora.* This green, tapering 2-foot-tall grass dominates marshlands, and each blade provides a home for up to a half dozen periwinkle snails. Touch the grass to your tongue, and you will taste salt. The grass filters the water of the creek, transforming salt water to fresh, and secreting the excess minerals from its cells. On slightly higher ground, 1 to 2 inches above the cordgrass, grows black needle rush. Unlike the flat-leafed grass, black needle rush is round and sharply pointed. The contrast between the olive-black coloration of the rush and the green-yellow cordgrass defines the brackish and saltwater marshes. However, there are several more species growing upland of these two dominant forces. One of these, the aptly named big cordgrass, towers overhead with its strong, 10-inch-long flower head plume. This cluster is called a panicle, and its green summer coloring turns tan in the autumn. Less visible to the kayaker is the salt meadow hay, which lies low to the ground several inches above

The headwaters of Mulberry Creek

Osprey

Osprey live all over the world, from Europe to South America to Asia, but the highest concentration of these agile hawks is in the Chesapeake Bay, which has over two-thousand mating pairs. It is an exception *not* to see an osprey during a summertime paddle. Their large nests are visible everywhere you look, on duck blinds, channel markers, nesting platforms, and even on top of the osprey's natural habitat—dead trees. They are easy to identify, because they are the only hawk with a primarily white underside, with black backs and black eye bands, and their wings are distinctly pointed at the mid-point, creating an M shape when they fly. You can often hear them before you see them, as they chirp their loud *kee-yoo* cry, sounding like an overgrown songbird.

The osprey eats only live fish, thus earning the nickname of *fish hawk.* They have keen eyesight and hover up to 100 feet over the water searching for fish below. When they spot their target, they fold their wings back, plunging headfirst toward the water. They flip position at the last second, hitting the water feet first, so they can deftly spear the fish with their sharp talons. Osprey sometimes submerse themselves entirely during this plunge, while other times they only get their claws wet. As they fly back out of the water, the proud birds flip the fish so that it faces head first into the wind, allowing for an easier flight back to the nest or a nearby branch.

the black needle rush. The salt meadow hay and big cordgrass are all members of the same *Spartina* family, and all of these grasses are important food and habitat for the native Chesapeake birds and other animals.

It is a 4-mile round trip, upstream and back, from the kayak landing. This can be the perfect length for beginners or birders, or if you are just in the mood for a short paddle. However, if you want to paddle farther, there is plenty more to see along Belle Isle.

Mulberry Creek continues to broaden as you head west toward the Rappahannock. Along the northern shore, the first two side creeks on the way out are wild and worth exploring. They are microcosms of the headwaters of Mulberry, with even more healthy marsh and more visible beds of salt meadow hay. This soft hay can be a fun break spot,

Like most bird species, osprey are monogamous and stay with the same partner for life. They mate in the spring and then work together rebuilding the same nest year after year. Once the eggs are laid, the female will not leave the nest because to do so would leave the eggs vulnerable to snakes, raccoons, and the elements. Instead, she is dependent upon her mate to bring her food. Osprey are extremely tolerant of humans, but they are much more sensitive and protective against human encroachment during the spring breeding season. During April, while the eggs are in the nest, the female will rise up onto her talon tips and scream at you, but if the eggs have hatched, she will fly up and more aggressively warn you away from her nest. The male will also warn you away from his family, and besides screaming his angry chirp, he will fly back and forth across the water, dragging his talons with a show of force. He will even dive on you if you do not take the hint and paddle away from his home.

Young osprey grow from little balls of fluff to acrobatic fliers in a short eight weeks, leaving the nests empty by July. All of the Chesapeake's osprey migrate south in the autumn, leaving shortly after Labor Day for Central and South America. After working together all spring and summer to raise their families, the parents take separate vacations and will not see each other all winter. But, every spring, right around St. Patrick's Day, the osprey return to Virginia, reuniting for another six months of raising a family.

especially if you are with other people. Have one person jump while everyone else stands still, and you will feel the ground roll and shake beneath you. If you removed the grass, there would be no land beneath it. Marshes create their own land: the detritus they grow in is formed through their decomposition every winter. Their roots contain their detritus and trap the sediment that washes in from the upland areas, cleaning and filtering it before it ever reaches the water column, creating an important buffer between land and water.

The second two creeks are more populated but can also make for interesting paddles for those who want to engage in a thorough investigation of Mulberry Creek. Once you reach the open Rappahannock, head to the left/south to travel along the wild shore of Belle Isle. Just around the point, there is a shallow crescent cove, with a small beach and a grassy clearing above. There are two picnic tables here and a trash can, making this one of the most comfortable lunch spots you could ever hope to find.

There is a thin strip of marsh along this shoreline, which is backed primarily by pine forest. There are occasional sandy rest spots hidden among the marshland, and I saw an eagle roosted in a pine tree about ½ mile south of Mulberry Creek. Deep Creek is at the end of this 1½-mile-long stretch of open water, and you can add over 9 miles to your day by exploring all the various side creeks of this waterway. Or, you can choose to do what I did, and paddle the open shore for a while, and then head back to Mulberry Creek, content with an 8-mile paddle.

I did pursue one more diversion on my way back, which was to explore the small side creek that is just downstream from the landing. After about ¼ mile, the creek splits into two forks. While they do not look like they go far on a map, in reality these guts wrap back toward the woods in the center of the creek valley, enchanting you with their beauty so that you follow them ever deeper into the marsh. While I was traveling on the center fork, I tried to see how silently I could move, working so that I did not cause the smallest splash with my paddle. I was apparently successful because, as I swung around a bend, I nearly impaled a great blue heron on my bow, causing him to fly up with his loud, prehistoric pterodactyl squawking.

Alternative Trips

There is a boat landing at the end of CR 606 that provides access to Lancaster Creek, which is just upriver of Mulberry Creek. The upper section of this creek is stunning, but the lower section of the river is a popular boat cruising spot for vacationers staying all along the Rappahannock in riverside cottages.

8.

Fleets Island

Features: An island circumnavigation with miles of wild beach, expansive salt marshes, and a combination of open- and small-water paddling. Herons, egrets, brown pelicans, cownose rays, and terrapins.

Length: 9 miles.

Put-in site: This is a beach launch off a small community beach, which is open from sunrise to sunset. There is limited parking, but in such a remote area, the parking should be sufficient even on a beautiful summer weekend day. There are no facilities at the landing. About 2 miles before the beach, you will pass by a small bait shop that sells sodas, snacks, ice, bait, and so on. Just past this shop is the Camp Little Bay campground, which welcomes both RV and tent campers and is open from April 1 to November 30 (804-435-6455).

Directions: If traveling from the south, cross over the VA 3 bridge, and in about 1.5 miles, take a right onto County Route 695 (CR 695) in the small town of White Stone at the junction of VA 3 and VA 200, and follow it for 7.5 miles to the Bay. If traveling from the east, follow VA 3 south to White Stone, and at the traffic light take a left onto CR 695, and follow it for 7.5 miles to the Bay. Pay attention to the marsh to the left of the first bridge that you cross—that is your ultimate destination.

FLEETS ISLAND was named for Henry Fleete, who was a legislator in both Maryland and Virginia from 1633 to 1661. He lived and died on this island. During the War of 1812, the British also made their last raid

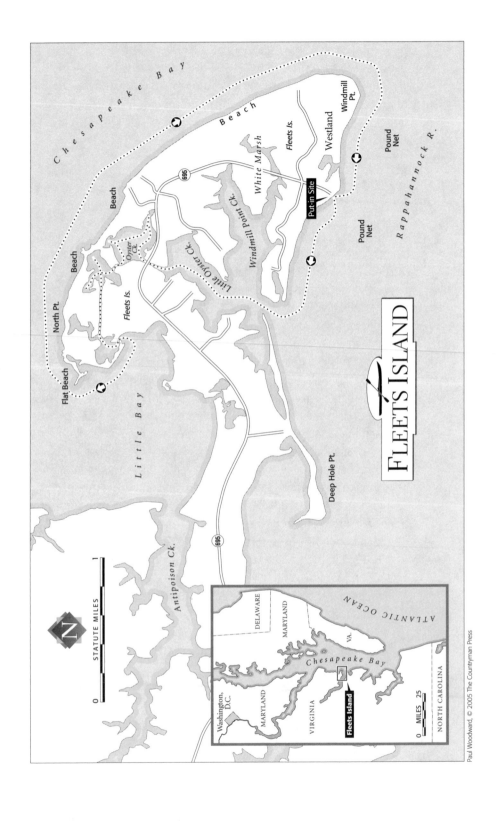

FLEETS ISLAND

in Lancaster County on this island, robbing a poor resident of all his worldly possessions. But this is all information you can learn from the historical markers by the beach. What is important about this trip is its beauty. The island is lightly populated, and for most of the circumnavigation, you will be paddling alongside wild Chesapeake beach or within wandering salt marsh, far away from any other boaters. The gut that allows passage all the way around the island does not even show up on most maps, and I would never have imagined that a circumnavigation was even possible if not for Jay Rohmann, the master boatbuilder of the Reedville Fishermen's Museum. It is this very sort of hidden trip that makes Chesapeake paddling so unique. With its soft edges and changing marshes, kayakers can paddle where there should be land and then find land where there should be water.

Trip Description

Over half of this paddle is on open water, so plan a route that will put the wind at your back for the end of the paddle. The wind was blowing from the north when I scouted, so I headed to the right from the landing, going west and then north in my clockwise circumnavigation of the island. There is a pound net immediately to the right of the landing. It stretches far out into the water, but there is a small space between the net and land that is deep enough and wide enough to provide passage for your kayak. Pound nets are installed, owned, and maintained by watermen and are permanent installations the locations of which are marked on navigational charts. It is an ancient and effective method of catching schools of fish that takes advantage of a fish's natural instincts. As fish move up or down the Chesapeake, they generally turn out to deeper water to move around an obstacle. When they meet the long net and swim out toward the open Bay to avoid it, they end up following it and swimming into a heart-shaped funnel. Confounded about how to swim back the way they came, the fish continue to search for a way into deeper water, thus making their way into a square false pound. Once in this enclosure, they have one more funnel to try to escape through, but this puts them into a second square pound. Here they wait, trapped until the waterman comes to fish them out. With this live catch method, fish that are too small or out of season can be separated, and only the keepers are transported to market. Most watermen visit their pounds early in the morning, so you need to be out paddling by sunrise if you want to watch them fish out their catch.

The southern shoreline is a 1-mile strip of beach, with summer cottages and houses overlooking the water. Most of the trees are loblolly, with one giant live oak near the point. Paddle toward the last stand of loblolly by the sandy point, go around the bulkhead, and follow the shoreline up toward the creek that separates the island from the mainland. There is a break in the bulkhead, with a small inlet behind the houses that shows on charts as a wetland. Then, the shore is riprapped. The Bay's bottom is firm sand, and the water is a clear green-blue—I could see my paddle blade even when its full 230 centimeters length was submerged.

The entrance to the creek is shallow, and a sandbar stretches nearly all the way across the point. There is deeper water near land, but kayaks can float over the sandbar during mid- to high tide. Straight ahead, to the northeast, is the wetland and loblolly-covered point that separates Little Oyster Creek from Windmill Point Creek. Windmill Point Creek is forested on all sides, with a salt-marsh buffer. Houses are scattered all around the creek.

As I paddled northeast into Little Oyster Creek, I scared up a half-dozen herons from the point. It is about 1 mile from the creek's mouth to the bridge, with houses dotting both edges. The current under the bridge can be strong, particularly during an ebbing tide, but paddle hard and push your way through to the other side of the bridge. This is your entrance to paradise. The water on the northern side of the bridge is called Oyster Creek, and aside from a couple of houses on the southern shore, this side of the creek is wild. You can see a white beach straight northeast from the bridge, and you can either paddle straight there, or do as I did and follow the right shoreline around to the beach. I watched egrets and kingfishers as I coasted along a lush salt marsh of cordgrass, black needle rush, and marsh elder bushes, which bloom with a silver-white flower from August through October.

Cownose Rays

If you spot two dorsal fins slicing through shallow brackish water, mere feet from your kayak, do not be alarmed. You have not stumbled into a real-life Jaws movie but have more likely come upon a cownose ray, cruising the shallows with wing tips exposed. Look sharply because rays swim in large schools, and you may soon be able to spot a dozen or more pair of wings dotting the water's surface. Rays live and feed in the shallows, rarely venturing into water deeper than 10 feet. You can paddle among them, watching as they patrol the muddy shallows in search of soft-shell crabs, completely oblivious to your passing as they knock and thud harmlessly on the hull of your boat in their single-minded pursuit of food.

The cownose ray is a cartilaginous fish, and thus is in the same class as sharks and skates. It has a broad wing disk formed by its two pectoral fins, with a wingspan of up to 3 feet, although more commonly between 2 and 3 feet. Its head rises above the wing disk, contains powerful, flat, grinding jaw plates, and vaguely resembles a cow's nose when viewed through squinted eyes. The ray's long, thin tail continues behind its body at a length that is slightly less than the width of its wings. There is a small dorsal fin on the base of the tail, along with two serrated venomous spines. However, despite this venom, rays are never aggressive or hostile. The only way to be injured by one is to handle it; thus fishermen are the only people that generally need to be wary of the fish's painful sting. The top of the ray is a smooth brown and the bottom is white, effectively camouflaging it when viewed from above or below.

Cownose rays are bottom-feeders, uncovering shellfish from the mud with their wings and then grinding them up in their jaw plates. They fill the Bay from May through October, schooling by sex and age and migrating as far north as Annapolis to birth their pups in early summer. The rays retreat to the ocean in late autumn, wintering in offshore waters. Several years ago a school of an estimated 5 million rays was spotted just offshore of the Chesapeake's mouth. The schools of up to a hundred rays that have passed underneath my kayak have left me dumbstruck but have not managed to capsize me. I do not think I'd have such luck among a million.

When my boat scraped up on the white sand of the beach, I knew I had arrived at the best beach in the Bay. It is crescent-shaped, with a steep slope and bleached white, soft sand. There is a scattering of grasses and shrubs on its flat crest, with a wind-sculpted bush that could have been a topiary carved by Dr. Seuss. A sole loblolly pine stood sentinel next to the strange bush. The open Bay is on the other side of the dune, with a long sand beach to absorb the crashing waves. After an hour of paddling against the stiff headwind, I fell upon this beach like I had been at sea for days. With my back against the warm, sloping bank, I enjoyed the sound sleep of someone who had arrived in paradise while the rest of the world was still stuck in a Monday-morning commute to work.

I finally coaxed myself back into action and paddled along the north shore, following it southward to the thin gut that leads to a small, protected bay. Here I found an even better beach than before—remote and out of sight of houses or the road; it is the secret cousin of the beach from the morning. The thoroughfare out to the Chesapeake is almost straight west from the entrance to this little bay and is only concealed by a small point of marsh. However, unless you are in a hurry to finish the paddle, take the time to explore some of the fingers of this creek. The guts and inlets wander throughout the salt marsh. One inlet on the northern shore nearly leads you back to the beach; other guts almost seem to lead you to the thoroughfare before tapering off into impenetrable mud.

Cordgrass bears the fruit of periwinkles, a type of snail that lives on this vegetation, moving up and down the stems of grass to escape predation by the blue crab. Periwinkles eat microscopic detritus and algae off the surface of their hosts. If you pluck one off its home and hum close to its shell, you can coax it to reach out and clasp onto your finger or your boat.

The thoroughfare is edged by salt marsh, and in ⅓ mile it opens up to wide water, with the open water of Little Bay to the left. There is a sand spit across this opening, with two poles marking the deepwater channel. Paddling northward along the shore, there is a half-moon small cove, with a white sand beach that envelops the island's point. The flat sand plateau was covered with gulls, bitterns, and pelicans. This beach is evidently a popular spot with powerboaters; a couple of beer cans and a tattered volleyball net lay scattered about on the flat sand. The water along here is as clear as before, with the shade and the color changing depending on the composition of the bottom—darkening to a deep blue over underwater grasses, and lightening to an aqua green over clear sand.

It is a little over 1 mile to North Point. From there you will paddle for about 3 miles southeast to Windmill Point. The entire exterior of Fleets Island is wild beach. As I paddled this section, I met long rolling waves, which were fun to surf as I made my way along the open Bay. Despite the waves and wind, the only time I came near to capsizing was when a cownose ray swam beneath me. While these rays are nonaggressive, the unex-

Periwinkles

pected sight of an animal directly beneath my paddle startled me enough to instinctively lunge in the opposite direction, nearly upsetting my boat. Windmill Point marks the northeastern side of the mouth of the Rappahannock River and is 4 miles to the north of the southern edge of the mouth, Stingray Point. Captain John Smith named the point after he speared a stingray and was subsequently stung.

After rounding Windmill Point, you will pass another pound net before crossing the inlet to the marina. Cormorants and gulls typically line the poles of these pound nets, and I watched as one brave pelican dove into the midst of the net, scooping up fish after fish in his private dining room. The landing beach is another mile from here, bringing to an end an enchanting 9-mile island circumnavigation. Fleets Island is a land where worlds meld. Aquatic and terrestrial merge, salt marsh blends with sandy beach, river blends with Bay, and water spills over land, creating passages where none should exist. I am glad that Jay Rohmann clued me in to its existence.

Alternative Trips

Gwynn's Island lies south of Stingray Point, on the southern tip of the mouth of the Piankatank River. It is one of the best known paddles in Mathews County and is a centerpiece of the "Mathews County Blueways Water Trail Guide." It is a larger, more populated version of Fleets Island, and the trip alongside its protected western shore brings the kayaker along a scenic watermen hamlet and past a wild landscape of marshes and beaches. You can launch on the island from the Milford Haven Landing at the Seabreeze Restaurant on the right after crossing over the island's bridge. Or, you can paddle the mainland side of the area by launching southwest of the island at White's Creek Landing, (the end of CR 682), or from Haven Beach Landing (the end of CR 643).

Part II — Middle & Lower Peninsula

9.

Piscataway Creek

Features: Tidal freshwater marsh, hawks, eagles, herons, and excellent fishing.

Length: 8 miles.

Put-in site: This is a small, informal landing with a gravel ramp and very limited parking. The creek empties into the Rappahannock 2.5 miles downstream of historic Tappahannock, with nearby hotels, bed & breakfasts, and camping.

Directions: Follow US 17 South, 2.5 miles south of the town of Tappahannock and the VA 360/US 17 split. Cross over Piscataway Creek, and then take the first right, 0.1 mile south of the bridge, onto County Route 663 (CR 663)/Ferry Landing Road. Follow this for 0.1 mile and then stay straight on the gravel road for another 0.1 mile to the boat landing. If traveling from the south, slow down and get into the left lane when you are approaching the Piscataway Creek bridge, and take a left onto CR 663.

THIS IS A TYPICAL CHESAPEAKE RIVER: subtle in its beauty, astounding in its variety, and graceful in its slow tidal flow. The Piscataway is a tributary of the Rappahannock, which means "where the tide ebbs and flows," and even though the creek is many, many miles from the ocean, it is still influenced by the strong tidal pull of the Atlantic. Thus, every day the waters rise and fall, in six-hour cycles, with two high and two low tides a day. While the ocean's influence is strong enough to dictate

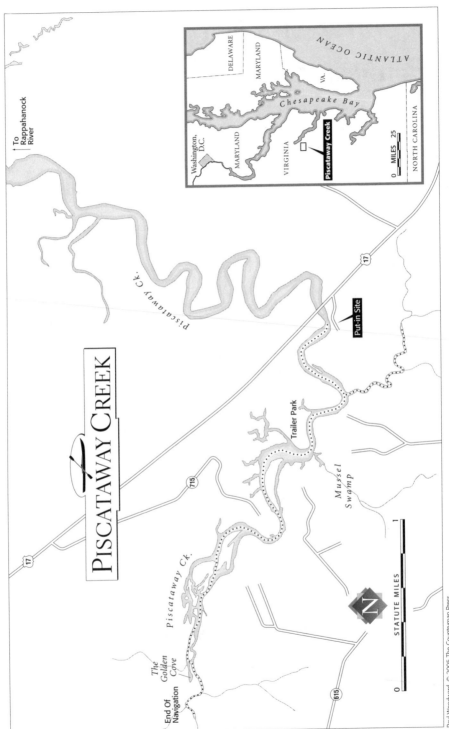

PISCATAWAY CREEK

To Rappahannock River

Piscataway Ck.

17

Put-in Site

Trailer Park

Mussel Swamp

715

Piscataway Ck.

The Golden Cove

End Of Navigation

17

615

N

STATUTE MILES

0   1

Washington, D.C.

MARYLAND

DELAWARE

MARYLAND

VIRGINIA

VA.

Chesapeake Bay

ATLANTIC OCEAN

Piscataway Creek

NORTH CAROLINA

0   MILES   25

Paul Woodward, © 2005 The Countryman Press

the tides, it is not powerful enough to taint the flow of freshwater that is pouring downstream, thus resulting in a unique ecosystem that overflows with life. With dozens of species of vegetation, the marsh's palate of colors is constantly shifting with the seasons; new flowers bloom from April through October. I wondered about this waterway for years as I drove between my house in Maryland and my sister's house in Norfolk, and longed for the time to stop and throw my boat into the water. The creek did not disappoint.

Trip Description

Bear left to paddle northwest, upstream and away from the US 17 bridge. There are a couple of houses on the southern shore by the landing, and also a couple on the northern side of the river. When the river bends to the left, it reveals a landscape of merging lines of marsh, forest, and water. After a small dock on the left side, as the river bends back to the northwest, you will pass the small opening to an inlet. This small creek is worth exploring, but I would recommend saving this exploration until the end of your trip. That way it will serve as a sweet dessert, leaving its wonder fresh in your mind as you finish your trip.

After passing the small creek, the river bends again and again, and there is an inlet off the top of each bend, with each gut framing in the point, enveloping the trailer park that is tucked away on the creek's shore. After the second inlet, you will pass an island of pickerelweed that is passable on either side. Like many Chesapeake waterways, the creek is enveloped with low-lying wetlands. The woods grow on the higher ground to frame the valley. The transition from low to high ground is subtle, with a 6-inch elevation change resulting in a new spectrum of species. Pickerelweed is a type of emergent vegetation that grows in the borderline, with stems that are rooted a foot or more underwater, but with leaves and flowers that live 1 to 2 feet above the water. They grow one dark-green, inverted heart-shaped leaf that is about 6 to 8 inches long and bear a blue-purple sprig of flowers from May through September. Ducks eat the seeds of the flowers, and muskrat eat their interconnected rhizome roots.

Pickerelweed is sometimes confused with two other emergent species, the arrow arum and the arrowhead—and if you look carefully, both plants can be found along the creek. As their name indicates, both of these species have arrow-shaped leaves. They are larger than pickerelweed, with arrow arum generally being the largest. Arrowhead has a distinctive white venation pattern, with all of the veins fanning out from where the stem joins the leaf. They also grow stalks of white flowers. While arrow arum is inedible to most animals, the arrowhead gained the nickname of duck potato for the nutritious tubers that grow from its roots, and the plant is an important food source for migratory waterfowl. Duck potato was also gathered and eaten by the Native American tribes in the region, such as the Rappahannock, who used to live all along the Rappahannock River Valley.

After passing another little dock, the river bends to the west and is passable on either side of a large marsh island. The land above the emergent vegetation is the middle marsh and is dominated by wild rice, which is the primary food of red-winged blackbirds. Native Americans used to harvest this wild crop by canoeing into the marsh and shaking the rice into their boats. Many other species intermingle with the rice, creating a well-balanced ecosystem. The sprawling vines of the triangle-leafed tear thumb are particularly noticeable. The plant is descriptively named, because what looks like a soft furry covering on the leaves and vines is actually thousands of little barbs that can easily rip the skin.

After the marsh island, the creek bends back to the north. The forested land on the southern shore falls away, opening up a wide pasture of wetland that explodes with yellow flowers in autumn. The non-poetically named sneezeweed, which has small flowers with delicate yellow petals and brown centers, enveloped and overwhelmed the borders of the creek with its sunniness. While the marsh is wild and healthy, there are constant small reminders of humans on the creek. Several small docks line the water's edge; and after passing the marsh island, there are two radio towers visible in the distance. There is also a house on top of a hill on the right side, and the clear-cutting for some new construction had just begun along some of the left side. However, despite the human presence, the marsh vegetation grows more diverse

Piscataway Creek, where the tide ebbs and flows

and abundant with every bend; and despite the docks, I doubt that you will find many boaters on the creek even on a hot midsummer weekend. It is simply too narrow and winding for anybody but fishermen or paddlers to want to travel.

The passage dramatically narrows about ⅓ mile above the large marsh island and gets lost among a series of small marsh islands for the next ½ mile. Some sloughs are less than 2 feet wide, others, 20 feet. Some guts dead-end; others lead you in loops back to the main passage. The northern bank slopes steeply to the river, with little undergrowth below the dense canopy of trees. There is a partially submerged powerboat at the base of the hill, providing a foundation for more marsh vegetation. This hill is one of the few spots of dry land in the creek, so it can be a good place to get out for a rest on your way back down the creek. It is not posted as private, but be respectful of the land and obey any signs that you see.

After wandering among the little islands, I followed the right shoreline on my way upcreek, and struck gold. Waving fields of wild rice softly framed a small creek, with a sea of yellow flowers at its end. My passing discharged hundreds of red-winged blackbirds into the air, and they circled around me as I drifted into a round cove of golden flowers. The colors were as vivid as a Disney cartoon, and I was stunned into stillness by the absolute beauty. It was Shangri-la. My trip was complete.

While I had no hope of finding anything that equaled the beauty of my golden cove, I eventually backtracked to the main passage and continued to follow it upstream. It was still as beautiful as before, but now it paled in comparison with what I had just seen. My sadness at reemerging into the normal world was confirmed in 100 yards as I came abreast of a clear-cut on the left side. It has been replanted, but many years will go by before it has a canopy of trees, and that canopy will be a monotone sea of loblolly green.

My upcreek journey ended about 1 mile from the golden cove, where downed trees blocked the passage. However, the wonderful thing about there-and-back paddling is that once you paddle as far as the creek will take you, you still have at least half of your trip left to go, giving you twice the opportunity to truly see the world around you. On the way back downstream, I was able to lift my gaze from the dazzling sight of the wetlands to the majesty of the forest and the openness of the sky. Thus, I saw dozens of live oak that I had not noticed before and watched a northern harrier hunting the marsh. This small hawk, also known as a marsh hawk, is a fast and agile predator.

Before I ended my trip, I detoured up into the small creek that I had passed on my way upstream. After leaving behind the lone dock by the creek's mouth, I rounded the first bend and approached a fallen loblolly that nearly blocked the whole passage. The silence of the afternoon was broken by the cacophony of dozens of turtles plunging into the water at once. At least 30 turtles had coated the tree, but it was empty by the time I passed the tree's tip. Then, after following the creek around a couple of small bends, I rounded a tight hairpin from south to north and scared up a bald eagle from its roost. I made it about ¾ mile upstream before being stopped by an impenetrable raft of yellow pond lily. Also known as spatterdock, this is another common type of emergent vegetation, with each of the flat lily pads growing one yellow flower during the summertime. Like the pickerelweed and the arrow arum, spatterdock dies back during the winter, and thus it may be possible to paddle even farther that time of year, perhaps allowing passage all the way to the mill pond that lies another ¼ mile upstream. The creek's water was clear, with the long, thin strands of wild celery clearly visible beneath my boat. I had thought that I was saturated with more than enough beauty for one day. However, the small creek unveiled even more riches, proving that every side detour can be worth traveling, no matter how far it goes.

Alternative Trips

By land, the Colonial town of Tappahannock is less than 3 miles from the Piscataway Creek, but by water it is about 7 miles away. This can make for an ambitious there-and-back paddle or can be paired with a car shuttle. Leave a car at the boat landing on Hoskins Creek in the midst of Tappahannock, which means "the town that sits where the tide ebbs and flows." Or, for a different there-and-back trip, you can launch on Hoskins Creek and explore the waterfront of Tappahannock before heading upriver, which is like a shorter version of the Piscataway.

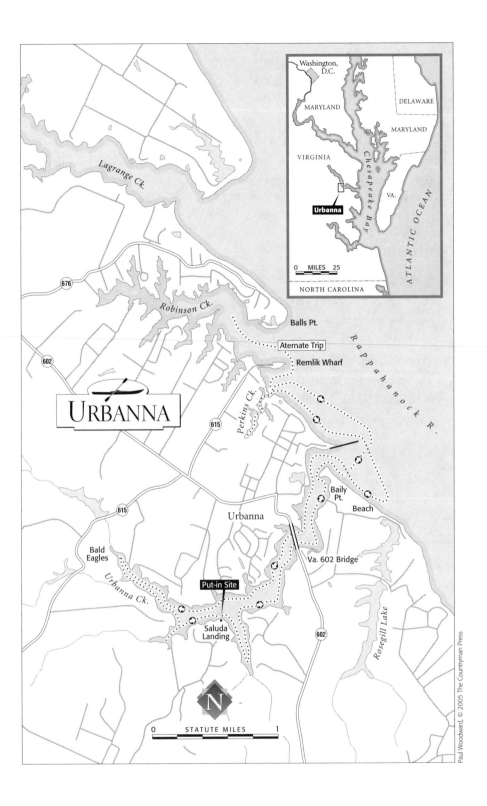

Washington, D.C.

MARYLAND

DELAWARE

VIRGINIA

MARYLAND

Chesapeake Bay

VA.

Urbanna

ATLANTIC OCEAN

NORTH CAROLINA

0   MILES 25

Lagrange Ck.

676

Robinson Ck.

602

Balls Pt.

Aternate Trip

Remlik Wharf

Rappahanock R.

URBANNA

Perkins Ck.

615

Baily Pt.

Beach

615

Urbanna

Va. 602 Bridge

Bald Eagles

Put-in Site

Urbanna Ck.

Saluda Landing

602

Rosegill Lake

N

0   STATUTE MILES   1

Paul Woodward, © 2005 The Countryman Press

10.

Urbanna

Features: Historic town, osprey, bald eagles, good swimming beach.

Length: 7 miles (with Perkins Creek, it is close to 10 miles).

Put-in site: Saluda public landing. There is limited parking by this sand-covered ramp and no bathroom facilities. There are bed & breakfasts in and around Urbanna, and the Bethpage Camp-Resort is a huge private campground in the area (804-758-4349).

Directions: If traveling on US 17 South, take a left at the junction with VA 33 onto County Route 618 (CR 618) at Saluda. If you are traveling north on US 17 from West Point, continue straight across the junction with VA 33 onto CR 618. Or, if you are traveling west on VA 33 from Mathews County, take a right onto CR 618. Follow CR 618 for 1.5 miles until it ends at the boat landing.

URBANNA IS A FAVORITE DESTINATION of many Virginians, and for good reason. It is a small, historic town, nestled along the water, with good restaurants, funky shops, a lot of antiques, and plenty of character. Every year about 75,000 Virginians pack the small town for the Urbanna Oyster Festival, a November tradition since 1958. (For information on the festival, visit www.urbannaoysterfestival.com.) Founded in 1680 by the Act of Assembly, this town was created as a tobacco port, and it remained a commercial center for many years. While its prominence as a trading harbor has faded, the town still retains a strong link with the water, as is evidenced by the sea of sailboat masts in the marinas below the CR 602 bridge. It is a populated creek, but that does not diminish its beauty. There are still wild creatures, clear water, and sandy cliffs, even in the middle of civilization.

Trip Description

Big, modern houses are scattered along both sides of the creek. Paddle straight away from the boat landing in order to head downstream. For populated creeks like this, it is best to paddle near the edge of the waterway, allowing powerboaters to have the center of the channel. Even if there are no boats around, the nearer you are to shore, the better chance you have of seeing animals. I stayed along the right/eastern shore for my paddle downstream and returned along the western shore.

In about 20 paddle strokes from the landing, you will be able to see the CR 602 bridge and the masts of the Urbanna sailboats. All houses on the right side fade away after you pass the short creek to the east of the landing. The shore is a series of small, brown sand beaches at the base of sloping, tree-covered hills. Houses continue along the left shore all the way to the bridge.

It is slightly less than 1 mile to the bridge, and once you pass under the bridge, you will be in the world of the sailboats. The Dozier Port Urbanna Yachting Center is on the west side of the creek, and the east side is covered with new homes, each with a corresponding marina below it. The amount of boat traffic can increase dramatically here, with both local sailors and transient boaters coming into the creek for the weekend. Stay well clear of the channel, and paddle along the edges of the marinas. Many of the boats are beautiful, and it is always fun to fantasy boat shop. Then, past the new homes on the east side, the Rosegill Farm remains, leaving the rest of the shoreline wild and forested after its faded white boathouse.

The water depth by the sandy tip of Bailey Point drops off steeply, allowing you to pass quite near this corner. There is a wide, wild beach all along the eastern side of the mouth of the creek, with a 20-foot-high cliff separating the beach from the farm. The Rappahannock's river

Sailboats in the historic town of Urbanna

bottom here is firm sand, and this is an excellent swimming beach, which is a worthy destination in itself. Powerboaters all over the Bay spend entire weekends anchored off beaches like this one. While we kayakers are devoutly logging mile after mile, they sit, contented to soak up the sun and swim in the clear waters. While I love paddling many miles, there are also some days when nothing feels quite as right as loading a camp chair, a book, and a collapsible cooler into my kayak and just paddling to a beach. This is one such spot. Between the point and the cliffs, there is a wide, flat section of beach, which is perfect for a game of sand soccer.

If you feel like paddling on the open river, there is plenty of water around here to explore. Paddle out beyond the long riprap breakwater that extends from the creek's western edge. When you reach the end of the breakwater, look both ways before crossing the channel that parallels it, and then cross over to paddle to the west of the breakwater and the creek. There were large herring gulls and cormorants all along the edges of the riprap, and as I rounded the breakwater's corner, a cormorant swam beneath my boat, surfacing to the right of me with a splash of his wings and giving us both a fright.

There are several creeks to explore to the west of Urbanna. I poked around into Perkins Creek, which had a narrow opening, was scattered with houses, and ended abruptly in a salt marsh. The next creek up, beyond the white Remlik Wharf building, is Robinson Creek, which is quite a bit larger, with a lot of finger creeks to explore. You could even continue farther upriver on the Rappahannock and explore Lagrange Creek. This creek is about twice the size of Urbanna Creek, with some beautiful wandering sections at the end. The choice is up to you and depends on how many miles you want to cover.

When you head back up Urbanna Creek, follow the western side for a change of scenery. There is a little inlet about ⅓ mile up the creek, and the tidal current can really rip through here during an ebbing tide. You need to duck low to pass under the bridge, and the inlet only leads to a small pond, but I like to squeeze into places like that, just because I can. It makes for a small, fun diversion.

After you paddle back up the creek, persevere past the lure of the landing and continue for another ⅓ mile. When the creek splits, follow the main body of water up to the right/west. There are a few more houses along the right/northern shoreline, but the southern shoreline is all forested. The creek narrows, and the wild beauty of this little waterway begins. After the last house on the right, the creek slims even more, and the wilderness increases. A mature bald eagle flew over my head and onto a branch that was already occupied by an immature eagle. They rose up and clashed in the air, grasping claws together and dropping out of the sky before releasing and resuming their mutual perches along the branch. A harrier hawk flew nearby, and then just a few hundred yards beyond the first two eagles, another flew in from the west. This is what makes suburban creeks so wonderful. You do not need to drive for hours to escape to the wild. Instead, right next door to houses and summer resorts, eagles and hawks go about their business, and as kayakers, we are lucky enough to be able to bear witness to it all.

I followed the creek all the way until it ended in a beautiful brackish marsh, just feet away from CR 616. The shorter northern branch of Urbanna Creek was beautiful as well, and I saw a fourth eagle while paddling alongside its broad marsh. I included Urbanna in this book for several reasons. First because of its association with the town, and every paddle on the creek should be paired with a stroll through Urbanna's streets. Second, it is an example of the beauty that can be found on a typical suburban creek. Despite the unique town inland of its shores, in all other ways the Urbanna Creek is the same as hundreds of other populated creeks in Virginia. It has houses scattered along its banks, sailboats and powerboats move up and down its center channel, and there are not magnificent forests or marshlands. Rather, the beauty is in the details. It is found in the bald eagles battling for territory, and in the cormorants swimming below the water's surface. This creek is just like the creek outside my back door, and that is my favorite waterway of all, because I can paddle it every day. Familiarity need not breed contempt; it can instead increase beauty and deepen love.

Alternative Trips

There are hundreds of little creeks, islands, and bays to explore all around Virginia, and on the lower Rappahannock, you can paddle in several anonymous creeks. Upriver from Urbanna, on the southern shore, you can launch on Parrots Creek from the landing at the end of CR 606 and explore such creeks as Harry George and Weeks. East of Urbanna you can launch in Whiting Creek from a small boat landing off VA 33. Just downriver of the VA 3 bridge is Parrot Island, which is sometimes called Peanut Island due to its nutlike shape. It is a fun little island to paddle around, with excellent fishing, and you can launch from the end of CR 626 onto the mouth of Mill Creek.

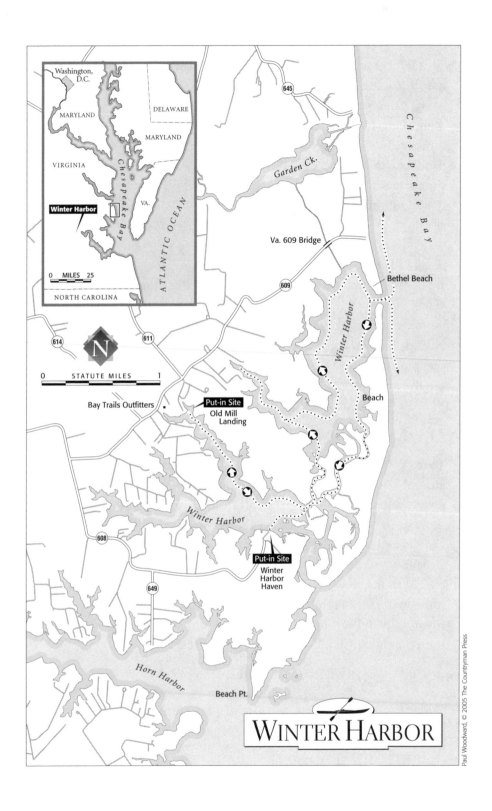

Washington, D.C.

MARYLAND

DELAWARE

MARYLAND

VA.

VIRGINIA

Chesapeake Bay

ATLANTIC OCEAN

Winter Harbor

NORTH CAROLINA

0   MILES   25

645

Garden Ck.

Chesapeake Bay

Va. 609 Bridge

609

Bethel Beach

Winter Harbor

Beach

614

N

611

0   STATUTE MILES   1

Bay Trails Outfitters

Put-in Site
Old Mill
Landing

Winter Harbor

608

Put-in Site
Winter
Harbor
Haven

649

Horn Harbor

Beach Pt.

WINTER HARBOR

11.

Winter Harbor

Features: Salt marsh and wild sandy beaches.

Length: 8 to 18 miles, depending on side routes explored.

Put-in site: There are two equally suitable boat landings for this trip. Old Mill Landing is actually a small watermen's dock but has a small marsh ramp on one side. The alternative is Winter Haven, which has a proper gravel ramp and is next door to a small private marina. Both are free public landings, and the trip description is based from Old Mill Landing, although it could easily be adapted for use from Winter Haven. I chose Old Mill because I like launching from smaller, sheltered areas before entering larger harbors, but it makes for a slightly longer paddle. Neither landing has bathroom facilities. Bay Trails Outfitters run trips throughout Mathews County and sell and rent kayaks from their Winter Harbor Farm. They are located on the same creek as Old Mill Landing, and you need to call ahead for reservations. The owners of Bay Trails helped create the "Mathews County Blueways Water Trail Guide."

Directions: *For the Old Mill Landing:* From VA14 East, take a left onto County Route 608 (CR 608) (there is a brown BETHEL BEACH NATURE PRESERVE sign at this turn), just past Port Haywood. Follow CR 608 for 1.6 miles, and then take a left on CR 609/Bethel Beach Road (again, follow the brown sign to the nature preserve). Follow CR 609 for 1.2 miles and take a right onto CR 611/Old Mill Landing Road (this turn is 0.2 mile past the Bay Trails Outfitters farm). Follow CR 611 for 0.2 mile until it ends at the water.

    For the Winter Harbor Haven Landing: Follow the directions above to CR 608 but stay straight on CR 608 instead of turning on CR 609. You will follow CR 608 for 4.3 miles until it ends at the boat landing.

ALTHOUGH IT ENCOMPASSES only 105 square miles, Mathews County has 240 miles of waterfront. No spot on land is farther than 2 miles from navigable water, and Winter Harbor is in the center of this water kingdom, with a riddle of guts, creeks, and coves enveloped by sprawling pastures of salt marsh. Residents of Mathews have a well-developed and intimate knowledge of their watery home, so they can navigate shallow bays that would mire down any other boater, and find hidden passages to deepwater holes rich with fish and crabs. The most famous exploiter of this local knowledge was John Taylor Wood. The grandson of President Zachary Taylor, he was an officer and instructor at the Naval Academy in Annapolis when the Civil War began. His father was from the North and his mother was from the South, and like so many Virginians he struggled with a torn allegiance. Ultimately, he chose his mother's land and resigned from the navy to fight for the South. He built small raiding vessels that could be transported by cart but that looked like small whaling ships. Then, he employed the services of Peter Smith, a local waterman, to learn the intricacies of the water maze. With his small force of men, he hurt the Union navy severely, taking much larger ships and robbing them of their contents. They would then escape into a creek, gut, or bay like Winter Harbor where no outsider could ever hope to find them. He was never captured, and Union sailors continued to chase his ghost even after he was promoted to commander and transferred farther to the south.

Trip Description

The water of Winter Harbor is split into countless fingers, guts, and passages, with the main open water being bisected by marshland into two distinct sections. This paddle begins in the inland section and travels south, then east and north into the upper harbor area by Bethel Beach. Paddle straight out from Old Mill Landing to head southward down the creek to the open harbor. Bay Trails Outfitters is just west of

The watermen's Winter Harbor dock at the boat landing

the landing, so it is easy to use this trip description if you are leaving from their store. There are a few houses scattered on the upper part of this creek, which is mostly wooded with loblolly pine. As the creek broadens, paddle nearer to the eastern/left side of the creek. After about ½ mile, the forests of the eastern shoreline stop and an expanse of salt marsh begins. You will pass by a small gut on the left, which is one of many side diversions that the harbor provides. Explore these guts now, on your return, or later, saving them for your many future visits to the harbor—all are good options. The wide water of Winter Harbor is directly in front of you, and the white buildings of the small marina at Winter Harbor Haven are visible on the opposite shore.

About 1 mile from the landing, you will reach the mouth of the creek, at the harbor proper. If you are paddling from the Winter Harbor Haven landing, you may wish to paddle straight across the harbor to the creek mouth in order to join up with the rest of this trip description. This will allow you to quickly leave behind the deepwater channel that is out from the landing. While there is plenty of water to explore to the west, head east from the creek toward the wild beauty of the coastal marshes and save the inland waters for later in the trip if you still have the time and energy.

The primary ecosystem for the remainder of the paddle will be salt marsh, with cordgrass dominating the landscape. You will pass a gut on the left, and then continue for another ¼ mile past that until you come to the next opening in the marsh. The passage is about 50 feet wide, and in less than 100 yards, you pass back through to more open water. Just before I paddled out of the passage, I heard the unmistakable whine of an outboard engine, so I slowed and waited along the marsh edge. In a few moments a waterman skimmed past in his skiff, with brimming baskets of crabs on his bow. The watermen know this marsh as intimately as the fish and the turtles, and their pots dot any channels that are deep enough to float their boats. However, you can always hear the watermen during their approach, so it is an easy thing to move to the side and let them pass. You will rarely find a more courteous and able boater than a Chesapeake Bay waterman.

You have many options once you reappear on the broader water of the other side of the passage. Like all trips in this book, my route is only a suggestion, and nowhere is that more true than in Winter Harbor. Explore, explore, explore. Take any passage you want, the worst that will happen is that it will end and leave you stranded in paradise. However, for a sure passage to the upper harbor, paddle to the left/north and take the first left. It is a wide opening with a small marsh-clump island in the center. There is a duck blind visible over the marsh grass to the right, and after a big looping bend to the right, there is a duck blind visible on the left. When the gut bends back to the left, the waterway narrows by half, from about 60 feet wide to 30 feet wide. The triangle noses of terrapins continually popped in and out of the water all around me, and egrets and herons rose up at every bend of the marsh. The gut bends to the right, with a duck blind and a gut cut-through on the left. Stay with the main passage, follow it as the water bends again to the right, and flow back onto the open water of the northern harbor. It is breathtaking and wild. The white sand of Bethel Beach is visible to the northeast.

There was a small marsh island in front of me, and although the water is shallow, it was passable on either side at mid-high tide. I paddled along the shoreline in order to continue to watch the birds, fish, turtles, periwinkles, and fiddler crabs that populate the edges of marsh and water. You can continue paddling the left shoreline all the way up a side creek toward the little settlement on Onemo. The creek begins as salt marsh, but as it heads inland, the shoreline elevation changes slightly, allowing for loblolly forest. There is a small amount of firm sand on the northern side of the creek's mouth, and because it is about 3 miles from the landing, it makes an excellent spot to stretch your legs before continuing on with your explorations. There is another patch of sand by the second, smaller creek to the north.

However, for a truly wild beach to explore, look toward the Bay. To your north is the long sandy hook of Bethel Beach, and straight east is a smaller beach that is only accessible by boat. You can reach Bethel by continuing to paddle along the shoreline and wrapping your way toward the inner side of the sandy hook. Or, you could take a shortcut across the harbor and head straight for the beach. The water is shallow in the open harbor, which can be both a help and a hindrance in windy conditions. The danger of shallow water is that waves quickly form and get steeper, up to 1 to 2 feet in even 15-knot breezes. The good news is that if you capsize you can stand up. I love rough water and had a fun time bouncing over and through the waves, but stay inland to avoid a wet ride during windy conditions. A sandbar runs perpendicular to the harbor opening to the Bay and is not passable during low tide, so paddle accordingly. Avoid paddling over areas where gulls appear to be walking on water.

The wild and beautiful Bethel Beach

The south side of the sandy beach of Bethel is slightly exposed to waves but is an easy landing with a gently sloped beach. The northern, inside part of the hook is completely protected, but the depth drops off dramatically from the beach, so be careful when stepping out of your boat. The sand of this hook is constantly shifting as new sand is carved and deposited here through the forces of wind and tide.

Bethel Beach is a natural area preserve that was purchased by the Nature Conservancy and the state of Virginia and is managed by the Department of Conservation and Recreation. It was marked for preservation due to the existence of the threatened northeastern tiger beetle that lives on the beach for its entire two-year life and to protect the beach nesting habitat of the least tern. Due to the nesting of these terns, do not land on marked portions of the beach from May 1 through September 15. The northern harrier hawk has also been spotted nesting in the surrounding forest, which is south of its usual range. There is an osprey platform on the southern end of the beach, and CR 609 ends at the northern end of the beach at a small parking area.

While the beetle, tern, and harrier may be why the beach was protected, what I found was a sandy site of unremitting beauty. It lulled me into a long lunch with beach-combing and snoozing. Besides the usual shells and driftwood, the sandy spit was also scattered with red beard sponge. Sponges are actually colonies of simple microscopic animals, and they live throughout the salty waters of the southern Chesapeake. There are several types of sponge in the Bay, but the most colorful and distinctive is red beard sponge, with its unmistakable, bright red color and intertwining fingers. The small openings throughout the sponge are where water is pumped in and out—bringing in food and oxygen and pumping out waste. They are beautiful and strange creatures, and I had never visited a beach with so many washed ashore.

When you are ready to become water-bound once more, you have several options. You may want to head out onto the open Bay on a flat day, exploring the coast to the north or paddling south to the entrance to the southern section of Winter Harbor. If you stay inland, you could head north into Garden Creek. The entrance to the ¾-mile-long canal that leads to the creek is visible to the north. After passing under the

CR 609 bridge, you will paddle in a salt-marsh passage, with loblolly pines backing the marsh on both sides. The pretty creek is about 1 mile in length and is only easily navigable at high tide.

You could also complete a full exploration of the northern harbor, and paddle back south from Bethel Beach on the interior of the eastern shore of the cove. Remember that the water is shallow at the mouth, and it is easy to run aground on calm days or flip on windy/wavy days, so you may need to duck inland slightly. The southern tip of the mouth has a small sandy beach with a duck blind on its point. Then, after about ½ mile of salt marsh, there is a little inlet on the left that leads to a small, white sand beach. The beach encompasses all of the land, from Bay to harbor, so while it is not long, it is wide and flat. The beach is only accessible by boat, and would be a much more private area for lunch on a weekend day when there are more day users on Bethel Beach.

While the map shows a passage to the southern harbor through an entrance about midway up the marsh edge, with an entrance that was conveniently marked by a duck blind, other guts on the map appeared to be navigable as well. Take the opportunity to explore. Plunge off the beaten path. I took a left into the first passageway I reached, which led me into a small round cove. There was a large, sun-bleached tree root ball in the end of the cove with an osprey nest on top. As I made my way toward this target, I floated in water that was so shallow that I had to stow my paddle and walk my kayak with my hands. However, perseverance paid off. I found a little entrance to a gut on the top/southern side of the cove and the water deepened to about a foot, which was enough for me to start using my paddle again. The gut paralleled the Bay, and I could hear the waves crashing on the beach. Trees were visible straight ahead, with the northernmost tree bearing an osprey nest at its top. These are the types of enchanted areas where only kayakers can venture.

Eventually the small gut bent to the right and joined with the main thoroughfare, which is deep and varies in width from 20 to 100 feet. With slight serpentine bends to the left and right, the passage took me southward, past little guts and a lot of cordgrass, with dozens of more ways to explore the marshland. Then, just after the marina buildings came into view in the distance, I passed the western passage that I had used in the morning. It is easy to see how John Taylor Wood was able to evade the Union navy in Mathews County's maze of marshes. You can paddle in Winter Harbor all day and see only a small fraction of this water wonderland, which is a good reason to visit this small county over and over again.

Alternative Trips

The owners of Bay Trails helped create the "Mathews County Blueways Water Trail Guide," which is a group of maps that outline an interconnected system of five different trip locations with over 90 miles of one-way mileage. The guide can be purchased from the Mathews County Visitor and Information Center or from Bay Trails (see Appendix B). Winter Harbor, New Point Comfort Lighthouse, and the alternative trips for both of these areas are all included in this excellent paddler's resource.

The Piankatank River forms the northern boundary of the county and is the northernmost trail. There are launch sites in Mathews County off CR 628 at Ginney Point Marina, at the end of CR 630 at Roane Point Landing, at the end of CR 632 at the Piankatank River Landing, and on Queens Creek at the end of CR 662 at Rose Creek Landing. There are also two launch sites in Middlesex County. Twigg Ferry Landing is on the north side of the VA 3 bridge; and Stampers Wharf, at the end of CR 630, provides easy access to paddle around Berkley Island. All of these trips are at the eastern end of the Piankatank, where the river is deep and wide. Another popular canoeing and kayaking spot is westward in the narrow and winding passages of Dragon Run. Access to this upper region is sparse, and there are numerous fallen trees blocking the passage. However, this area is wild and scenic, making it well worth the effort of portaging over logs on a one-way trip. Contact the Friends of Dragon Run for more information about paddling the river, or to join one of their biannual paddle days.

12.

New Point Comfort Lighthouse

Features: Third-oldest lighthouse in the Chesapeake, primitive camping, beach and salt-marsh ecosystems.

Length: The paddle to and from the lighthouse is short, about 4 miles. There is much more paddling to be done in the area.

Put-in site: The landing is beside the New Point Comfort Nature Preserve observation platform, in the southern tip of Mathews County. The nature preserve protects all the shoreline from the observation platform to the point. There are no bathrooms. There is a trash can, but they have considerable problems with raccoons digging out the trash, so it is best to pack out whatever trash you bring with you. There is primitive camping along the route of the paddle, and the New Point Campground is also nearby.

Directions: You will follow VA 14 East through Mathews County all the way until it ends in Bavon. When you reach the T-intersection in Bavon (there is a small green store on the right corner and a sign to let you know that you are in a town), follow the brown historical marker sign and take a left to continue on VA 14. Follow that for 0.3 mile, and then continue straight on County Route 600 (CR 600) as VA 14 forks off to the right. Follow this for 0.7 mile, and take a right on Lighthouse Road (there is a wooden, brown NEW POINT COMFORT NATURE PRESERVE sign marking this turn). Follow for 0.3 mile until it ends at the water.

WITH AN AVERAGE DEPTH of about 21 feet and a coastline without many distinguishing landmarks, the Chesapeake Bay has always been dangerous to navigate. Beginning in 1792 with the Cape Henry Lighthouse

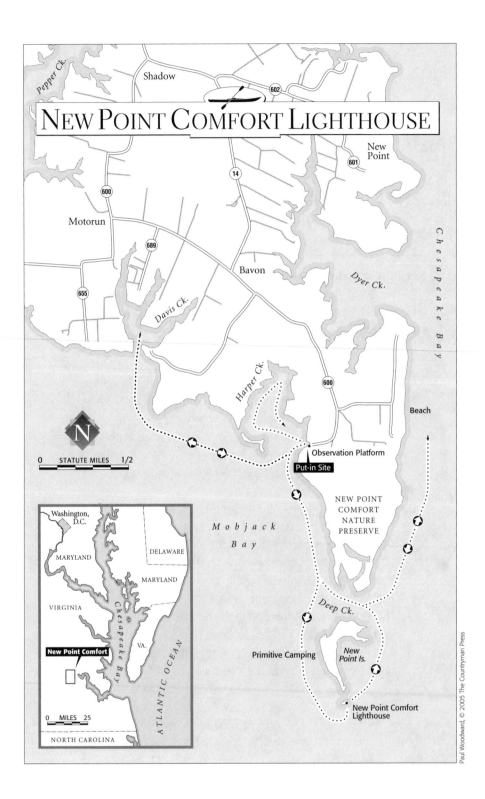

NEW POINT COMFORT LIGHTHOUSE

Shadow

602

New Point

601

14

600

Motorun

689

655

Bavon

Davis Ck.

Dyer Ck.

Pepper Ck.

Chesapeake Bay

Harper Ck.

600

Beach

N

0   STATUTE MILES   1/2

Observation Platform

Put-in Site

NEW POINT
COMFORT
NATURE
PRESERVE

Mobjack
Bay

Deep Ck.

Primitive Camping

New
Point Is.

New Point Comfort
Lighthouse

Washington,
D.C.

DELAWARE

MARYLAND

MARYLAND

VIRGINIA

Chesapeake Bay

VA.

ATLANTIC OCEAN

New Point Comfort

0   MILES   25

NORTH CAROLINA

Paul Woodward, © 2005 The Countryman Press

in Virginia Beach, the federal government began to commission light-houses as vital to the safe navigation of the Bay. Elzy Burroughs, a stonemason, built Old Point Comfort, the second lighthouse on the Bay, in 1802 in Hampton, Virginia. He then received the commission to build the Chesapeake's third lighthouse, New Point Comfort, which he began in 1802 and finished on January 17, 1805. He was paid $8,500 to build the lighthouse and light keeper's house, and upon completion of the job, President Thomas Jefferson personally appointed him as the light's first keeper. Originally lit by fish and whale oil, the light aided boaters in finding safe passage north and south along the Chesapeake for over 150 years, warning them away from the point's shoals, and guiding them into the safe harbor of Mobjack Bay.

Trip Description

The lighthouse is visible from the observation platform, making the navigation of this trip straightforward. The landing is on the mouth of Harper Creek; and as you head out from the landing, bear left/south along the marsh. You are paddling along the broad waters of Mobjack Bay, which is formed by the junction of the East River and the North River. This broad bay is continually growing through the slow erosion of the shoreline. Evidence of that exists in the old pilings of a menhaden (fish) processing factory that used to dominate the shoreline. The pilings now stand about 50 yards west of land.

The shoreline here is a typical salt-marsh combination of cordgrass and black needle rush, with a loblolly forest behind the broad marsh. I paddled away from the marsh in my rush to reach the lighthouse and then meandered along its edges on my way back to the landing. The water is clear, and the sand of the bottom is mostly hidden by a lush growth of grasses. In the shallower water near the shore, you can also see red beard sponge as you watch large and small fish dart beneath your boat. You will pass three duck blinds in your southern passage and paddle past a large overturned bleached root with an osprey nest built on top.

While the lighthouse was built on the mainland, the site was slowly being separated from the peninsula by the erosive power of storms throughout the 1800s. Then, in 1933, two hurricanes devastated the Chesapeake, flooding towns, destroying homes and wharves, and re-shaping much of the Bay. Two islands were carved out of the point, and on the farthest island stood the lighthouse, a proud testament to the solid craftsmanship of Elzy Burroughs. The channel between New Point Island and the lighthouse is about ⅓ mile wide and was dubbed Deep Creek. Despite the name, the channel is mostly shallow, which can be dangerous during high winds. The day I paddled out to the light-house the wind had been blowing about 15 knots from the northeast for over 24 hours. This was sufficient to stack up breaking waves about 2 feet high, causing some fun and wet paddling for my approach to the lighthouse. While I enjoy kayaking in those conditions, it was less than optimal for viewing the structure and was disastrous for taking photos. I would never bring a novice kayaker out in such wind. Pay attention to the forecast when you are planning your trip to the lighthouse; you may want to avoid the high-wind seasons of autumn and early spring.

The lighthouse is an off-white octagonal tower, built of sandstone from the same Pennsylvania quarry that provided the stone for the con-struction of the White House. The foundation is sunk 5 feet below ground, with a wall thickness of about 5 feet at the base, which tapers to a width of 2 feet at the top of the tower. The lighthouse stands a total of 58 feet above sea level. The high vantage point of the light proved to be strategically important to the British, who occupied the tower and light keeper's cabin during the War of 1812 and used it as a base of op-erations for their numerous raids in the Mathews County area. War came to the lighthouse again in the 1860s, when it was sabotaged by the Confederacy in order to hinder Union shipping activity. Unfortunately, some sabotage of the light continues today, and the local preservation-ists had to install bulletproof glass in defense against frustrated hunters who use the light as target practice.

In 1919 automatic gas lights replaced the lighthouse's oil-fueled lanterns, and the keeper's house was torn down. The coast guard took control of all the Chesapeake lighthouses in 1939; and in the early 1950s, they replaced gas light with electric lamps, ending the need for any res-ident light keepers. In 1960 the New Point Comfort's spit light beacon was constructed about 1,000 yards southeast of the lighthouse, and the lighthouse was abandoned in 1963. Over the next dozen years, it was vandalized, its lenses were stolen, birds and bats made it their home, and it was hit by lighting sometime during the years between 1963 and 1976. Then the lighthouse's luck turned. A committee of concerned Mathews County residents acquired it; and through the combined efforts of the state, county, and citizen committees, the tower was restored. While it remains decommissioned, a decorative light was installed in the tower three years ago so that it once again illuminates the night.

After looking at the light, I had fun surfing my kayak for a while along the southern tip of land. I finally paddled around the tip of New Point Island and pulled up in the flat water of the leeward side of this little sand stop-off. This island is part of the nature preserve, and it is permissible to camp here. In order to preserve the beauty and ecology of the spot, you must pack everything in and out of this island, including your personal solid waste (use non-clear, tightly sealing Tupperware containers or double Ziploc bags in a dry bag). It might seem a little gross, but it is a better than polluting the island. The island is all sand, with the higher portions of land including some scrub grasses and vegetation. Be aware of the tide, whether you are setting up camp or just leaving for a long stroll along the beach. Pull your kayak well above the high-tide mark and pitch your tent on the upper section of the island. If camping overnight, you might want to take the extra precaution of anchoring your kayak. Tie a line to the bow and the other end of the line to piece of driftwood; then bury the driftwood about 2 feet deep. I learned this trick in Mexico, and on a number of occasions, this saved my kayaks from floating away on unusually high tides.

The eastern tip of the island was filled with a mixture of brown pelicans, gulls, and cormorants. The channel between the island and land is shallow but should be passable at high tide—you can easily wade across the channel in order to explore the long beach of the mainland.

From here, you can continue paddling in the open Bay northward along the eastern shoreline of the county. The land between the light and Dyer Creek is all beach, with the southern section of the beach belonging to the nature preserve and the northern section is part of a

Observation platform at New Point Comfort Nature Preserve

private waterfront of summer cottages. You could also head up Mobjack Bay, past the landing, to explore Harper Creek or Davis Creek, which is about 1 mile north of the boat landing. Davis Creek has a public landing off CR 689, and many workboats are moored and docked along its edges. About 1 mile north of Davis Creek is Pepper Creek, which is at least twice the length.

All of these creeks have a combination of salt marsh and a maritime forest that is dominated by the loblolly pine. The loblolly is a somewhat opportunistic species of tree and has replaced the original forests of oak, chestnut, maple, and live oak, which were cut for the boatbuilding industry that once thrived in this county. For a hundred years, between the mid-1760s and the Civil War, boats of all sizes and intentions were crafted along every creek and cove of Mathews, with upwards of a hundred ships being built each year. The largest ship of the Revolutionary Virginia Navy, the *Gloucester,* was built in 1777 in Pepper Creek. According to a survey of the county in 1835, the county residents' focus was so completely on boatbuilding that for many years most of the clear-cut land laid fallow and corn needed to be imported for food. Joseph Martin, the surveyor, makes note of this lack of agriculture as a failing of the residents, but I differ with his estimation. I like the fact that until 1951 there were only two roads into this county.

I like that the majority of the county is uninhabitable because the water permeates the land in expansive salt marshes. In my estimation, this seems to me to be the way one should live alongside the Bay.

Elzy Burroughs was first in a line of over 20 light keepers, and he served the light for 10 years, laying deep roots in the county in the process. When I wrapped up my morning paddle, I met his great-great-great-grand niece, Mrs. Trusch. She is a retired schoolteacher who lives in Bavon and cares for the light with a sort of maternal pride, coming to the observation tower at least twice a day to make sure the platform is free from trash and that the lighthouse is lit at night. It is easy to understand her pride. It has withstood two centuries of storms, two wars, and years of neglect—yet it still stands, as deeply rooted in the Bay as the residents of this small and proud county.

Alternative Trips

The East River has miles of paddling above the lighthouse, with much of the route taking you alongside historic homes and traditional watermen settlements. There are just two launch sites on the river. One is the William's Wharf landing, which is at the end of CR 614. The other is Town Point Landing off CR 615. Both roads are off VA 14. If you paddle south from William's Wharf, you will pass a tide mill that was once used to grind grain with the power of the tidal current. If you head eastward up the creek from Town Point Landing, you can paddle toward Mathews County Courthouse, which is the center of the county's historic district. There are numerous bed & breakfasts in the East River area.

As with the Winter Harbor trips, there are many trip alternatives listed in the "Mathews County Blueways Water Trail Guide." Horn Harbor is to the north of New Point Comfort, and it has an excellent landing at the end of CR 699 that will put you onto Doctors Creek. You can also launch from across the harbor at the end of CR 698. This is a deepwater harbor with a clearly marked channel. The edges and scenery are more of the same beautiful, pastoral landscape you find on the East River.

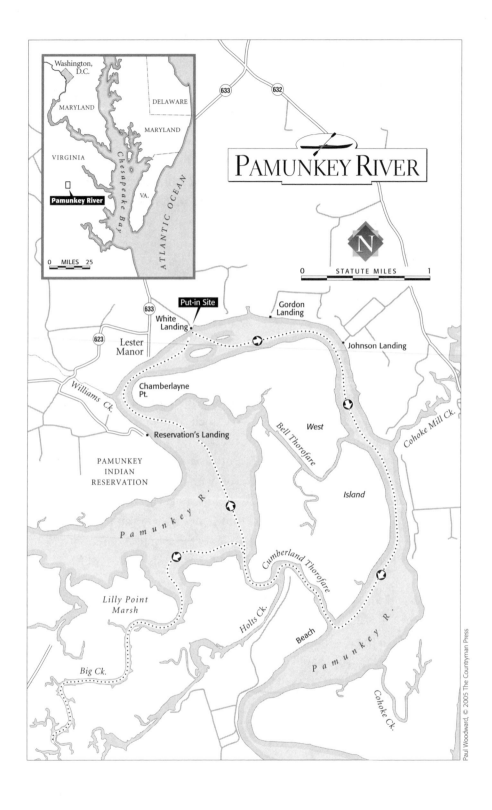

13.

Pamunkey River

Features: Pamunkey Indian Reservation and an island circumnavigation.

Length: 7-mile circumnavigation, 12 miles with Holts Creek exploration, 17+ miles by adding on other side explorations.

Put-in site: White Landing is a public boat landing just east of the Pamunkey Indian Reservation and has a concrete ramp, a short pier, and limited parking. The Pamunkey Indian Reservation also has a boat ramp, but you need to call ahead (804-843-4792) if you want to use it, so the public landing is the easier alternative. To visit the reservation and its pottery school, gift shop, and informative museum, follow the directions below but continue straight on County Route 633 (CR 633) rather than turning on CR 672. The town of West Point is downriver, where the junction of the Mattaponi and Pamunkey Rivers forms the York River. There are many places to shop and eat within West Point's historic district. The Mattaponi Canoe and Kayak Company guide trips here.

Directions: From US 360 (accessible southeast of Richmond by I-295), exit onto VA 30 South. Follow for about 8.5 miles, and then take a right onto CR 633 (Powhatan Trail). There is a sign for the reservation here. Follow for 7.6 miles and then take a left onto CR 672. Continue for 0.4 mile, over the railroad tracks and down the hill, to the small public landing.

FORMED BY THE JUNCTION of piedmont rivers like the North and South Anna, the Pamunkey River runs deep as it powerfully carves its way to the York River. Borrowing the strength of this freshwater river's tides, a kayaker can enjoy a nearly effortless circumnavigation of an island, paddling along shores that are a mixture of forest, marsh, and swamp, and spotting a variety of wildlife, including bald eagles and osprey. The river has hosted paddlers through much of its ancient history. The Pamunkey Indians have been stewards of this land for over twelve-thousand years, and many still live along the river's banks, fish its waters, and create pottery from its clay. Nestled in a horseshoe bend of the river, the small 1,200-acre Pamunkey Indian Reservation was established by a 1677 treaty with King Charles II of England, making it one of the oldest reservations in the United States. The Pamunkey Indians were once the most powerful tribe in the Powhatan Confederacy. Although this cooperative union included over 30 tribes in the coastal plain of Virginia, the common language of Algonquin united it. This lost language now mostly exists in the place names of Virginia like Potomac, Poquoson, Mattaponi, and Chesapeake. The Pamunkey tribe was home to the ruler of the confederacy, Chief Powhatan, and his three brothers; and the leaders and council members of the confederacy traditionally came together along the shores of the river to rest and restore their spirits. The Pamunkey River still holds these restorative powers today, with serenity provided to all that take to the river's waters, whether by kayak or dugout canoe.

Trip Description

The Pamunkey River's strong tidal current is too powerful to paddle against for a sustained period, so the direction of the tide will decide your route when circumnavigating West Island. If you fail to plan well, the tide may change mid-trip and force you to repeat a part of the circumnavigation, missing an entire section of the island. The current was in full ebb when I left, so this route description travels to the east and south first, creating a clockwise circuit. You will need to reverse these directions during a flood tide.

From White Landing, paddle straight across the Pamunkey. You may want to try borrowing a white-water technique for this crossing and ferry glide your boat across. Just angle your bow slightly upstream (into the current) at about a 45-degree angle while you paddle. This technique takes some practice, but it allows the currents to work for you, sliding your boat effortlessly across the waterway. If you are not pushed too far south during your crossing, the first land you will reach will be that of two small marsh islands that stand a little way off from West Island. These are about two-thirds of the way across the ¼-mile crossing. As you near the shore of these small islands, the eddy forces of land will slow the current, and then you can spin your boat to face downstream. I paddled between the two islands and then closer to the low marsh that creates the northern shore of West Island.

The mainland shoreline is heavily wooded with fairly tall banks. An occasional house is visible through the trees, but mostly you are in the midst of a wild landscape, with the wooded mainland on your left and the island's mixture of swamp and marsh on your right. Stay along the edges of the island, clear of the main navigation channel. This will keep you out of the way of any powerboat traffic and bring you closer to the beauty and wildlife, which includes bald eagles, kingfishers, osprey, and wood ducks. The river bends to the south about 1 mile from the landing, and this mileage can go by much faster than you may be used to, due to the strong current. As I rounded this bend, I passed within a couple of feet of a very surprised muskrat.

In about ⅓ mile you will pass a little gut, and then another in about the same distance. There are a fair number of duck blinds all along the island. Marsh mallow was in full bloom in the summertime, and the scrub vegetation of the edges was a rich mixture of dark browns and greens. I also noticed the small triangles of turtles' heads popping out of the water throughout the length of this paddle. While the Pamunkey Indians have a strong agricultural tradition, they also used to fish the Pamunkey's deep waters, hunt its forests, and harvest the swamp edges for all its offerings. The roots of arrow arum were eaten, the beautiful, white-flowered marsh hibiscus (or marsh mallow) was made into a sweet confection, and turtles were caught, with every part of the reptile being consumed or used. Even the turtle's shell was used as a shield.

Spatterdock along the edges of the Pamunkey River

On the western shore the woods give way to a green pasture, which rolls down to the bank of Cohoke Mill Creek. When I was there in the summer, the creek's entrance appeared to be completely choked with spatterdock. On the island side of the river, directly across from Cohoke Mill, you will come upon Bell Thorofare, which is the first major gut that bisects the island. It is an excellent passageway to explore, or you could follow the waterway all the way to the other side of the island, shortening your circumnavigation.

Depending on the level of the tide, you may need to stay several yards away from shore to avoid running aground on the tidal flat. Here I saw large fish rolling in the shallow water all along these flats. From their long dorsal fins, I identified them as carp, which are often found wallowing in the mud like freshwater pigs. Cumberland Thorofare will come into view as you round the bowed out section of marshland. The mouth of this wide gut is impossible to miss, with a 25-yard opening that is about 1¾ miles from Bell Thorofare, at the fattest part of the Pamunkey River. The current's power is evident at this mouth, with small whirlpools being spawned by the force of the tide. While this is definitely not a good swimming hole, there is a brown, gravel sand beach on the far bank of the passageway that is one of the best spots to stop during this paddle.

The Cumberland Thorofare is the southern boundary of West Island, so you need to paddle through the thoroughfare in order to continue the circumnavigation. Paddling will be a little more difficult because you will be pushing against the tide. In about ½ mile, you will see some large duck blinds on the right, as the gut bends to the left. The water rips strongly around this corner, forming small whirlpools that will whip and tug at your kayak—paddle farther away from shore to avoid the full brunt of the water's strength. By continuing along the left bank, you can head up Holts Creek, which is about 2½ miles long. It has a gentle current and is wooded on the left shore with marshland on the right. I did not explore the whole length of the waterway because doing so would have caused me to miss the tidal change, forcing me to return to the landing the same way I had just come. However, the creek appears to be a wild and gentle side diversion.

The gut is about 1¼ miles long, and once you are through to the other side, the ebbing current will catch you, bringing you back toward home. If you want to extend your paddle, you can defy the current and paddle upstream into Big Creek, which is about ½ mile west of Cumberland and is slightly longer than Holts Creek. However, if you only have the time or energy to paddle one side route, choosing Holts Creek will allow you to avoid the hard work of paddling upstream against the current of the Pamunkey.

The river is large here, about two to three times the width of the river on the east of the marsh. There is an osprey nest on the corner of the opening, and you can paddle alongside the island for a while on the return route home. The swamp forest is thick here, and you are likely to spot a lot of osprey, eagles, and ducks. However, be careful not to stray too close to the island because the tidal flats extend deep into the

Shad

Shad are anadromous fish, which means that they live in the Atlantic Ocean but come to the freshwater rivers of the Chesapeake Bay to spawn. They are valued both for their tender flesh and for their roe (eggs), and have been an important commercial fishery on the Chesapeake since Colonial times. They are traditionally cooked over an open fire on cedar planks, and George Washington's troops in Valley Forge were reportedly saved from starvation by eating a diet of dried shad. However, beginning in the late 1800s, the fishery began to buckle under the pressures of overharvesting. With remarkable foresight, the Mattaponi Indians began a hatchery program in 1916, and the Pamunkey Indians followed suit two years later. In this way the Native Americans continued a long tradition of giving back as much as they received from the land and water, ensuring a healthy, self-sustaining fishery. As shad levels in the rest of the country plummeted due to overfishing, dams, and pollution, the shad population in the Pamunkey and Mattaponi Rivers remained comparatively healthy.

In the 1970s biologists began to catch on to the idea of restocking wild populations of fish, and many came to the Pamunkey Reservation to learn how the delicate job is done. The spring run of shad is still caught with nets, in much the same way as it was when the Virginia Indians taught colonists how to fish hundreds of years ago. Because

river, especially on an ebbing tide. Also, the northern tip of the island extends more than ½ mile out into the river with the long, low grass marsh of Chamberlayne Point; so for the most direct route of travel, angle toward the duck blind. As you near the blind, head more to the left, straight toward the buildings of the Pamunkey Indian Reservation and the shore of the mainland. It is about 1½ miles from the Cumberland Thorofare to the reservation.

After passing several homes, you will come to the reservation's boat landing. This may be a convenient spot to get out and walk around the reservation; however, the ramp is private property, so you will need to call ahead to get permission. The reservation is currently home to only about 75 people. Until desegregation in the 1960s, the tribe's children were forced to leave for boarding schools in Pennsylvania because the

the fish run with the tides both day and night, lanterns often illuminate the nets so that they can be put to use even during the darkest nights. The live fish are milked into common buckets for their eggs and sperm, and this mixture is poured into the holding tanks of the hatchery, where the young fry/fingerlings (fish) are kept for 16 days before being released in the river. Some of the shad and roe are also caught for food and market, with the tradition that fish caught in the afternoon are harvested for the hatchery, while the fish caught in the morning are sent to market. In 2000, 3.2 million fingerlings were returned to the Pamunkey.

Through the years, other rivers on the Bay have been reopened to shad, including the Susquehanna, whose giant obstacle of the Conowingo Dam was circumvented with a fish elevator. In 2004, the Embry Dam on the Rappahannock was destroyed in order to open the upper parts of that river to shad and herring. However, the fish will not return on their own because, after they spend three to six years in the ocean, they unwaveringly return to their birth waters. Thus, the young fingerling shad from hatcheries, including the Pamunkey, are used in stocking these reopened waters. These restocking efforts have been successful, bringing hope that traditional shad planking feasts can once again become an annual spring tradition throughout the Bay.

reservation schools only taught up to the sixth grade and the local Virginia schools would not accept them. Most of these displaced children stayed away, and although some of them and some of their children returned as they grew older, the reservation's population has not recovered. However, the traditions and pride of being Pamunkey still flow strongly among this community, both on and off the reservation. The reservation's shad fishery is one such example of this modern native pride. The shad hatchery is to the north of the landing and is only active during the spring spawn.

Beside fishing, the other current traditional use of the river is pottery making. Reservoirs of clay lie beneath the rich mud of the riverbanks. The location of these clay seams has been passed down through the years among the Pamunkey, as have the laborious techniques for harvesting and preparing the clay. The three-thousand-year-old coil-style tradition of pot making was passed on from woman to woman over the years and was known as "blackware" for the dark shades of gray that it developed when it was cured over an open fire. Then in 1932, in the midst of the Great Depression, the Pamunkey Pottery School was established by the state of Virginia to educate more tribal women in pottery making, and to hopefully allow the Pamunkey to make money on the craft. The school was successful, and with the introduction of modern kilns and techniques, the tribe was able to make enough pottery to sell to tourists. In later years the potters have turned back to the old way of pottery making, so that currently both modern and traditional methods are in use by the handful of craftsmen who use the pottery school workshop.

The narrow, spatterdock-filled entrance for Williams Creek is just above the reservation, on the top of the river's bend to the east. Because I was loath to end my day, I poked my kayak into the small waterway to see what I could find. One bend after passing a small house on the left, I came upon two barred owls. One flew away immediately after my arrival, but the other stayed and watched me watch him. It was dark, rainy, and overcast, and while I have never seen an owl during a sunny day, this was my third or fourth time spotting an owl during the false twilight of an overcast afternoon. I enjoyed his company for at least 15 minutes before I slowly backed out the way that I came. During high tide, it may be possible to paddle the creek all the way to the main river on the other side of this long horseshoe bend. However, as my encounter with the owl proves, it is not always necessary to paddle far to see a lot.

Paddling by myself, with a strong current, I covered water quickly and was back at the boat landing a little over three hours after beginning my trip. I certainly could have extended my journey by exploring farther up Holts or Big Creeks, or by simply taking longer breaks. However, while I love to spend a day on the water, it is also nice to combine a shorter trip with time spent on land. We kayakers are amphibious creatures who need both land and water. I spent at least an hour on the reservation that afternoon. A wonderful and informative woman named Isabelle was running the museum while I was there, and later on, a potter's apprentice, streaked with clay from a morning spent harvesting a seam, gave me a personal tour of the workshop. Thus, it was only by leaving my kayak behind that I was able to gain this fuller view of the Pamunkey. *Pamunkey* means "people who look for new land." They found that unique and special land here, and now so have I.

Alternative Trips

The Pamunkey's sister river to the north is the Mattaponi. The Mattaponi's tides are even stronger than the Pamunkey's, and with no islands to circumnavigate, a trip on the Mattaponi needs to be a one-way shuttle trip. Depending on the tidal flow of the day, launch in either Aylett or Walkerton, and then paddle with the flow for the 10-mile trip. The Mattaponi Canoe and Kayak Company offers rentals and shuttles from their home base in Aylett. Upriver of the Pamunkey are two moving water rivers, the South and North Anna. The water is primarily not whitewater and is thus suitable for sea kayaks. Information on these routes can be found in one of the whitewater books listed in appendix C. There is a York River Water Trail that covers most of the length of the York and the two tributaries of the Mattaponi and Pamunkey. The trail includes 10 access sites, covering 120 miles of water, from the Pamunkey Indian Reservation to Yorktown. Information can be found by contacting the Mattaponi and Pamunkey Rivers Association (see appendix B).

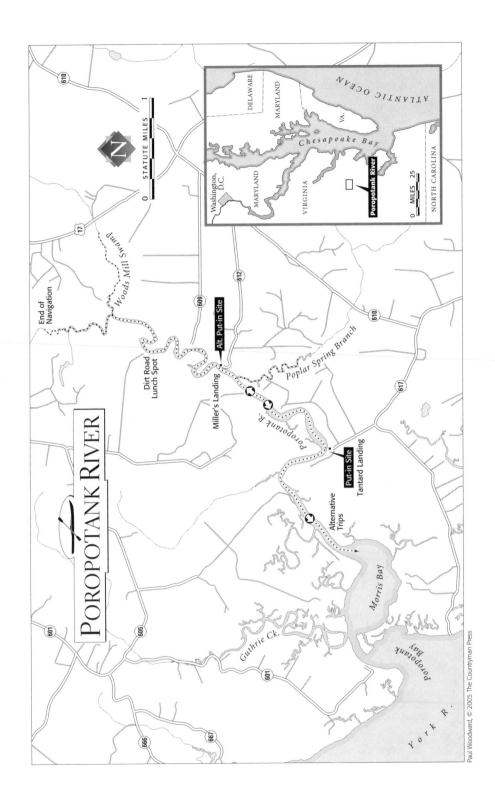

POROPOTANK RIVER

Paul Woodward, © 2005 The Countryman Press

14.

Poropotank River

Features: A largely unpaddled, meandering, and protected river, with eagles, waterfowl, deer, and muskrat. A good beginner trip.

Length: 9 to 11 miles (depending on side trips).

Put-in site: Tanyard Landing is a free ramp that is managed by the Virginia Department of Game and Inland Fisheries (804-367-1605). This is a small, quiet landing with limited parking and no facilities. Upstream houses add to the security of the landing. No outfitters paddle this river, and Gloucester is the nearest city, so it is best to arrange for kayak rentals in whatever city you are driving from.

Directions: Tanyard Landing is approximately 10 miles north of Gloucester. From US 17, exit onto County Route 610 (CR 610) (Davenport Road) at Woods Crossroads. This will be a right turn if traveling southbound, or a left turn if traveling northbound. There is a brown sign for a public boat landing at the turn. A general store and post office are at this small junction. Follow for 3 miles, and then take a right at the T-intersection onto CR 617 (Tanyard Landing Road). Follow for 1.5 miles until the road ends at the landing. *For the alternative landing (Miller's Landing):* Follow CR 610 for about 0.75 mile and then take a right on CR 612/Miller's Landing Road. Follow for about 1.5 miles until it ends at a cul-de-sac. The landing is to the right, down a sandy/paved driveway. Parking is plentiful in both the cul-de-sac and by the landing. There are no facilities, and it is managed by The Virginia Department of Transportation (VDOT) (804-758-2321).

THE POROPOTANK RIVER is an unheralded gem that is easily overlooked in surveying the Bay's waterways, but it is just this sort of simple tidal river that defines the Chesapeake and creates the subtle grandeur of the region. Fiddler crabs swarm among the marshes, muskrats crisscross the river, and each bend reveals new scenic views. I kayaked this river on the first warm day of April and was completely alone, except for two bald eagles, one mature and one immature, both of which soared overhead for most of my trip. I cannot think of a better way I could have spent my day than in this area of little environmental or historical importance. I emerged from my paddle with that odd sensation of having missed time, of having stolen several hours from the usual pace of life and taken them completely for my own. This is the sort of gift that rivers like the Poropotank can give to any paddler willing to stray from the crowds.

Trip Description

Paddle right from the landing to head northeast, upriver. There are a number of houses along the right side of the river during the early section of the trip, but the left side is wild marsh, with a forest buffer that mostly conceals the pasture and farmland farther inland. The river is broad here and will remain so for the first mile of your journey. After the first bend to the left, the marsh broadens even more on the northwestern side, with a farm field visible straight ahead. On the left/northwestern bank of the river, you will pass the first of numerous small guts, all of which are ripe for exploration. While most of them run out of water quickly, exploring them may offer glimpses of muskrat, or at least a closer look at their tracks and lodges.

After rounding the second bend, the river straightens out for close to 1 mile, and the houses thin out considerably. The opening to Poplar Spring is tucked in on the right, just south of a couple of boathouses, about 1½ miles from the boat landing. While the creek entrance is inviting, I generally recommend saving major side-creek exploration for the trip back downriver, thus allowing for new water to explore on

Canada Geese

Autumn has not truly arrived in the Chesapeake region until you hear the musical noise of honking and see the distinctive flying V pattern of Canada geese overhead. The Chesapeake Bay is an important part of the Atlantic Flyway, a migratory route that stretches from the Hudson Bay to Florida, and Canada geese use the Chesapeake both as their flyway and as a final destination and primary wintering ground in a round-trip migration of 3,000 miles. The geese mate for life, usually when they are three years old, and breed in northern Quebec, where they generally have four or five goslings. They remain in Canada all summer, until the shortening days alert them that it is time to lead their young on the long journey back to the same wintering grounds that they use year after year. From 1986 to 1996 the geese suffered from a combination of poor environmental breeding conditions in Canada and increased hunting pressure in the United States. To help the population rebound, goose hunting was closed all along the Atlantic Flyway in 1995. The moratorium will continue until the population has returned to normal; and when hunting does return, better management and stewardship regulations will be put into place.

These migratory geese are different from those you see nesting along Virginia's shorelines in the spring, or wandering around farm fields and roadsides during the summer months. The latter are a completely separate population of resident geese, which remain in the Chesapeake region year-round. The resident geese phenomenon began in the 1930s with the release of tamed geese used as live decoys for hunting. Government and private sector stocking programs also contributed to the population. The majority of the resident geese populate the eastern shore, where they are well fed all year due to the dependable food supply offered by the agriculture of the mid-Atlantic. The resident goose population is somewhat problematic due to the increased feeding and pollution pressures that they bring to the Bay's waters.

A side note about geese and grammar. They claim no nationality and are not citizens of Canada. Thus, they are called Canada geese, not Canadian geese.

the return journey. When you do paddle the spring, it will not disappoint, offering up a paddle of almost 1 mile before running out of water.

About ¼ mile above Poplar Spring, you will pass Miller's Landing on the right-hand side. This is an alternative launch spot that is especially good for beginning kayakers, allowing for a shorter, less exposed paddle. It is a primitive, carry-in landing, a popular local fishing spot, and an excellent place to stretch your legs.

Above Miller's Landing the river bends to the left, and then to the right again. A duck blind is situated upon a raised hillock in the midst of the marsh. The path of a river is ever changing, and this high spot was likely separated from the mainland by an ancient meander. The river is gradually narrowing at this point, with the frequency of the bends increasing. All human habitations disappear and are replaced by an abundance of muskrat houses—mounded piles of marsh grass and mud, usually built in the rounded dimensions of about 4 feet tall by 3 feet wide.

On the end of one meander, I passed by a goose that had made her nest on top of a muskrat house. I had never before seen such a phenomenon—usually goose nests are low depressions in the marsh grass, hidden from sight. The expectant mother resolutely stayed on her nest as I passed by, watching me silently with her neck low, behavior that is common among birds when they are still incubating their eggs. Do not pause too long or paddle too near any nest because you might irritate the bird so much that she would abandon her eggs. Furthermore, geese mate for life, and her partner will probably be nearby, ready to defend his mate and her nest fiercely with a rousing display of hissing and charging.

About 1½ miles from Miller's Landing, a dirt road comes down to the river on the northwestern bank, allowing for a more secluded break spot. After another bend to the right and the left, the river straightens back out and passes by Woods Mill Swamp. This is an excellent side exploration either now or on your way back downriver. Do not be discouraged if downed trees block the entrance, as they did when I paddled it in 2004. By navigating around and under them, you can enter a creek where no other type of boat can travel. There are some

The meandering Poropotank River is a seldom-paddled Chesapeake gem.

houses on the left bank with a good rest stop by the mouth. While not posted, a neighboring resident may own the land, so be courteous and stay below mean high tide. The navigable stretch ends near the trees, with the entire detour lasting 10 to 30 minutes, depending on how long you linger within the peaceful waters.

While the marsh grasses on the lower banks of the creek were tough to identify in the early spring, the area is likely to be mildly brackish. However, as you come to the upper stretches of the creek, the water turns completely fresh, with native marsh species like arrow arum and pickerelweed dominating the transitional area. After rounding the first bend beyond Woods Mill Swamp, you will pass a cliff with steps and a NO TRESPASSING sign. The bends come even more rapidly, and the river begins to lose itself, with the passage splitting into three branches and small marsh islands scattered everywhere. The middle passage is the true river, the right option is blocked by trees, and the left option ends in a cove.

The river continues to twist around a series of marsh islands with many inviting places to wander and drift. There are several duck blinds in the final mile and one small house with an accompanying canoe.

Once you enter the trees, the island maze drops away, and the river steadily narrows. There is an empty duck blind on the left that offers a good, sandy spot to pause. The water is clear, a little tannic, with a firm sandy bottom about 3 feet below, creating an inviting midsummer soaking spot. This is a place of overhanging trees and speckled shade, with many turtles sunning on logs, including the smallest turtle I have ever seen, likely no more than a couple days old. Within hearing distance of VA 14, the passage is blocked by multiple downed trees, forcing the end of the upriver journey about 4½ miles from the trip's beginning. However, the downriver journey still lies before you, including the explorations of Woods Mill Swamp and Poplar Spring, both of which allow you to experience your Poropotank journey all over again in miniature, thus further delaying your reentry back to the real world.

Alternative Trips

Using the same landing as in this trip, you could paddle downstream, into Morris Bay, and then up into Guthrie Creek, which lies on the northwest bank of the river. For another scenic river, use one of the landings on the Ware River, either at Warehouse Road (Virginia Department of Game and Inland Fisheries) or on Payne's Landing Road (Gloucester County, 804-693-2355). This will give you access to paddle upstream on the Ware River and downstream to the Bay. There are also several access points for exploring the broad waters of Mobjack Bay on Severn Wharf Road, Johns Point Road, and Browns Bay Road (VDOT).

15.

Chickahominy Lake

Features: Near Richmond, with excellent largemouth bass fishing
and bird-watching. Cypress and freshwater marsh, a lot of
marsh mallows.

Length: 4 to 20 miles.

Put-in site: You can start this trip from one of two put-in sites.
Eagle's Nest Landing (2142 Landing Road; 804-966-9094),
the larger of the two, has a marina store and offers canoe
rentals. Trail's End Marina operates on the honor system and
consists of an old dock with a small ramp beside it. Both are
privately operated, and thus you need to pay a fee for their
convenience. They generally charge by the car rather than by
the boat, but this can change. The current fee for launching is
between $3 and $5.

    The Chickahominy River was a strategic site for many battles
during the Civil War, including the Battle of Cold Harbor. The
Confederacy used the deep swampland as a natural defense,
building trenches and embankments to further mire down the
advancing Union army. Nearby battlefield sites are preserved
on private land and in the Richmond National Battlefield Park,
and many of the trenches and mounds are still visible.

Directions: From US 60, turn onto County Route 650 (CR 650)—
take a right if traveling east, about 4 miles east of VA 155/Prov-
idence Forge, or take a left if traveling west, about 10 miles
west of the junction of VA 30 and US 60). Follow CR 650 for
0.25 mile, then take a 90-degree left turn and follow for a little
less than 0.25 mile before taking a right into Eagle's Nest
Landing. Or, follow for another 0.25 mile until the road ends at
Trail's End Landing.

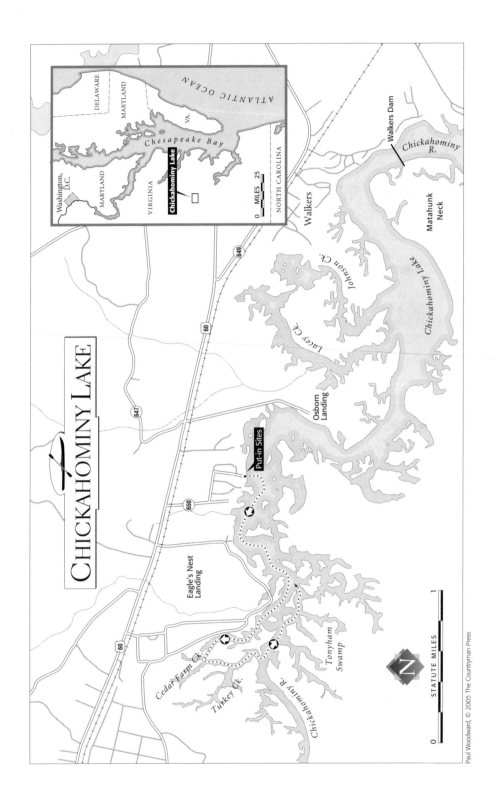

CHICKAHOMINY LAKE

Walkers Dam

Chickahominy R.

Matahunk Neck

Chickahominy Lake

Johnson Ck.

Walkers

Lacey Ck.

Osborn Landing

Put-in Sites

Eagle's Nest Landing

Cedar Farm Ck.

Tunkey Ck.

Chickahominy R.

Tonyham Swamp

60

649

647

60

650

60

N

STATUTE MILES

0   1

Chesapeake Bay

ATLANTIC OCEAN

DELAWARE

MARYLAND

MARYLAND

MARYLAND

Washington, D.C.

VIRGINIA

VA.

Chickahominy Lake

NORTH CAROLINA

0   MILES   25

Paul Woodward, © 2005 The Countryman Press

THIS IS A ROUTE I never intended to scout. The long, narrow lake escaped my notice as I scoured maps and charts of Virginia for trip ideas, and no outfitter or guidebook made mention of this cypress-rimmed reservoir. However, while I stayed a night with friends outside Richmond, they mentioned "Chick Lake" as one of their favorite local fishing holes, so the next day we headed out to explore what it had to offer kayakers. Nestled between Richmond and Williamsburg, we found a water world rich in cypress, osprey, bass, and herons. While most man-made reservoirs drown out all traces of the former habitat beneath their flood of water, the Chickahominy Lake is an exception to this rule. Dammed in 1943 to provide water for the Newport News area, the lake has become a rich new ecosystem in its own right with a labyrinth of side passages that entice the paddler to explore and become lost in their depths. The swamp is densely populated by a variety of birds, including a multitude of osprey, and it is renowned for its excellent fishing. The route that my friends shared with me is one option out of dozens in this entrancing cypress swamp hidden at the edge of Richmond.

Trip Description

Paddle right from the landing to head west on the lake. There are some houses on the northern shore, and cypress-filled islands dot the water to the south. While the reservoir was a surprise to me, bass fisherman love this lake, and they will be your primary company during the day. In general, fishermen are some of the nicest and safest boaters you will ever meet, and they only move fast when they are heading to their fishing spots. This high-speed travel is mostly confined to the center of the lake, and once the fishermen reach their destination, they creep along at a third of a kayaker's speed as they hunt the edges as carefully and thoroughly as great blue herons. Beside largemouth bass, the lake's waters are full of yellow perch, catfish, crappie, and chain pickerel. Shad and rockfish also migrate into the lake, making good use of the fish ladder by Walkers Dam.

After you pass an old farmhouse, the shore bends to the right. Be sure to stay along the right edge, but do not go up into the first side creek you see, unless you are looking for a brief diversion. The lake splits off here as you enter what is known as the Four Corners. To the left you can see a wooden bridge walkway, with a tall arched passageway in the center for boats. As you paddle along a continual bend to the right, you will pass old wooden summer cottages that are mostly abandoned. Just past these cottages, about 1¼ miles from the boat landing, follow the creek that branches off to the right. This is Cedar Farm Creek, and it is a slightly meandering waterway, with a lot of short fingers. This creek is the whole point of the paddle—its wandering passages filled with trees, lilies, and marsh grass. With every dip of your paddle, great blue herons, egrets, kingfishers, ducks, geese, and osprey are stirred into flight. In the summer months, the water in the upper section of the creek is coated with a dense, bright green blanket of duckweed, which is the smallest flowering plant in this region. Beneath this layer of green is an even denser mass of submerged aquatic vegetation. These grasses can be a considerable hindrance to navigation, making this route an excellent autumn and spring trip.

About ½ mile from the lake, you will reach a point where the passage straight ahead is blocked by swamp, and it looks as if the main passage is to the right. Go against your instinct here and bear left through a little passage between the marsh and a clump of trees to the right. This turn is easy to miss, so it is important to pay attention to your paddling pace in order to judge your distance/location. After about 20 feet the way to the left becomes clear. You may hear some traffic noise from I-60, and you will know you are paddling in the correct direction if you are heading away from the traffic.

Even if you are careful, you may still miss the turn. Don't worry. Allow time for getting lost because that is really the point of this kind of paddling. Once you make the left, in less than ¼ mile you will join up with Turkey Creek, which flows in from the right. The water becomes much broader and deeper with the addition of this creek. You can either paddle the remaining ¼ mile back to the lake, or you can investigate the interesting diversion of Turkey Creek.

You have many excellent options once you have completed the 1-mile horseshoe loop and are back on the main lake. Many paddlers may want to head back to the put-in after the loop, with the 4-mile distance serving as a comfortable introduction to kayaking or a quick paddle after work. On your way back to the landing, you can paddle on the outside of the little clump of islands that you paddled on the inside of during the beginning of the trip, thus allowing you to see new scenery for almost the entire route. Those with more time can continue paddling upstream, following the water as it narrows from lake back to natural river. Or you can poke into the other side creeks of the Four Corners area. Use a compass to help you find your way back, and definitely bring along a good map. Or, just get lost for a while—that is often my favorite way to explore deeply. You can also head back downstream, past the landing and toward the dam. The water is much wider here, with countless osprey nests that have been solidly built in cypress trees. Paddling up Lacey Creek and down Johnson Creek can make another good loop. The possibilities and combinations truly are endless.

The day we scouted this route was gray, cold, and rainy, yet we found unrelenting beauty. Furthermore, we saw this route through the eyes of fishermen, and although we each cast our lines a hundred times without once reeling in a fish, the day was

The cypress-rimmed Chickahominy Lake

a success. The true beauty of fishing is that it gives you an excuse to stop and stare at the water. It allows you to see a place intimately, as you notice every log, tree, root, and plant in your quest to find the fish. I first discovered this power of seeing while on a National Outdoor Leadership School (NOLS) backpacking trip. While we backpacked over 100 miles in the month-long trip, the only places that I still see clearly in my mind are the places I explored with my fly rod. Drop me on any one of the unnamed creeks that I fished a dozen years ago, and I would still be able to pinpoint my location on a map without a problem. So my advice is to take up fishing if you want to really learn to see, or at the very least copy the pace of the fishermen that you pass during your journey. The other lesson that I have learned over and over from fishermen is that you need not travel deep into the wilderness to find beauty—it is anywhere and everywhere, often lurking just a few miles from where you live and work. I need to thank Cindy and Scott Deffenbaugh for reminding me of this, and for sharing this great little trip with me.

Alternative Trips

Other good trips in the Richmond area can be found on the James River. You can launch south of Richmond, off the Osborne Turnpike on the river's northern shore, and from the end of Deep Bottom Road. I have paddled from the Deep Bottom location, and it is fine during the off-season but can have a lot of powerboats during the summer. You can also launch on the Appomattox River from the Hopewell Yacht Club and explore the river upstream, or paddle downstream to the James River. You can reach the beautiful marshes of the Presquile Isle National Wildlife Refuge by paddling downriver from Deep Bottom, or upriver from the Appatomattox. It is about 4 miles from either landing to this marshland, and there can be quite a bit of powerboat traffic, making these good weekday or off-season trips. The Chesapeake Bay Gateways Network is in the process of creating a Lower James River Water Trail from Richmond to the Chesapeake. Information on the developing trail can be found at www.jamesriverassociation.org.

16.

Morris Creek

Features: Primitive kayak camping, area of extreme beauty.

Length: 8½ miles for upstream portion of the trip, 13½ miles when paddling the entire creek.

Put-in site: The boat landing is in the Chickahominy Wildlife Management Area, which is a 5,200-acre park managed by the Virginia Department of Game and Inland Fisheries. Primitive camping is available anywhere in the park, as long as you are 100 feet from the nearest road. There are no bathrooms, but there is plenty of parking at the boat landing.

This trip could easily be combined with visits to the historic Colonial towns of Williamsburg and Jamestown, or with a stay in Richmond, which is about one hour to the north. Additionally, stretched along VA 5 is a series of privately operated historic plantations, many of which are open to the public (for a fee), and information can be found about these tours at www.jamesriverplantations.com.

Directions: From VA 5 South (from Richmond), 3.5 miles before the bridge over the Chickahominy River, take a left onto County Route 623 North (CR 623 North)—or, if traveling on VA 5 North, take a right. Follow this for about 4 miles, and then take a right onto CR 621. In 2.8 miles, you will come to a cul-de-sac, where you need to take a right onto the gravel road (this turn is clearly marked). Follow the gravel road for 0.8 mile, bear right where the road splits, and continue for another 0.6 mile until the road ends at the boat landing.

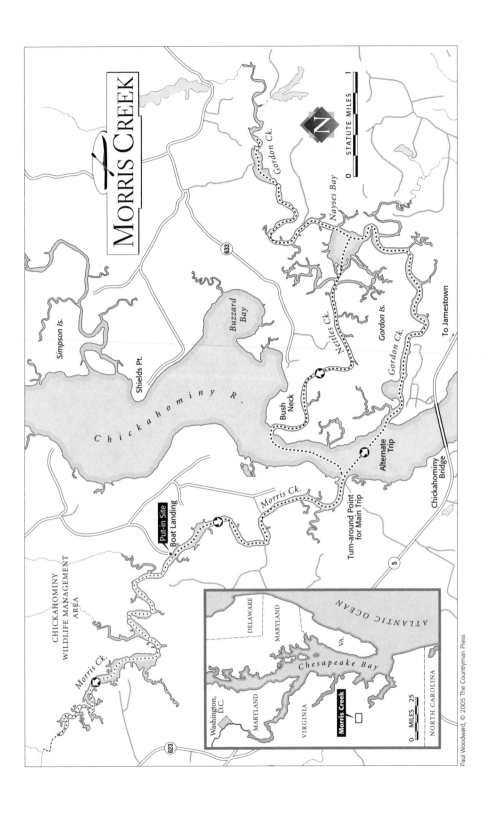

MORRIS CREEK

STATUTE MILES

CHICKAHOMINY
WILDLIFE MANAGEMENT
AREA

Morris Ck.

Put-in Site
Boat Landing

Morris Ck.

Chickahominy R.

Buzzard
Bay

Simpson Is.

Shields Pt.

Bush
Neck

Nettles Ck.

Gordon Is.

Gordon Ck.

Gordon Ck.

Nayses Bay

To Jamestown

Turn-around Point
for Main Trip

Alternate
Trip

Chickahominy
Bridge

5

Morris Ck.

633

623

Washington,
D.C.

MARYLAND

MARYLAND

MARYLAND

DELAWARE

VIRGINIA

VA.

Chesapeake Bay

ATLANTIC OCEAN

NORTH CAROLINA

Morris Creek

MILES   25

Paul Woodward, © 2005 The Countryman Press

IF YOU WANT TO get novice paddlers hooked on kayaking, bring them to Morris Creek, which is a wandering tributary of the Chickahominy River. Do not worry about paddling downstream, and banish all distance goals from your mind. Instead, just lead them upcreek at a gentle pace and allow them to become entranced. This creek begins beautiful, only to become more glorious with every bend. The power of the creek's majesty is so great that while I was within it, all other places in the world disappeared from my memory. I was confounded in any effort to conjure up a single place that was equal in beauty to Morris.

Trip Description

The put-in starts you out in the center section of Morris Creek, with the Chickahominy River about 2½ miles downstream. However, for this route, paddle right to head upstream, away from the Chickahominy and into the meandering beauty of Morris Creek. The creek is relatively broad, and the big looping bends of the waterway are well spaced, with about ¼ mile of straightaway between each bend. This entire creek is a pristine example of a healthy freshwater marsh ecosystem. Marsh mallow, cattails, pickerelweed, and wild rice fill the lowlands of the creek valley, with a dense riparian forest of cypress, pine, and hardwoods along the highlands. Like the Chickahominy River, during non-glacial periods of history, Morris Creek was a broad waterway, filling the creek's valley from bank to bank, carving wide meanders out of the land. The water receded to a narrower passage during the last ice age, exposing wide stretches of dry land on either side of the creek. When the ice melted and the sea level rose, the water backfilled the creek, creating the expansive marshes that frame the river today.

Side guts and creeks crease the marshland, allowing access to minor valleys and ecosystems. I usually paddle these side routes on my way back, when my pace has slowed, when my curiosity about what I will find upstream has been satiated, and when I am looking for any excuse to linger longer on the water. Some of the side guts will be impassable due to vegetation, and I was unable to even find the entrance to the first one, ¼ mile above the put-in, due to the dense vegetation of the summer. Other guts will be choked by submerged aquatic vegetation, which will cause your kayak to slide to a stop as you become entangled in an underwater meadow. Like all plants, the grasses are dependent on the sun for photosynthesis and only grow in the shallow areas where the sun's rays can reach them. Thus, while the center passage of Morris Creek always remains clear, the edges and side creeks can become choked, particularly at low tide. These hindrances of vegetation provide good reason to paddle in all seasons—while the fecundity of the marsh is glorious in late spring and early summer, the dormant vegetation of autumn and winter exposes clear edges and boundaries, opening and transforming the waterway.

There are two guts that are always passable and well worth exploring. The first is on the right side of the creek, about 1¼ miles upstream of the landing, after the third bend. It is long and meandering and is quite broad in its beginning bends. After this gut, when rounding the next bend, you will see a white house up on a bluff that will disappear from sight as you grow near, only to reappear as you reach its bank. There is an entrance to a gut on the left, and this is the second side gut that is always passable. It is shorter than the downstream gut, but it is a beautiful replication of Morris Creek in miniature. As the creek narrows, there are many snags hanging into the water, with turtles occupying every available spot. While I was there frogs filled the shoreline and seemed to make sport of jumping over, around, and occasionally on top of my kayak.

There is a marsh island in the center of the main stem of the creek, just above the second side gut, and both sides are passable. After the island and a wide looping left turn upstream, you will pass a large boathouse and dock on the left, followed by a smaller boat lift and an even smaller dock. You will see a couple of houses, then the creek will begin to narrow, with yellow pond lilies filling in the edges, effectively halving the navigable space at low tide in the summertime. Each plant has a single dark green leaf pad that is round and flat, with an accompanying yellow flower. They are submerged by high tide, and when the water recedes, the lily pads are mottled with sediment, which is why these plants are locally known as spatterdock.

In the earlier section of water, I saw a fair number of osprey and great blue herons. As the creek narrows, with the wooded edges closing in, the birdlife increases and diversifies. I saw an immature bald eagle on one bend and then a mature eagle on the next. Herons, kingfishers, and turtles all become more plentiful. You will pass by another island; the left side is the more direct passage of the two options. There are some more houses on the left. The creek narrows and narrows, and the bends come more and more quickly.

Then, at a bend to the left, you will pass a wood duck box and the small, narrow, wooded portion of the paddle begins. This section lasts for less than ½ mile and should be savored. When I guide groups in areas such as this, I often institute a practice I call the silent, separated paddle. The basic idea is to separate each kayak by as much time and space as possible, staggering each person's departure into the section by at least a minute, if not more. That way, rather than miss the intimate and quiet beauty of these upper reaches with the distraction of conversation, each person can experience the wonder of the area in solitude. They can allow themselves to be seduced by beauty, can pause to watch a dragonfly alight upon their bow, and can stalk herons along the edges. I have used this paddling technique with people aged 7 to 70, and they unfailingly report it as their favorite experience on the water.

At low tide you will come upon a series of snags just below the bridge for CR 623 that prevents further passage upstream. At high tide you may be able to explore slightly farther upstream, even getting a little way past the bridge. There are many good rest areas along the creek, especially in the upper section where you can beach your boat and gain easy access to low bluffs with a quick climb up the soft banks. You may notice signs of campfires at your lunch spot, and that is because all of the Chickahominy Wildlife Management Area is open for primitive camping. This sort of kayak camping is a rare luxury in Chesapeake country and should be savored and utilized. If you do take advantage of this opportunity, make sure to observe Leave-No-Trace paddling practices, and leave the campsite just as you found it (or even better than you found it, by removing any trash or damage done by earlier campers).

If you still have time or energy when you reach the landing, continue your paddle by heading downstream toward the Chickahominy.

The space between the bends lengthens, with only two major curves in the creek. While upstream the banks are muddy, downstream of the landing the creek bottom is a mixture of hard sand and gravel. The first bend begins with a right-hand turn about 1 mile downstream of the landing, with a high sand bluff on the outside of the turn, overlooking a sea of marsh grass. The creek bends back to the left, completing a hairpin turn before the waterway returns to its southeastern/downstream flow.

After a ½-mile straightaway, the river begins to bend to the right; and on the outside of the turn, the left bank ends with a high, two-story cliff. The rest of the creek flows through marsh grass from here to the river. There is a small spot here where you can beach your kayak, allowing you to climb up for a great view of the surrounding countryside, especially in the wintertime. This would make a superb campsite, especially because it allows good access for downstream paddling on the Chickahominy. You can see the VA 5 bridge over the Chickahominy from here, along with the mouth of the creek, which lies another ½ mile downstream. I had my fill of paddling by this point, but if you need a total sense of completion for your

Morris Creek, one of the most beautiful places in the world

day's journey, you can reach the mouth of the river by pressing on for another ½ mile.

While usually home to a shooting range, the area downriver from the boat landing was closed to vehicular access while I was scouting the area. Hollywood apparently agrees with my assessment of the creek's unique beauty because a major studio film, called *The New World*, about the colony at Jamestown, was being shot while I was there—its release in 2005 timed to celebrate the 400th anniversary of that settlement in 2007. The location of the film is accurate, not only because it is several miles north of the true settlement, but also because Captain John Smith was captured by members of the Chickahominy tribe while he was exploring the river. They turned their captive over to Powhatan, chief of the Powhatan Confederacy, a conglomeration of tribes that covered most of the coastal plain, not including the Chickahominy. That capture is the genesis of the legend of Pocahontas, who is said to have begged her father, Chief Powhatan, to spare the captain, thus allowing the English to settle in Virginia.

Chickahominy means "coarse pounded corn people," and they had a long-standing agricultural tradition that allowed them to build stable communities, with stationary homes and lives that were much different than the teepee culture of the western tribes. Their intimate relationship with the cultivation of corn is evident not only in their name but also in their calendar of seasons. Nestled between summer and fall is a fifth season, *Nepino,* which means the "earing of corn." While the Chickahominy's pardoning of Smith makes for a good movie, it was really the sharing of their traditions, particularly the cultivation of corn that allowed the English to settle successfully in Virginia. Over a thousand members of the Chickahominy tribe still live in Virginia, making it the largest tribe left in the state.

An avid movie buff, I have long regretted the lack of true Chesapeake beauty on the big screen. I do not have to see the Jamestown movie to know that any film made along Morris Creek will amply fill that void. My expectations for Morris Creek were high, and as was so often the case in my explorations of Virginia, my hopes for this waterway were well exceeded. I know this is an area I will return to again and again, and if I had to pick a favorite trip in Virginia, this would certainly be at the top of the list.

Alternative Trips

An excellent addition to this route is to paddle downstream from Morris Creek, across the Chickahominy. Head up Gordon Creek, through Nayses Bay, and then back down Nellie Creek to the Chickahominy, just upstream of Morris Creek, thereby completing a circumnavigation of Gordon Island. It is about a 12-mile paddle and is a variation of a route that John Page Williams mentions in his book *Exploring the Chesapeake in Small Boats.* Another area paddling opportunity lies just downriver on the James, around the historic settlement of Jamestown. Tamsin Venn provides a good description of this paddle in her book *Sea Kayaking Along the Mid-Atlantic Coast,* and this route is also covered by the Powhatan Creek Blueway Water Trail. For more information visit www.james-city.va.us.

17.

Poquoson

Features: The largest saltwater marsh on the western shore, and the absolute best trip on the western shore for birding, with brown pelicans, oystercatchers, and black skimmers, along with a variety of herons and egrets.

Length: 10½ miles (with considerable variations of this length and route available).

Put-in site: The boat landing is on the edge of the town of Poquoson. In 2003 the city made national news due to the devastation it suffered during Hurricane Isabel, when half the town's 4,300 homes suffered some sort of damage. The landing is free and public, with no bathroom facilities but with plenty of parking. There are two long, broad cement ramps. The docks and ramps seem to be well used by commercial watermen for loading and unloading, and many watermen also keep their large crabbing skiffs tied up to pilings in deeper water, using little john boats and punts to get to and from their boats. Tidewater Adventures occasionally offers trips here.

Directions: From US 17, exit onto VA 171 East (take a right if traveling northbound, or a left if traveling southbound). It is 3.7 miles to Wythe Creek Road. Cross over that, and staying on the main road (which will change names from Little Florida to Poquoson Avenue), continue for another 3.2 miles and then take a left onto Messick Road. Follow this for almost 2 miles to the boat landing, which is near the very end of the road.

THE CITY OF POQUOSON borrowed its name from the Algonquin word for great marsh, and it would be difficult to come up with a more apt

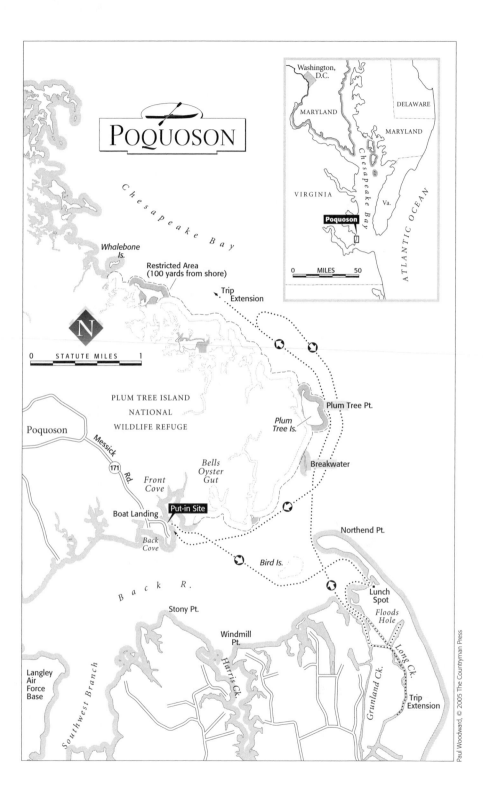

POQUOSON

Washington, D.C.

MARYLAND

DELAWARE

MARYLAND

VIRGINIA

Chesapeake Bay

Va.

ATLANTIC OCEAN

Poquoson

0   MILES   50

Chesapeake Bay

Whalebone Is.

Restricted Area
(100 yards from shore)

Trip Extension

N

0   STATUTE MILES   1

PLUM TREE ISLAND

NATIONAL

WILDLIFE REFUGE

Poquoson

Messick Rd

171

Front Cove

Bells Oyster Gut

Plum Tree Is.

Plum Tree Pt.

Breakwater

Boat Landing

Put-in Site

Back Cove

Northend Pt.

Bird Is.

Lunch Spot

Floods Hole

B a c k   R.

Stony Pt.

Windmill Pt.

Langley Air Force Base

Southwest Branch

Harris Ck.

Grunland Ck.

Long Ck.

Trip Extension

Paul Woodward, © 2005 The Countryman Press

description of the area. East of the city is the Plum Tree Island National Wildlife Refuge, which is the largest salt marsh on the western shore, providing habitat for a diverse array of wildlife. The irony of this abundance of wildlife is that much of it has been preserved through some of the most destructive forces that mankind can muster. From 1917 to the late 1950s, the wetland was used as a bombing and gunnery range, with aerial bombs exploding craters deep into the marsh, creating small circular ponds while sending showers of detritus high into the air. This 3,275-acre area became the Plum Tree Island National Wildlife Refuge in 1972, and has been forever closed to development, primarily due to the high number of bombs that failed to explode. This dormant ordnance makes the refuge off-limits to travel by land, but that does not matter much to the kayaker. This trip is neither destination nor goal driven. It does not matter if you paddle 3 or 30 miles in this area, it is all beautiful and worthy of exploration.

Trip Description

The boat landing puts you on Front Cove. Paddle straight across from the put-in to the other side of the pilings where some of the local fishing fleet is moored. Once there you will be out of the main channel and near the beauty of the shoreline. Bear right (south) and follow the shoreline to the open water of the Back River. Once you are on the river, look to your right to see the large military and NASA complexes that dominate the upriver shoreline. While Poquoson used to be primarily a farmer and watermen community, it is now home to the civilians and military personnel who work at the numerous local military installations, including Langley Air Force Base, NASA's Langley Research Center and the army's Fort Monroe.

As you round the curve into the main part of Back Creek, bear left to paddle toward the open Bay. You will see a duck blind straight ahead and a tall lookout tower in the distance on the marsh's edge. Spaced along the refuge edges are blue-and-white NATIONAL WILDLIFE REFUGE signs reminding you that entry is prohibited. You will likely be escorted for some of your journey by groups of fighter jets that launch from

The long, wild beach of Grandview Nature Preserve

Langley Air Force Base. The flight path of these gas hawks takes them directly down the river; and although they rapidly gain altitude, they are low enough at Plum Tree that you can see the pilots.

You will reach the opening to Bell's Oyster Gut about ¼ mile from Front Cove. There is a low duck blind in the center of the opening, and it is a relatively common type of simple blind, in which the low-slung john boat serves as the platform, and the surrounding structure works to camouflage the boat and its hunters. Looking in toward the gut, you can also see a large concrete bunker on the island's interior. The refuge is scattered with these bunkers, which were used to observe the bombing and gunnery exercises. The watchtower was used for this purpose as well. At this point you need to direct your boat away from the island. The area from Bell's Oyster Gut to Whalebone Island is a designated danger zone, which means in addition to not getting on the island, you must also remain 100 yards away from the island's shoreline. This rule is absolute. This distance from the island might seem extreme, but the water surrounding the marshland is shallow, and bombs have a funny way of working their way up out of the sediment, so your safety is guaranteed only when you keep a football field between you and the wetland.

Do not let this bomb talk scare you, the birds and scenery make paddling by this former bombing range well worth the intimidating regulations. The restrictions in no way hinder the paddle because to the southeast, in the middle of the river, is a little island. It is surrounded by channel markers, which are necessary to allow powerboaters to navigate the shallow shoals of the river's mouth. Head across the sand flats to this island. If you are paddling any time from midspring to midautumn, the sheer volume of birdlife that populates this stretch of sandy marsh will stun you. In mid-July the air was filled with arctic terns, oystercatchers, and skimmers, with plover and gulls patrolling the sand. This is a delicate and rare piece of nesting habitat, and thus it has been heavily posted with AREA CLOSED—BIRD NESTING signs.

When I originally was planning this route, I had intended to stay alongside Plum Tree Island, paddling 100 yards off the edge of the marsh as I followed it out into the Bay, toward Whalebone Island. However, once I had reached the satisfying diversion of the bird-filled island, I noticed exposed sandbars between that center island and the southern shoreline of Back River. Each of these sandbars hosts its own population of birds, with the largest of the bars containing a sizeable grouping of brown pelicans. Once I reached the last of these flats, I was only 100 yards from the long wild beach of Northend Point, which is protected by the Grandview Nature Reserve, a Hampton City park. This beach is an excellent rest spot, except during the nesting season, which runs from April through June. During these months you should stretch your legs away from shore, taking advantage of the generally shallow depths of the river's edges.

While eating lunch on the beach, I idly watched a workboat headed up Long Creek. My interest was piqued when it had not returned a half hour later. The creek was off my map, but I decided to turn my back on Plum Tree in order to follow the boat into new areas. Entering the creek you'll see three antennas at about 2 o'clock and a watertower at 1 o'clock. Hug the left/east shoreline when entering the creek and pass by the east side of the largely wooded island that dominates the creek's mouth. It is a broad and straight passage that is tree-lined on both sides, providing a nice vacation for the eyes after so much open water and marshland. Many great blue herons and green herons hunt along this shoreline, and

Bay Bombers—the Brown Pelican

I have often been awakened at a waterside campsite by the early morning bombing of pelicans. These large, 4-foot-long birds plummet out of the sky and head first toward their target, slamming into the water with such force that the splash spins them around 180 degrees, often submerging them entirely. The concussion of these mighty splashes carries far over the water, alerting everyone around that the pelicans are working.

Pelicans eat up to 4 pounds of fish per day, all of which they catch with these powerful dives. They fish whenever the fishing is good, which is usually during the cooler morning and early evening hours, when the fish come nearer to the surface of the water. Pelicans have excellent eyesight and can see fish while flying 60 feet above the water. They enter the water with their mouth open so that a large pouch distends from their long, straight bill. They can hold three times more in this bill than their stomach can digest, but most of that volume is water, which they push out, leaving behind only fish. A fish or two sometimes escapes during this straining but is usually gulped up by the gulls that accompany the pelicans everywhere. Sometimes the gulls are even so bold as to sit on the pelicans' bills while the straining is taking place.

Much like osprey and bald eagles, pelicans were once victim to DDT poisoning, and their eggs' shells were too thin to survive. However, since the banning of DDT in 1972, the numbers have rebounded, making them another conservation success story. Brown pelicans are the only nonwhite species of pelican, and Virginia is the northernmost state where pelicans live year-round. You will find them

in about ½ mile you come to a three-way split. To the left is a beautiful cove known as Flood's Hole, which is absolutely full of birdlife. At the far, eastern end of the cove you will come within 100 feet of the open Bay, with just a narrow strip of marsh between you and open water. I saw night herons, green herons, great egrets, bitterns and sandpipers—all are common on the Chesapeake, although not usually in such abundance. Terns and gulls filled the air above the marsh and water. I saw at least a hundred individual birds in this ¼-mile-long detour.

You will find pelicans on most trips in Virginia's open water.

on most trips in the open waters of Virginia, with their numbers increasing as you travel south in the state, toward broader and saltier waters like Poquoson and the Virginia Coastal Reserve.

Pelicans are gregarious and social creatures, and you will rarely find one without a companion. They fly together in groups of at least two to three birds, often gliding inches from the water, with their 6-foot wingspan fully extended so that the feathers on their wing tips almost trail in the water. They also nest in large colonies, laying two to four eggs in beach nests, which is one of the reasons that areas like Fishermen's Island and the Grandview Nature Preserve are restricted during the spring and summer. In fact, since the banning of DDT, the main stress on the pelicans' continued recovery is the loss of beach breeding habitat, so it is easy and understandable why you can't land on nesting beaches during the spring and early summer.

Back on the main creek, it is possible to follow Long Creek for another 2¼ miles upstream, past the little town of Grandview. It may even be possible to navigate a small inlet from Long Island back onto the open Bay. It looked absolutely beguiling, but Plum Tree Island was calling my name, so I took the western option at the three-way juncture, to see if I could paddle around the marsh island on my way back to the river. I stirred a dozen egrets into flight, filling the air with a graceful white dance. When you reach a T-junction in the water, take a right to head back to the river. The western side of the island contains a broad marsh that buffers the trees in its interior. As I reached the head of the island I surprised a doe that was feasting on the marsh grass—I do not know which one of us was more startled.

Back out on the Back River, I paddled straight across its mouth. This open-water crossing is relatively safe, especially because most of the area is comprised of sand flats that keep powerboats confined to well-marked channels. Just do not stray into the outer edges of the sand flats, or you may experience some small dumping surf where the shallows first occur.

Stay on the open Bay by paddling to the right of the lookout tower and the long breakwater of double pilings. These pilings are usually covered with long rows of cormorants, gulls, and pelicans. A string-of-pearls chain of marsh islands protects the Bay-exposed shoreline of Plum Tree Island. It seems as if you could paddle along this exposed shore forever. In about 3 miles of paddling from Plum Tree Point, you will reach Whalebone Island, after which you can paddle closer to the refuge, although landing on the island is still prohibited. I did not paddle this far, having seen enough beauty for one day. Instead, I turned around after a while to make my slow way back to the landing, drifting for stretches of time to enjoy simply gazing upon this expansive sea of marsh.

Alternative Trips

John Page Williams describes a trip around Cow's Island in his book *Exploring the Chesapeake in Small Boats*. This island is in the northern portion of the refuge. The easiest access is from Ren's Marina, and the water around Cow's Island is less restricted. The refuge even occasionally allows foot traffic on the island under a special-use permit.

Part III — Southeastern Virginia

18.

Blackwater River

Features: Swamp paddling, good fishing, wild turkey, longnose gar, and miles of solitude.

Length: 6 miles (with more mileage available up and downstream).

Put-in site: The Joyner's Bridge boat landing is a state-managed, free boat launch with plenty of parking in a large gravel lot above the landing. Tidewater Adventures occasionally runs trips north of here, through the Blackwater River Preserve.

Directions: Travel 1.5 miles east of the Blackwater River in Franklin, on US Business 58, and exit onto US 258 North. Follow US 258 for about 3.5 miles, and then take a left onto County Route 611 (CR 611). Follow that for about 2.5 miles. The landing is on the east side of the bridge, on the left (south) side of the road. A brown public landing sign marks it.

MY DAY ON THE BLACKWATER RIVER did not go according to plan. I began the day at a small boat launch off CR 621, with the aim of paddling downriver through an ancient stand of old-growth bald cypress trees. Some of the trees are over 800 years old and protected by the Nature Conservancy's Blackwater River Preserve. That was the point of the paddle—or so I thought. However, ¼ mile downstream, my plan was thwarted by a large tree that blocked the whole river, with several more downed trees visible beyond that first obstacle. The downstream current was strong, and it was with much struggling that I freed myself

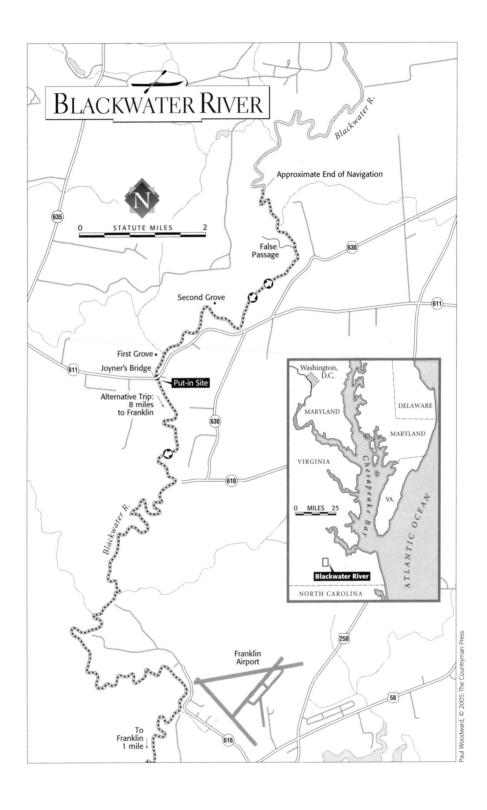

from being pinned against the log and turned back to the landing. Three more times I went to landings; three more times I was turned back by downed trees or nonexistent entry spots. While I had expected to find the occasional tree felled by 2003's Hurricane Isabel, the damage along this river was beyond my expectations. However, just when I had given up hope, I found a stretch of river that was free of obstacles, leaving from the landing off CR 611. Then the river took over the day, erasing the morning's frustrations with its beauty as I stopped looking for a point to the paddle and just enjoyed the river for what it was.

Trip Description

Like all trips in this book, this is a there-and-back route that requires no vehicle shuttles. Whenever possible, I prefer to paddle against the current in the morning so that I am working the hardest when I am at my freshest and using the power of the river to aid me in my journey home. Therefore, I paddled to the right to head upriver, away from the town of Franklin, which lay about 8 miles to the south. The current is usually rather weak in the wider areas, but the entire river can become non-navigable when the river is in a flood stage, so pay attention to the local weather—you may want to avoid this there-and-back route after a heavy rain.

As I paddled underneath Joyner's Bridge, I was still wrapped up in the frustration of the morning's thwarted attempts, and I glared straight ahead, daring the river to throw another obstruction my way. Then I rounded the first of the river's many gentle bends and encountered a flooded forest of trees that stunned me into stillness. It was a mixture of tupelo, cypress, elm, and maple, all with trunks that were fluted out at the bottoms, buttressing them against the instability of growing in water. I wandered among the towering trees, feeling like a child among giants. This grove reminded me of the architecture of a great cathedral, and my mind settled as I slowed to join the pace of the river. I left the aggravations of the road behind me, feeling clean and new for the remainder of my journey upstream.

After several gentle river bends, about 1 mile from the landing, you will round a sharper bend toward the right. The main flow continues along the right bank, while off in the left bank, there is another cove of trees, even deeper that the last. While I had begun the day by searching for 800-year-old cypress, it is these groves that turned out to be the point of the paddle—it was about meandering through beauty. There are several sandy islands among the trees, and your day would not be wasted if you brought a camp chair and a blanket, a book and a journal, and spent the entire paddle right in this spot.

After rounding a sharp turn to the left, you will enter a long straight section. There were explosions of water all around me as I made the turn, and I found myself surrounded by longnose gar. These fish measured about 2 to 3 feet in length, but can grow as long as 5 feet. They school near the surface and are a striking, primitive species of fish that date back to the age of dinosaurs.

After a little over ½ mile, the straight section comes to an end. The main passage of the river continues up to the left, past two false passages to the right. Neither of these side sloughs go far, but both are beautiful diversions.

Despite its name, the Blackwater is not black but rather a dark amber brown, stained by the tannic acid of the cypress trees. Called bald cypress, because unlike most conifers it sheds all of its needles every winter, this tree defines not only the color of the Blackwater River but also the shape of its swampland. Cypress dominate the mixed forest of trees and can live to be 1,000 years old, looming tall above the modern history of the United States. While their reddish, wide, and stringy trunks are easily identifiable, their most distinctive trait is their "knees." These are shoots that branch up out of the water from the roots, and it is thought that the thinner bark on these knees helps the submerged roots of the trees emit their oxygen.

The banks will begin to rise and all traces of road noise will disappear. Unlike many swamps, there are small, flat sandbars and banks scattered throughout the river, creating many good places to stop for a rest. This sandy soil is common in the area. The nearby city of Suffolk was built upon such soft soil, and the Colonial city faced the constant problem of pedestrians sinking into the town's sandy streets. The solution—to fortify the roads with tar and turpentine—worked to prevent sinking citizens, but it also further polluted the already unclean and unhealthy environment of Colonial Suffolk. I chose a lunch spot on an unsinkable sand bank just north of the false coves and passed my time watching hummingbirds and damselflies in the air, and water striders and whirligigs on the water.

The current, which was barely noticeable by the landing, becomes stronger as the river narrows, much like the effect created by pinching off a section of garden hose. This narrowing increases the likelihood that a single fallen tree will block your passage. I came upon such a snag just above the straight section, following a side cove off to the left to avoid the hindrance. This detour led me ¼ mile into a forest before I was eventually blocked by a giant blowdown, which exposed the massive and shallow root mass of these swampland trees. Through some creative navigating, I was able to weave my way through the forest back to the main channel of the river, entering it 100 feet above the downstream snag.

Often where there is one snag, there are others not too far away, and such was the case with the Blackwater. It was possible to paddle around some, but eventually a giant cypress blocked all passage. The banks here are flat, allowing for an easy portage

The Blackwater River offers miles of swamp paddling and solitude

around the dams; however, decide what your goal is for the day before you proceed. If you are doing a one-way, downstream paddle, then you should portage around every log. However, for there-and-back paddlers, portaging may not be worth the effort. Do not be afraid to leave your boat and hike for a bit. Walk upstream to see if the way clears up in 100 feet. Or, embrace the possibilities of the day and go for a true hike—just make sure you drag your boat well clear of the water.

The many old logs and snags I saw that had been trimmed back with a chainsaw told me that this section of the Blackwater River has some good patrons. The right-of-way trimming is most likely the work of rangers from the Virginia Department of Parks and Recreation, in combination with local fishermen who tend to be good stewards of their fishing holes. I scouted the Blackwater River only nine months after the destructive wrath of Hurricane Isabel, and barring another hurricane, I would not be surprised if all the passageways are clear in another nine months.

Be careful when paddling back downstream around partial snags. Your velocity can be deceptively fast, and it can be quite challenging to maneuver your boat around the obstacles. If you have to choose between keeping both hands on the paddle to steer and getting whacked in the face by a stick, choose the latter. If you stop steering you may broach against a snag, which at best will get you stuck and at worse will knock you underwater, holding you and your boat down with a tangle of submerged branches. Rudders are a hazard in areas like this, as the steering cables can easily become snagged and hung up in overhanging shrubbery—the number of clients that I have disentangled from trees must be in the hundreds. So if you are doing a lot of paddles like this, buy a non-rudder or a skegged boat (paddling with the skeg stowed in environments like this). Or, if you exclusively paddle rivers like the Blackwater, buy a short gunkholers boat, or even a canoe. Canoes give you more flexibility with portages, enabling you to step onto a log, pull the boat over, and then step back into the boat, all without ever pulling over to shore.

I saw a wild turkey on my way back downstream, and I will have to agree with Benjamin Franklin in his high estimation of the bird—while bald eagles are nice, the wild and wary turkey would have made a fine national emblem. The gar were still rolling in the river, and the groves still seduced me in stillness. Thus, by the time I reemerged at the landing, I had spent five hours on 6 miles of river. Joyner's Bridge was the sight of several Civil War battles, and I sometimes find it interesting to try to picture the old conflicts, imagining the soldiers seeking cover in the surrounding trees. However, on that day I stayed away from all historical fantasies. The silent groves of trees were simply and entirely enough for the day—and I was wholly satisfied.

Alternative Trips

There are many alternatives for paddling the Blackwater River, especially if you have two cars available for a shuttle trip. The upstream launch that first thwarted me was off CR 621, and after some portaging you should be able to reach the Blackwater River Preserve. The downstream pick-up point for this is 8 miles south, where CR 620 crosses the river—this is an unofficial launch site with minimal to no parking. There is also an official public landing off CR 603. The upstream portion was heavily blocked with snags, but it is about 9 miles south to the landing at Joyner's Bridge. Or, you can launch from Joyner's and paddle downstream about 8 miles to the boat landing in Franklin. Franklin made national news in 1999 when Hurricane Floyd flooded the Blackwater, drowning the town with a record 500-year flood.

There is a tidewater creek off the North Landing River that shares both name and scenery with the Blackwater River but does not have as many fallen trees. The Blackwater Creek is a tributary of the North Landing River and is accessible off VA 165/Blackwater Road.

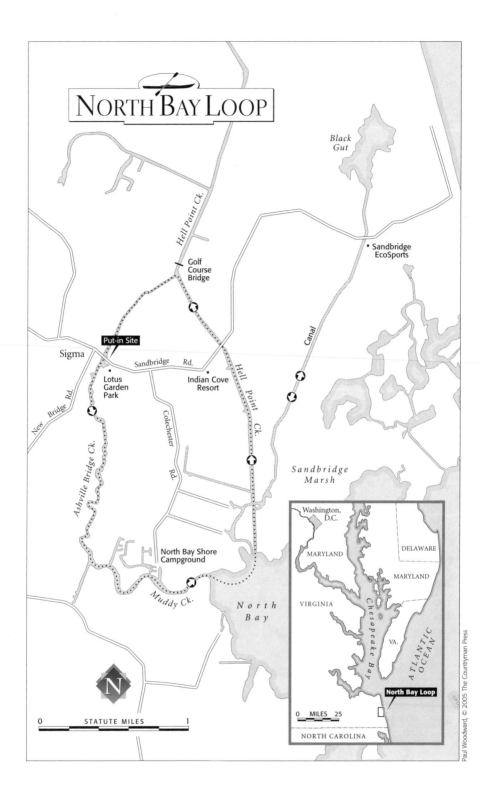

NORTH BAY LOOP

Black
Gut

Hell Point Ck.

Golf
Course
Bridge

Sandbridge
EcoSports

Canal

Put-in Site

Sigma

Sandbridge   Rd.

Lotus
Garden
Park

Indian Cove
Resort

Hell   Point   Ck.

New Bridge Rd.

Ashville Bridge Ck.

Colechester

Rd.

Sandbridge
Marsh

North Bay Shore
Campground

Muddy Ck.

North
Bay

Washington,
D.C.

MARYLAND

DELAWARE

MARYLAND

VIRGINIA

Chesapeake Bay

VA.

ATLANTIC
OCEAN

North Bay Loop

0   MILES   25

NORTH CAROLINA

0   STATUTE MILES   1

N

Paul Woodward, © 2005 The Countryman Press

19.

North Bay Loop

Features: Good beginner or sunset paddle. Deer, river otters, muskrat, herons, osprey, and a multitude of songbirds abound.

Length: 5½ miles.

Put-in site: The launch spot is in the Lotus Garden Park, a small roadside oasis established by the Cape Henry Women's Club in 1955. The wild lotus that gave the park its name later died, likely damaged by either herbicides or temporary draining of the area for road construction. While the lack of lotus is a shame, the park remains an excellent launching spot for this round-trip journey. There are picnic tables but no bathroom facilities.

The North Bay Loop is the home route for Sandbridge EcoSports, a rental and tour company. The shop is located on a spur off the creek, allowing you to paddle your rental kayak right out the back door and around this route. This is also a popular Wild River Outfitters trip, and Tidewater Adventures offers a similar trip, although they launch from Horn Point, which is south of the loop on the western shore of North Bay.

A good addition to the trip is to end with a visit to Marge and Rick's Restaurant. It is located 100 yards east of the park on Sandbridge Road and serves up good, cheap seafood, making it a local favorite for years.

Directions: From I-64, exit onto I-264 East. Take exit 22, turning right at the end of the exit ramp onto Birdneck Road. Travel for 2.8 miles and then take a right onto General Booth Boulevard. Follow this for about 5 miles, and then take a left onto Princess Anne Road. At the next traffic light, proceed straight (in the middle lane). The road now becomes Sandbridge Road. Follow this for about 2 to 3 miles. After the road makes a hard, 90-degree left, you will pass New Bridge Road on the right and then cross Asheville Bridge Creek. The park is on the right, on the other side of the bridge.

ON ROAD MAPS OF THE AREA, the three-creek North Bay Loop seems stunningly uninspiring, with the entire route lying within the crowded developments of Sandbridge. I would have overlooked this paddle entirely had it not been for the impassioned intervention of Lillie Gilbert, owner of Wild River Outfitters, who named the trip as one of her favorites. A friend who lives in Sandbridge vehemently agreed with Lillie's assessment, so I arranged to paddle this route with her, tagging the exploration on to the end of a day spent paddling the nearby Great Dismal Swamp, thus ensuring that the day would not be a complete loss if the loop proved to be overhyped. All of my doubts were assuaged within two minutes as it was once again proven to me that you need not travel hundreds of miles to find wilderness. Rather, all you need is a kayak and an open mind. The route circles through a wide variety of environments, from cypress and freshwater marshes to brackish wetlands and riparian pine forest land. Its short length makes this an excellent route for novice paddlers, or for any kayakers who wish to extend their day with an evening paddle into beauty.

Trip Description

As in all circumnavigations, you must choose your direction of travel. My friend and I chose to head south, paddling left from the landing on Asheville Bridge Creek. This arbitrary decision yielded great results, beginning the trip with the astounding beauty of the downstream creek, while allowing us to end the journey with the quiet and intimate passage of the upper creek.

The first mile on Asheville Bridge Creek winds through a healthy, diverse freshwater marsh with a wide assortment of native grasses and plants, combined with the cypress and pine trees that punctuate the shoreline. The creek meanders through a paradise of marsh hibiscus and cattail, pickerelweed and arrowhead, revealing new landscapes of beauty with every turn. Because this route is in the middle of a populated area, you will see the occasional house tucked within quiet coves, but they are too few to detract from the quiet glory of the creek. Some property owners are more private than others, and the owners of the first house we passed protected their cove by hanging a string of barbed wire low across the water.

Take the gorgeous first part of this journey as slow as you can, because after only about 1 mile of travel, Muddy Creek joins from the west and the direction of flow changes from generally southward to generally eastward. With the addition of this second creek, the width of the waterway increases markedly, and the quality of the marsh plummets as the diversity of the native marsh is overrun by the invasive species of phragmites. The grass towers overhead, blocking any views of the surrounding world. Shortly after the mouth of Muddy Creek, you will pass the entrance to a short, straight gut on the left/southern bank. Blue Pete's Restaurant is at the end of this gut. Blue Pete's welcomes kayakers but is fairly upmarket, so wear your better paddling clothes if you plan on including the restaurant in your trip. Back on the main stem of Muddy Creek, the second major gut you pass is on the left/north side of the river. This is the entrance to North Bay Shore Campground, which is the first of two campgrounds you will pass on this loop.

After you pass a house on the left/north side of Muddy Creek, trees begin on the outside corner of a bend to the right/south; and when you round that turn, you will see the broad waters of North Bay before you. Heading to the left/east, you will paddle in North Bay for only ¼ mile before you turn to the left/north into the broad cove indentation along the shoreline. The entrance to Hell Point Creek is on the far eastern edge of the cove. This is an old, man-made canal; and while it is not quite as wild and beautiful as Asheville Bridge Creek, it is certainly more diverse than Muddy Creek. We paddled at twilight and enjoyed a beaver escort for about 100 yards of our journey up the long and narrow creek. After about ¼ mile from North Bay, you will pass the entrance to a side canal on the right/east side of the waterway. Sand-bridge Eco Sports is situated 1¾ miles up this canal. They offer kayak rentals from the back of their store, which makes a great alternative launch site for those in the need of rental boats.

Continuing north on Hell Point Creek, in about 1 mile from North Bay, you will pass Indian Cove Resort. Numerous campers had fishing lines in the water as we passed, so make sure to be aware of this hazard, staying well away from the lines to keep the fishermen from growing nervous or disgruntled. You will pass under Sandbridge Road about ¼ mile above the campground, marking the 4-mile point of your journey. Past the bridge, the shoreline becomes entirely wooded, with a lot of herons fishing along the shaded shore. Once you see the golf course bridge, begin looking on the left/west bank of the creek for the secret passage back to Asheville Bridge Creek. The entrance is about ½ mile above Sandbridge Road and about 50 yards shy of the bridge. It is only about 10 feet across, so it is easy to miss among the overhanging trees.

Having begun the trip with the overwhelming beauty of Asheville Bridge Creek, it is fitting that the trip ends back on the upper section of that same creek. Here the beauty is more subdued, consisting of a narrow passageway with an overhanging mixture of trees, from pine to maple to cypress. Once you reach Sandbridge Road, you are faced with a final decision. Rather than an open passage under the bridge, the water is funneled through two culverts. While foreboding, these narrow tunnels are passable at a normal mid-high water level. Stowing your paddle under your deck lines and leaning backwards into a limbo, you can work your way through by pushing along the top of the tunnel with your fingertips. The intrepid paddlers who choose this route will en-counter a few spiders and their webs, but it is an interesting way wrap up a unique paddle. The alternative is to pull out on the north side of the bridge and carry your boats across the road—you'll avoid getting spiders in your hair, but it can be treacherous to portage your boat across Sandbridge Road.

While this journey would work during any time of day, it is perfect as a sunset paddle. Its protected waters shelter you from any evening wind or waves, and the loop provides the framework for a definable

The North Bay Loop is perfect for beginning kayakers and for paddling at sunset

3-hour paddle. We timed it so that the sun set as we paddled the final leg of Asheville Bridge Creek. While we still had light to find the hidden passageway, we lingered on the water just long enough to watch the world around us transform from day to night. In our reluctance to end the enchanted evening, our paddling pace slowed to a slothful drift as we absorbed the glowing sky's pastel pinks, purples, yellows, and blues. In our silence we noticed a doe grazing on the shore's tender grasses. She never paused in her eating, nor gave any sign of noticing our passing. I began the suburban paddle as a begrudging doubter. I ended the journey transformed with serenity. Such is the power of kayaking.

Alternative Trips

For another short paddle, but with a little more excitement, head out to the ocean to paddle with dolphins. This is a trip highly recommended by Randy Gore, and it is an excursion offered by his company, Tidewater Adventures. Wild River Outfitters and Sandbridge Eco Sports also run dolphin tours. According to Randy, if you head out onto the Atlantic from the beach at about 89th Street from July to September, you stand an 80 to 90 percent chance of seeing dolphins. This area along the point of Cape Henry is unique in that there is a constant eddy caused by the confluence of the ocean and the Chesapeake. Randy has dubbed the area the dolphin's fast-food alley. The dolphins feast on menhaden that live in these rich waters and use the area as their calving grounds. Only experienced kayakers should head into the ocean without a tour operator. Not only do the waves sometimes pound hard upon the beach, but there is also the hidden danger of strong winds from the south. When combined with the constant northwest-flowing current, these winds can send you straight off the tip of Cape Henry and into the open mouth of the Chesapeake Bay. All of the outfitters run their trips in sit-on-top kayaks due to the high possibility of capsize.

20.

Back Bay

Features: Large fall migration of waterfowl including snow geese, open-water kayaking among a maze of freshwater marsh islands. Kayak camping alternative.

Length: 8 to 16 miles (with possibility for much more).

Put-in site: Little Island City Park (3820 South Sandpiper Road, Virginia Beach, VA 23456; 757-426-0013, www.vbgov.com/parks). The launch location is in Little Island City Park. The carry-in kayak landing is across the road from the parking lot, and it is a short carry over the sand trail, so plan to paddle with a buddy or bring a cart if you have one. From Memorial Day to Labor Day, there is a $3 parking fee on weekdays, and a $4 fee on weekends and holidays. Parking is free for the remainder of the year. There are bathrooms, concessions, and an excellent oceanside beach for swimming after your paddle.

If you need to rent a boat, you should go to Back Bay Getaways, which is located about ¼ mile north of Little Island Park. They rent both tandem and single kayaks.

You can also launch kayaks from within Back Bay National Wildlife Refuge (4005 Sandpiper Beach Road, Virginia Beach, VA 23456; 757-721-2412), which is about ¼ mile to the south of Little Island. Their entrance fee is about $5.

Directions: From I-64 East, exit onto I-264 East. Take exit 22, turning right at the end of the exit ramp onto Birdneck Road. Travel for about 3 to 4 miles, and then take a right onto General Booth Boulevard at an intersection. Follow this for about 4 or 5 miles. After crossing Nimmo Parkway get into the left lane and take a left at the next traffic light onto Princess Anne Road.

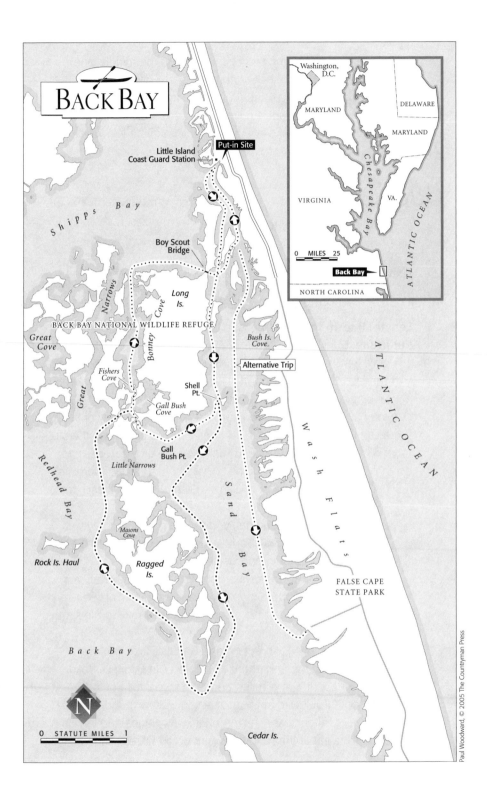

BACK BAY

Put-in Site

Little Island
Coast Guard Station

S h i p p s   B a y

Boy Scout
Bridge

Long
Is.

Narrows

Bonney Cove

BACK BAY NATIONAL WILDLIFE REFUGE

Great
Cove

Great

Fishers
Cove

Bush Is.
Cove.

Alternative Trip

Shell
Pt.

Gall Bush
Cove

Gall
Bush Pt.

Little Narrows

Redhead Bay

Masons
Cove

Sand   Bay

W a s h   F l a t s

A T L A N T I C   O C E A N

Rock Is. Haul

Ragged
Is.

FALSE CAPE
STATE PARK

B a c k   B a y

N

0   STATUTE MILES   1

Cedar Is.

Washington,
D.C.

MARYLAND

DELAWARE

MARYLAND

Chesapeake Bay

VIRGINIA

VA.

A T L A N T I C   O C E A N

0   MILES   25

Back Bay

NORTH CAROLINA

Paul Woodward, © 2005 The Countryman Press

At the next traffic light, proceed straight (in the middle lane). The road now becomes Sandbridge Road. Follow this road until you enter Sandbridge, and then take a right onto Sandpiper Road. Follow for about 4 miles until you reach Little Island City Park, which is an old coast guard station on your left, with a large parking lot.

ESTABLISHED IN 1938, the Back Bay National Wildlife Refuge is an 8,000-acre expanse of wilderness just below Virginia Beach. Despite the fact that only a sliver of dunes separates the bay from the ocean, Back Bay does not flow into the Atlantic until deep within North Carolina's Outer Banks, through the Oregon Inlet, which is over 60 miles away, making the bay a nontidal, fresh-water to mildly brackish ecosystem. This day trip explores the island-rich area just above Back Bay proper, with Shipps Bay to the north, Redhead Bay to the west, Sand Bay to the east, and Back Bay to the south. It is a well-protected area with a healthy variety of marsh and forest vegetation. Over 300 bird species have been identified in the area, including peregrine falcons, northern harrier hawks, and a variety of ducks and songbirds. The refuge was created to provide a safe haven along the Atlantic Flyway for these waterfowl, and it has been most successful in that purpose, with thousands of water-fowl passing through every year, including close to 10,000 snow geese. There is an endless variety of ways to navigate around the islands on this route. Getting lost among this maze of marsh is the entire reason for this paddle; and so rather than offer a detailed route to follow, this description merely suggests an easy base route, perfect for a beginner's paddle or as a springboard for a longer exploration.

Trip Description

From the parking lot at the Little Island Park, it is a short carry over a sand trail to the Back Bay launch site. While the trip takes place across the dunes on the back bays, the place where you are leaving your car is interesting in its own right. This was the site of the coast guard's Little Island Lifesaving Station, which was established in 1878 for the search and rescue of offshore shipwrecks. This area was infamous for shipwrecks, due mostly to False Cape, which is the mile-long strip of beach that protrudes slightly into the Atlantic just south of here. Captains commonly mistook the shape of False Cape for Cape Henry and would steer their boats toward what they thought was the entrance to the Chesapeake Bay, only to run aground on the low dunes that separate Back Bay from the Atlantic. The coast guard responded by building lifesaving stations all along the coast, with one station every 6 miles. The original Little Island Station was destroyed by a hurricane in 1933, but the buildings that you see today were built in 1925 and survived that hurricane. The station closed in 1964 and opened as a park in 1966. Take a good look at these buildings and be grateful for their continued presence because when you are heading back to the landing after your paddle, they will be your best landmark by which to navigate your way home.

While Back Bay is not affected by moon tides, it is governed by wind tides. It is not uncommon for much of the water to disappear whenever there has been a sustained southwesterly wind, so sometimes you may have to drag your kayak fairly far out into the inlet before you find enough water to float your boat. When you leave the landing, paddle straight out of the little inlet and into the open water of the bay. The unnamed extension island of Long Island is the land mass that is just slightly south of you, about ⅓ mile across the water, with a wooded hummock on its northern end. Although hunting is prohibited in the refuge, as you paddle toward that hummock, you will see duck blinds scattered

Little Island launch site

throughout North Bay, carefully placed to take advantage of the abundance of waterfowl that are drawn to the refuge's protected waters.

Like all wildlife refuges, the primary purpose of Back Bay is wildlife conservation. Thus, not only is hunting forbidden, but any human interference with the bay's protected lands is also prohibited, including trespassing on any of the islands of the refuge. Because of this, you need to be willing to get wet whenever you get tired of paddling or want to stretch your legs. Thankfully, the bay is quite shallow with a firm sandy bottom in most areas, so you just need to check the water for depth with your paddle and then get out for a soak. You can do this quite near any of the islands, just as long as you do not step onto them. Park your bow into the marsh, or just leave it to float freely next to you, making sure to keep track of it if there is any sort of wind. If you choose your rest spots well, you will only get wet up to your shins, although in hot weather you will probably want to get more than your feet wet anyway.

Once you reach Long Island, turn your boat left to paddle south alongside its eastern shore. The island is divided into two sections by a narrow inlet about a third of the way down its length. This first section begins with a hummock of trees and then has a low stretch of grass, then another hummock. Several marsh islands lay to your east, and shorebirds are prolific on all of these clumps of grass. Once you reach the second hummock of Long Island, you should begin to look for the bisecting inlet. It is located about 1 mile south of the tip of the island and is partially obscured by overhanging trees, making it hard to see until you are past it. There is a metal bulkhead on the southern side of the inlet, which is about 40 feet wide, with the uprights for an old Boy Scout bridge in the center of the passageway. Your first choice is now upon you, and you must decide whether to continue down the eastern side of the island or to switch over to the western. I chose the first option after poking my kayak around the corner to take a look at the alternatives. I was startled to find a raccoon just feet from my face, perched on top of the metal bulkhead that contains the west side of the island.

Continuing down the eastern shore, you will be paddling alongside a mostly wooded island. Long Island is the largest island in the bay and is thus more stable and able to accumulate and keep soil. It is the only island in the bay that contains more woods than marsh. The trees are a motley mixture of live oak, loblolly pine, and persimmon. It is about 1½ miles from the inlet to Shell Point, and another ¼ mile to the absolute end of the island. There continues to be a scattering of marsh islands to your east, and all of them might be fun to paddle around. Shell Point is a small island that stands a little offshore from Long Island. Its sand shoal makes for a good place to rest, especially in cooler weather because your ankles will barely get wet in this shallow spot.

From Shell Point, Ragged Island lies before you, appearing a bit like a mirage in the distance. For those looking for a longer journey, the paddle across to Ragged Island is an excellent choice. It is about a 1¼-mile crossing if you leave from Shell Point and land about mid-island, by the inlet into the interior. You can then explore all around this island, paddling the outside and interior sections of what seems like a waterlogged archipelago. Whereas Long Island is a generally solid and raised land mass, Ragged Island is exactly as the name describes—a ragged collection of guts, coves, and marshes cobbled together to create one island. It is about 6 miles around if you circumnavigate all of it, although you could certainly paddle much more or less, depending on the route you take. After paddling Ragged Island, you can head back north to paddle the other side of Long Island back home; or if you are burning with even more energy, you can bear northwest and explore as many islands as you desire. Just paddling Long Island and Ragged Island is about a 16-mile journey (more or less depending on how much interior versus exterior paddling you do). Adding on an exploration of more islands could result in a trip of 20 to 30 miles, certainly more than all but the craziest and fittest of us would want to attempt.

For a shorter, 8-mile roundtrip, bypass paddling over to Ragged Island and simply round the corner until you find the small inlet opening into Gall Bush Cove. Then look for the next small opening into Fishers Cove. You can now paddle back up the east side of Long Island, taking as many detours as your heart desires into and around the dozens of various-sized islands that lie to the west of Long Island. On your return around Long Island, you may want to weave your way to the inlet through the island or paddle all the way around the top. Either way, as you come up or around the northern tip of Long Island, you will see the white buildings of the trailer park to the northeast, but the small cove that hides the landing blends in well with the long strip of marsh shoreline. To find your way home, look for the lifesaving station, which is the last cluster of white buildings. Paddle toward them, steering toward the northernmost building of the group. As you draw nearer to land, make sure your boat is south of the point and then paddle straight in to the landing. After the labyrinth of the Back Bay islands, the paddle home will likely be the only straightforward paddling you will do all day.

Alternative Trips

A popular addition to Back Bay paddling is to extend the trip to camp overnight at False Cape State Park. Excellent primitive camping is available in four different areas of the park, with access to the campgrounds only by foot, kayak, or canoe. This area used to be home to Wash Woods, a true *Gilligan's Island* community that was founded by shipwreck survivors who used scavenged wood from their ship to build their homes and church. You can base several days of Back Bay exploration from False Cape, exploring not only Virginia waters, but also some of the islands of North Carolina. Additionally, you have an entire wild and pristine oceanside beach to explore and lounge upon. Reservations are required and can be made via the reservation center (1-800-933-7275). Both Wild River Outfitters and Tidewater Adventures offer fully supported camping trips to False Cape. Back Bay Getaways offers motorboat support to those who are paddling it on their own, but do not want to cram all of their gear into the small holds of their kayaks.

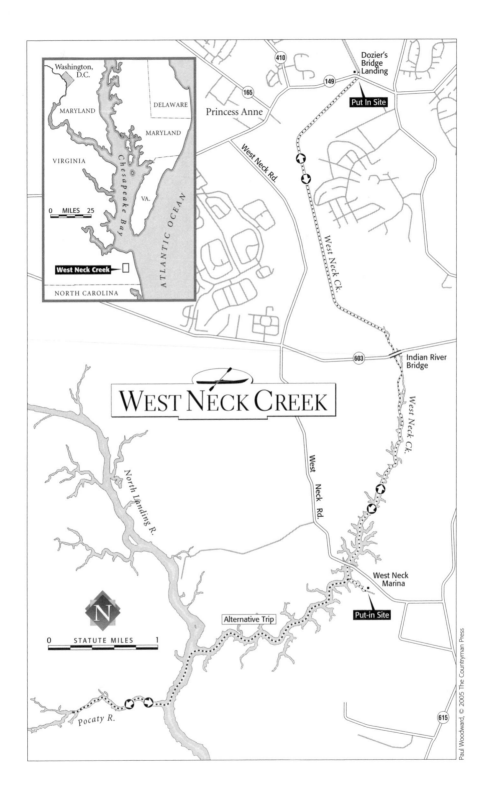

WEST NECK CREEK

21.

West Neck Creek

Features: Cypress swamp with otters, herons, gar, and cotton-mouths. Excellent bass fishing. A convenient vehicle portage allows for an easy one-way trip.

Length: 11 to 14 miles round trip, or 5½ miles one way.

Put-in site: There are two, equally suitable landings for this river, depending on the day's wind: West Neck Marina (3985 West Neck Road, Virginia Beach, VA 23456; 757-426-6735) and Dozier's Bridge Landing. West Neck Marina is a small power-boat marina with a boat ramp, bathrooms, picnic tables, and a marina store (cold drinks and bait). There is a nominal launch fee. Dozier's Bridge is a kayak-only launch with a low wooden dock and no bathroom facilities. This is a popular trip destination for Wild River Outfitters, but Tidewater Adventures also guides trips along this route.

Directions: *For West Neck Marina:* From I-264 East, take Independence Boulevard (exit 17A), toward Princess Anne. Bear left at the fork in the ramp and merge onto South Independence Boulevard. Follow this for about 3.5 miles and then take a left onto Princess Anne Road/VA 165 South at a traffic light. Follow Princess Anne for about 3.5 miles, and then take a right onto Nimmo Parkway and follow for about 0.5 mile. Nimmo becomes West Neck Road, and you'll need to bear left to remain on the road. Follow it for about 4 miles. Bear left over West Neck Creek, where the entrance to the West Neck Marina is on your right-hand side. For *Dozier's Bridge Landing:* Follow the above directions until the junction with Nimmo. Instead of taking a right onto Nimmo Parkway, continue following Princess

Anne Road. The landing is on the left, just before you cross
West Neck Creek.

WEST NECK CREEK originates 29 miles above the North Landing River
in Lynnhaven Bay in the middle of Virginia Beach. The navy dug the
canal (that you paddle in the northern section of this day trip) in the
1940s to open a route from the Atlantic Ocean to the Intracoastal Waterway, thus allowing small boats to travel from Virginia Beach to North
Landing. The passage fell out of use in the later half of the century, until
it was entirely forgotten. Then in 1980 a schoolteacher and competitive
canoe racer named Lillie Gilbert noticed the thin blue line connecting
the ocean to the river on a city planning map and decided to see if it
was navigable. She undertook the journey with a friend in a 17-foot
Kevlar canoe, armed with hedge clippers, a pocketful of dimes, and the
map. They were not sure if the waterway still existed as the map
showed, so every time the water crossed under the roadway, they would
each walk one direction of the road in order to determine where they
were, then use the dimes to call and report their location to a friend.
The hedge clippers were put into constant use to clear passages through
thick vines of poison ivy that choked off entire sections of water. Eventually, they came into the clearer downriver portion of West Neck
Creek, which this trip description covers, and were vindicated by
reaching the North Landing River. That journey was the beginning of
Lillie's quest to establish a scenic waterway system for Virginia Beach,
with West Neck Creek as the spine. She also became the owner of Wild
River Outfitters in 1980, and West Neck Creek is one of their most popular trips. Her company has adopted the waterway, and they sponsor
clean-up days every year.

Trip Description

The West Neck Creek is governed by wind tides, with the current and
water depth entirely dictated by the prevailing winds of the day or
week, so you should choose your launching site according to the wind.
If you are paddling a round-trip, you should paddle into the wind to
begin your day so that you can benefit from a free ride home on the way

back. If you arrange for a car portage, then you can use the wind for the whole of your journey. Because of the wind conditions at the time, I paddled the creek from West Neck Marina.

Dewey Mullins is the proprietor of the marina and is a reserved wealth of information about the area. He welcomes all kayakers, so even if you are paddling a round-trip from Dozier's Bridge, you are still welcome to land here to use the facilities—making the marina a great lunch spot, with the added perk of cold sodas. The fishermen who frequent his small store and landing are a friendly bunch of regulars. Make sure to be considerate of the launchings and landings of the bass boaters while you ready your kayak for the water.

Paddling straight/west out of the marina's small inlet, bear right to head north on the creek. You will pass under a bridge into an area worth lingering in. There are numerous side pockets and coves for the next 2¼ miles. You will likely pass several fishermen quietly working these side areas. One local said that he repeatedly spooks otters while fishing the sides, and he estimated that there are several otter families living in the area. While this creek is richest in bass, it is also full of most freshwater species including gar. Gar often linger near the surface unseen until your kayak comes alongside and startles them into an underwater dive with a noisy explosion of muscle and water. The splashing can be so loud and forceful that every time it happened to me, I had to throw a quick low brace in order to keep from capsizing.

The creek flows through a healthy cypress swamp, with clumps of small cypress islands throughout the passage. Be prepared to run aground, as the solidly black water keeps the submerged logs and stumps out of view until you are perched on them. About 1 mile upstream, after you pass the first of two duck blinds, the river becomes even richer with side coves and short passages. And in about another ½ mile, the river splits into two passages. Both are passable, with the east passage being the larger of the two options. Just before Indian Creek Road, the second largest cypress tree in the state is in the swamp on the east side of the river.

You will pass under Indian Creek Road in 2½ miles from the West Neck Marina. Shortly after this bridge you will enter the canal. While man-made, and thus unnaturally straight, this area is still beautiful.

The sprawling cypress swamp of West Neck Creek

There are overhanging trees, with a greater mixture of tree varieties, such as elm and beech. The cypress are younger and smaller than the trees downriver. I ran into several floating rafts of debris on this stretch, but all were passable. Some of the side canals run fairly deep into the swamp, and Randy Gore of Tidewater Adventures reports that by following some of them you can emerge into the open air of farm fields. There are occasional places where you could get out on the canal banks; however, exercise caution when doing so. In addition to the large amount of poison ivy in the area, I also saw several cottonmouths in the canal section of the creek.

The canal runs to the northwest for about ½ mile, almost straight north for another 1¼ miles, and then bends to the northeast for the final ½ mile, which will bring you to Dozier's Bridge. The low dock kayak landing is on the north side of the bridge. This is a good, solid place to get out and stretch your legs or eat lunch.

For a simple round-trip, turn around at Dozier's Bridge. However, if you are craving extra mileage you can continue north on the creek. After passing underneath a double pipeline, and then under a third pipeline about ½ mile upriver, you can follow the canal for another 1 mile until you rejoin with a natural waterway, bearing left to remain on West Neck Creek.

If you are paddling the round-trip, and still have energy when you return to West Neck Marina, continue south, past the marina, paddling toward the North Landing River. The creek here is natural and wild, with both the width of the water and the number of bass fisherman gradually increasing as you head downstream. In about 1½ miles you will reach North Landing River. You should turn around at this point unless you are looking to dramatically lengthen your day by traveling down to the Pocaty River (see Alternative Trips). The North Landing River is a part of the Intracoastal Waterway, and as such it is not designed for leisurely paddling. Be especially cautious about entering the river during "snowbird" season, which runs from April to May and from September to November every year. During these months powerboats disobey all speed limits as they race toward their summer or winter playgrounds. Every year bass boats are sunk by the high wakes of these powerboats, so this is certainly no place for a kayaker. Instead, remain in West Neck Creek, exploring all the nooks and crannies it has to offer.

Alternative Trips

Using West Neck Marina as your launch site, paddle south toward the North Landing River. Take a left to head south on the river, crossing it as soon as you are below the mouth of West Neck Creek. About ½ mile south of West Neck, take a right to head east into the Pocaty River. The Nature Conservancy protects the shoreline here, and they have a platform that is open to the public on the southern (left) bank of the river. There is a small carry-in boat landing a little farther upriver. This trip variation is offered by Tidewater Adventures. There are also a multitude of urban paddles available in the Norfolk/Virginia Beach area.

Snakes

The fear of snakes is primal and raw but mostly unfounded. These legless creatures are generally content to go about their lives without ever interacting with humans and will usually go out of their way to avoid contact with anyone paddling through their watery homes. There are four types of water snakes that you will commonly see in Virginia: the northern water snake, the brown water snake, the red-bellied water snake, and the cottonmouth. Of these, only the cottonmouth is poisonous.

Cottonmouths are pit vipers that live in the swamps of southeastern Virginia. They are also known as water moccasins, but many Virginians call all water snakes moccasins, so it is best to use the more specific name. Cottonmouths average between 3 and 4 feet in length, although they can grow even longer. They are generally a brownish, olive-black color, with dark, almost black bands. The older the snake, the darker it will usually appear. Cottonmouths eat fish, amphibians, crayfish, and small mammals like mice or young muskrat, which they kill by clasping the animal in their mouth and injecting venom until it dies.

As kayakers, we are larger than any of the cottonmouths' intended prey, and so usually they will avoid any contact. However, if you disturb a snake, it will hold its ground, typically shaking its tail and opening its jaws wide, showing the cotton-white interior of its mouth. It will strike at you if you insist on bothering it. The venom will not usually kill a healthy adult, but it can make you quite sick, so while on shore, watch where you are walking and do not swim where you see snakes. If you are bitten, get to the hospital immediately. If you are paddling with a partner, do not let the injured person exert themselves and keep the bitten limb immobilized while you tow them back to the landing. You can use a Sawyer Extractor kit to suction out some of the venom, but the best remedy is to get the bitten person to a doctor quickly.

The cottonmouths' range does not extend north of the James River, yet I have met hundreds of people who swear that they have seen

Carolanne Farm Park offers access to the Elizabeth River Water Trail (Virginia Beach Parks and Recreation, 757-536-1130). In Norfolk, the Haven Creek Landing, on Delaware Avenue, provides access to the Lafayette River, which allows for viewing some of the gorgeous homes poisonous moccasins in a river near them in Northern Virginia, along the Eastern Shore, or in Maryland. What they more likely have seen is the northern water snake, which has the greatest range of Virginia's snakes and lives in all of the freshwater rivers of the bay. These nonaggressive, nonpoisonous snakes can even be found in brackish water and in the coastal bays. The northern water snake can grow to be about 4 feet long, and it has a brown and beige coloration with oval-shaped bands that look quite similar to the markings of a cottonmouth. The easiest way to differentiate the species is by how they swim. Northern water snakes swim with only their head out of water. The cottonmouth swims entirely on top of the water, almost looking like it is slithering across ice. Also, if you see a snake north of the James, it is not a cottonmouth; it is a northern water snake. Snakes do not go on summer vacation; they stick to their home habitat.

Two other species common to the southeastern swamps are the brown water snake and the red-bellied water snake. The brown water snake looks similar to the northern water snake but has brown square blotches instead of bands and is about the same length as the northern water snake and cottonmouth. Although some have occasionally been spotted in the Pamunkey River, they are more common south of the Rappahannock. They are essentially the southern version of the northern water snake.

The red-bellied water snake looks entirely different from the other species. It has a solid brown body, with a bright red belly. It is the most terrestrial of the four snakes and is very common in the Lake Drummond area. The red-bellied water snake is rarely found north of the James River and is never found north of the York River. The brown and red-bellied water snakes share the northern water snake's diet of amphibians and fish, and all three species eat their food live by unhinging their jaw and swallowing their prey whole—no poison necessary.

in this area from the water. More information about the Norfolk area and the Norfolk Water Trail can be found through the City of Norfolk Bureau of Parks and Forestry (757-441-2435).

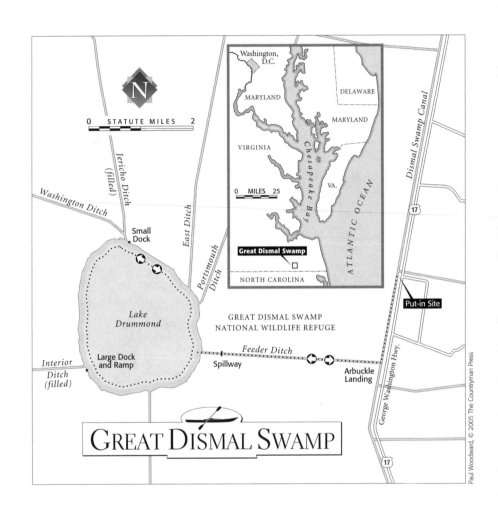

STATUTE MILES

0   2

N

Jericho Ditch
(filled)

Washington Ditch

East Ditch

Small
Dock

Portsmouth
Ditch

Lake
Drummond

Large Dock
and Ramp

Interior
Ditch
(filled)

Spillway

Feeder Ditch

GREAT DISMAL SWAMP
NATIONAL WILDLIFE REFUGE

Arbuckle
Landing

George Washington Hwy.

Put-in Site

Dismal Swamp Canal

17

17

Washington,
D.C.

MARYLAND

DELAWARE

MARYLAND

VIRGINIA

Chesapeake Bay

VA.

ATLANTIC OCEAN

Great Dismal Swamp

NORTH CAROLINA

0   MILES   25

GREAT DISMAL SWAMP

Paul Woodward, © 2005 The Countryman Press

22.

Great Dismal Swamp

Features: A 750-square-mile cypress swamp wilderness with kayak camping available. Long-distance paddle on shallow waters.

Length: 15½ miles total (8 miles of there-and-back canal paddling, along with a 7½ mile circumnavigation of Lake Drummond).

Put-in site: The Great Dismal Swamp National Wildlife Refuge (3100 Desert Road, Suffolk, VA 23434; 747-986-3705). The launch location is on the opposite side of the swamp from the refuge's office and is a 30- to 60-minute drive from the Norfolk/Virginia Beach area, depending on traffic. The landing is a narrow, board-lined slip at the south end of the parking area, with room for only one trailered boat at a time. There are no rest rooms or other facilities at the landing. There is kayak-accessible camping in the heart of the swamp.

Directions: From I-64 (south of Portsmouth/Chesapeake), exit onto US 17 South. Follow for about 8 miles (it is about another 2½ miles after you pass Douglass Landing on the left). The boat landing is on the right side of the road—it is a large gravel parking area with two entrances, so if you miss the first entrance, grab the second.

AWE IS THE WORD that best describes my state of mind when I first glided onto the still, black water of Lake Drummond in the heart of the Great Dismal Swamp. It was like unexpectedly encountering the overwhelming and unique beauty of a glacier hidden in the middle of a city park. Located in southeastern Virginia, an easy half-hour drive from Norfolk and Virginia Beach, the Great Dismal Swamp National Wildlife

Refuge is a 111,000-acre expanse of land, including the 3,100-acre Lake Drummond, which is the destination of this paddle. The swampland is an enigma—lying higher than the surrounding countryside, all water drains out of the swamp rather than into it, and yet despite the concerted efforts through the years of men like George Washington to ditch and drain it, the swamp never empties. It is a wilderness paddle that is unique in the world, with a beauty that astounds and amazes.

Trip Description

With a simple left turn from the boat landing onto the Dismal Swamp Canal, you have entered a registered historic landmark. While unassuming in appearance, this is the oldest continually operating man-made canal in the United States. The canal was constructed as part of a cooperative effort between George Washington and Governor Patrick Henry to create a safe and direct route between North Carolina's Albemarle Sound and Virginia's Chesapeake Bay. Beginning in 1793, the 22-mile-long, 50-foot-wide canal took 12 years to build, with almost all of the labor done by slaves who dug it out by hand. Before it was replaced with the construction of canals off the North Landing River, the Dismal Swamp Canal was an early part of the Intracoastal Waterway, which connects Miami to Norfolk with a string of protected inland waterways.

Within five minutes of leaving the landing in the morning, I paddled under a bridge and mentally logged it as the landmark that would tell me when I was nearing home at the end of the day. However, on my return journey I paddled and paddled with no sign of the bridge ahead of me. Just as I was beginning to lose heart, I noticed large pier structures on either side of the canal and discovered to my surprise and relief that the bridge was retractable. The bridge provides access to the farm fields in the swamp and is kept in the stowed position, allowing clear passage for tall vessels on the canal and keeping curious tourists or trespassers from wandering onto the fields.

After the bridge/no-bridge, there are twin docks on either side, with a small farm boat skiff tied up on the US 17 side, which would also give the farmer access to his fields. There are several other small docks, boathouses, and steps leading into the canal along this short stretch. Do not be surprised to see cows that have descended from the bordering pasture land to the canal for a drink.

About ½ mile from the boat landing, you will take a right into the feeder ditch. There is a sign high up on the right bank that welcomes you to the Great Dismal Swamp. This narrow canal is your home for the next 3½ miles of paddling. It is not a scenic paddle. Tall banks close you in on either side, displaying an unchanging backdrop of a motley assortment of trees, scrub brush, and vines, the monotony of which is interrupted only by several culverts that drain the surrounding swamp. However, there is the powerful carrot of Lake Drummond that serves to entice the paddler to venture forth into this uninspiring waterway.

The Great Dismal Swamp was dubbed "dismal" by William Byrd who, upon surveying it in 1729, reported it a "horrible desert unfit for respiration." However, George Washington surveyed the land in 1763 and disagreed with Byrd's assessment, summarily forming two land development companies that purchased 40,000 acres to ditch, drain, and develop. While Washington and others shrunk the swamp from 3,000 to 750 square miles, the heart of the swamp remained wild, defeating Washington's dream of creating expansive, fertile plantation land. Ever adaptive, Washington changed the purpose of his company from land development to logging, which remained the primary use for the swamp for the next 200 years, until the last of the virgin timber was logged in the 1950s. The rot-resistant timber from bald cypress was used for thousands of ships, while the swamp's Atlantic white cedar were used to shingle houses from Virginia to Maine. In 1974, 110,000 acres of swampland were declared a national wildlife refuge and will never again be commercially logged.

As a result of the draining and logging efforts, ditches, canals, and roads crisscross the wilderness. The feeder ditch that leads to Lake Drummond served a slightly different purpose than most of these ditches—it was built to provide water to the Dismal Swamp Canal so that it is always navigable. A spillway controls the water level, and as you paddle down the ditch, the white structure of the spillway tender's boathouse comes into view. Obey the signs and bear left when you reach

A lone tree on the Great Dismal Swamp

the spillway. This will bring you along the backside of a man-made peninsula. The slough ends at the Lake Drummond Railway, which is a simple boat trailer that is electrically winched up and over the land that borders the spillway. It is self-operated and is open from 8 A.M. to 3 P.M. I did not use this novel device, finding that dragging my boat the 25 feet was a simpler proposition. The land by the spillway is a campground, free and available to all who want to use it. There are docks for larger boats, picnic shelters, barbecue grills, trash cans, flush toilets, and plenty of space to set up tents. There is no potable water here, but beside that it appears to be a comfortable and inviting place to spend a few nights, although I have been told that the evening insects are supremely awful here in the summertime. It may be worth braving the insects, though, for a late-night paddle and the chance to spot the Lady of the Lake. The legend of the lake, immortalized by Thomas Moore's poem "The Lake of the Dismal Swamp," tells of an Indian woman who died just before her wedding, and who now paddles her ghostly white canoe over the lake at night awaiting her lover. The legend likely springs from the fox-fire luminescence certain fungus on decaying logs give off.

Once you splash down on the other side of the spillway, it only takes another ½ mile of paddling to reach the lake. No amount of pictures or anticipation will prepare you for the sight that will greet you as your kayak floats free of the tight boundaries of the canal into the expanse of the lake. At 3,100 acres, the lake is huge. Rimmed by cypress trees and with no sign of human development, I imagine the lake looks just as it did when Governor Drummond of North Carolina first discovered it while lost during a hunting trip. Not a breath of air stirred the water when I drifted into the lake, and the knowledge that I was absolutely alone in this expanse of water overwhelmed me. I was conflicted with the simultaneous urges to shout, sing, and sit in silence. Cypress trees are scattered around the entrance of the lake, some standing 100 feet or so from shore. Some are large, some are small, and some are twisted and stumplike while others are soaring and majestic. They reminded me of the grace of bonsai trees, with so much attention paid to every twist and turn and growth.

I paddled to the right, for no reason other than I had to pick a direction. If the wind is blowing, then let this dictate your direction, opting for a lee shore in the afternoon. As I made tracks on the mirror-still water, I felt like I did as a child, when I was the first skateboarder to glide over the perfect black asphalt of a freshly paved road. It has been a while since I have been affected like this by wilderness. I have swum with sea lions in Baja, danced my kayak over whirlpools off the coast of Brittany, and sailed through a pod of orcas, and yet I found myself stunned speechless in a patch a wilderness that is only 30 minutes away from my sister's home in Norfolk.

Be sure to mentally create landmarks for the canal's entrance before you stray too far from the feeder canal because, while it is marked with one yellow-and-black striped sign, it is still easily missed. Face your boat directly into the lake and then take notice of what landmarks you can find to mark your location—I used an expanse of dead trees that were at about 10 o'clock from my position.

The lake is one of only two natural lakes in Virginia, and its origins are a mystery. One of the most popular theories posits that the lake was formed in the crater of a meteor. Another claims that during a time of high drought the peat bog bottom of the lake burned down, leaving an indentation in the midst of the swamp. Scientists are fairly certain that at one point all the land from the swamp east was under an ancient sea and was only exposed by the last major shift of the continental shelf.

The water is shallow, reaching only 6 feet deep, and for much of my paddle around the edges, it only measured about 2 feet deep. The black tannic water is unusually pure and sterile, its acidity prohibiting bacteria growth. Many ship captains, including Blackbeard the Pirate, used to fill their kegs with the lake water because it would stay fresh during long sea voyages, never growing the algae or bacteria that would spoil other kegs of water.

There are many trees growing away from the shoreline near the entrance to the feeder ditch, but in ¼ mile or so, the numbers of these "pioneers" diminish. After you pass a line of about seven trees sticking out from the shoreline, you'll come upon only one more solitary tree across from East Ditch. After this, the cypress are mostly close to land until you begin to near the feeder ditch from the south. Do not worry if you miss some of the canals that are marked on the map; they can be hard to see, and many are no longer true canals, having been filled years ago. Only three shoreline spots are important: Jericho Ditch, Interior Ditch, and the feeder ditch you came in on. Jericho Ditch is 2½ miles from the feeder ditch and is actually the old entrance of both Jericho and Washington Ditches, both of which are now filled and are used as hiking/biking trails. There is an old weathered dock, with a bench and a mounted binocular—the kind that usually requires a quarter but this one is free! There is space to pull up onto land to the left/north of the dock, and this is an easy and well-timed place to stretch your legs after about an hour on the lake. There is an information sign here that tells about some of the natural history of the area.

About 2¼ miles from Jericho Ditch, you will reach t|
Ditch, which also is no longer a ditch but now a dirt roac
4½ miles back to the refuge office. There is a concrete ra
south side of the dock. Both Tidewater Expeditions and
Outfitters have permits to launch directly into the lake from this location, saving you from the long paddle on the canals. While this convenience is priceless, you will lose a bit of the wondrous experience of
paddling onto the lake after the monotony of the canals. While I love
to paddle with other people, I am so glad that I first experienced the
lake alone, without the distracting chatter of a large group. You will
need to weigh the plusses and minuses of paddling with a group before
making your own decision.

Although greatly damaged by years of ditching, draining, and
logging, the Great Dismal Swamp is still home to an abundance of
seldom-seen wildlife, including bobcats, deer, mink, and the largest
black bear population in Virginia. In the autumn, large rafts of migratory waterfowl can be seen, but during the summer months, the most
noticeable wildlife are dragonflies and butterflies. The lake has healthy
populations of catfish, chain pickerel, and sunfish. Throughout the
1800s, while many slaves were enduring a horrible existence in the
canal-digging efforts of the swamp, others were using the swamp as a
refuge, as it became an important passageway along the Underground
Railroad. Thousands of runaway slaves passed through the swamp,
living off the land, drinking the pure lake water, and pulling fish from
the darkness. Many chose to end their journey here, settling deep
within the swamp where they lived undetected for years.

As I became accustomed to the grandeur of the scenery, my mind
started to be bored with the sameness of the paddle, with none of the
small guts and wildlife surprises that my usual marshland paddling
provides me. However, just as I began to speed my pace to reach home,
a bald eagle joined my paddle and flew with me for the last mile of my
journey on the lake, soaring ahead of me for about 100 yards at a time
before perching and awaiting my approach. Each time the large bird
took flight, it circled the entire lake with ease, returning in a few

minutes. I was so entranced by the eagle that the feeder ditch reappeared too soon, seeming much closer than the 2½ miles it is from the Interior Ditch.

I have wanted to paddle in the Great Dismal Swamp since I first heard its name. I love the combination of the words *great* and *dismal* to describe the same area, and it has been my experience that one person's dismal is another person's wilderness. There are many other kayaking trips in this book with more visible wildlife, better fishing, or more challenging water conditions—however, none can equal the pure grandeur of Lake Drummond. My paddle back down the canals went by quickly, my mind fully wrapped in the memories of the beauty of the lake.

Alternative Trips

For a completely different experience, there is good open-water paddling in Broad Bay; launch from First Landing State Park (757-412-2300). While during the summer the water is overrun by jet skiers, the place is generally deserted by September, and for an off-season paddling perk, a pod of dolphins winters over every year. (Tidewater Adventures runs winter trips here).

23.

Northwest River

Features: Cypress wilderness with excellent car camping available. Good smallmouth bass and bluegill fishing.

Length: 10 miles.

Put-in site: Located on the border of Northwest River Park (757-421-7151), this carry-in boat landing is on the side of the road, with limited parking and no facilities. There is camping available at Northwest River Park, which is a well-managed, city-run (Chesapeake) park; and while their canoe rentals are mostly for their pond, experienced canoeists are sometimes allowed to bring rental boats onto the river.

Directions: From I-64, follow VA 168 (Battlefield Boulevard) about 15 miles and then take a left on Indian Creek Road (about 5 miles south of Great Bridge bypass). Follow Indian Creek Road for about 3.25 miles. When you cross over Indian Creek, the small roadside landing is on the right-hand side, adjacent to the bridge.

THIS IS THE SOUTHERNMOST trip in the book; and if you paddle just a few miles longer than the route description, you will pass into North Carolina. The Northwest River drains the Great Dismal Swamp, flowing through little more than 20 miles of the flat coastal plain in its slow southeastern journey toward the Albemarle Sound. Far from the ocean, and unhurried by topography, the Northwest's water level and current is governed entirely by the wind. The shoreline is thickly clothed with a deep cypress swamp, making the river one of the most wild and pristine wind tide waterways in the world.

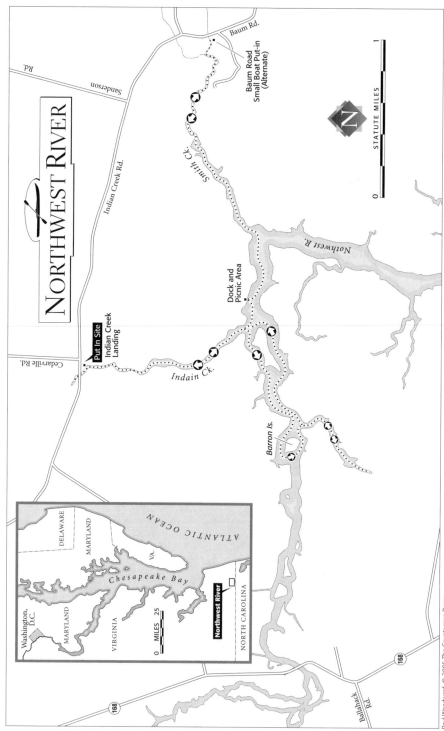

NORTHWEST RIVER

Baum Rd.

Baum Road
Small Boat Put-in
(Alternate)

Sanderson Rd.

Indian Creek Rd.

Smith Ck.

N

STATUTE MILES

0   1

Cedarville Rd.

Put In Site
Indian Creek
Landing

Indain Ck.

Dock and
Picnic Area

Nothwest R.

Barron Is.

168

DELAWARE

MARYLAND

MARYLAND

ATLANTIC OCEAN

VA.

Chesapeake Bay

Washington,
D.C.

MARYLAND

VIRGINIA

0   MILES   25

Northwest River

NORTH CAROLINA

168

Ballahack
Rd.

Paul Woodward, © 2005 The Countryman Press

Trip Description

From the Indian Creek landing, paddling downstream is the only option because a low clearance bridge blocks off upstream exploration. The creek is deep, making it navigable even during a northwestern wind, and it is entirely encompassed by a cypress swamp. Cormorants and green herons perch on fallen trees, and after the first big bend, the creek widens. There is a well-used fishing camp on the right side, and at the next bend the river comes into view at the end of a long stretch of creek. The shoreline is rippled, with peaceful shallow coves and indentations all along this straight stretch of water, and it is typical of all of the shoreline of this paddle. Just as there are few straight lines in nature, you will not find any hard boundaries in a cypress swamp, where the trees often stray far from land.

At the mouth of Indian Creek, the wide open water of the river lies before you, with the opposite shoreline almost ¼ mile away. To the right is the back inlet around Barron's Island, which will be explored later in the paddle. But for now, paddle left to follow the river downstream to the east. The entire northern shoreline in this section is owned and protected by the 763-acre Northwest River Park. Kayakers are welcome and shortly after you pass the observation platform, you will come upon a grassy picnic area with a dock. This dock was built with kayakers and canoeists in mind, and it is adequately low at mid-high water. There are restrooms, picnic tables, grills, and vending machines in this area, along with hiking trails from which a paddler can see the river from a landlubber's perspective. While you probably will not need a break when you first come to the picnic area, remember it for later because it can be a very comfortable lunch stop and midday distraction.

As you travel, stay near the edge, in order to avoid the numerous bass boats that frequent this river. Most bass fishermen move more slowly than a kayak while they are fishing, but they can move fast when they are changing fishing locations. There can also be some waterskiing in the area. In about ⅓ mile, you will come to the entrance to Smith Creek, which is at the northern elbow of the 90-degree turn that the river takes to the south. Smith is a small, quiet creek that is a popular resting area for migratory waterfowl in the fall and spring. There are a couple good guts for exploration. The first one on the left takes you almost all the way to the observation platform of the Otter Point Trail, and as the name indicates, river otter are sometimes spotted around here. About ¼ mile farther up Smith Creek, there is a small gut to the right with a wood duck box at its entrance—it is a short but beautiful side jaunt. This swamp is a rich habitat for many creatures, including snakes, and as I headed into the narrow section of this gut, a 4-foot-long black rat snake dropped out of a tree with a splash, directly in front of my kayak. The timber rattlesnake also finds a home along these secluded side waterways, as do cottonmouths and northern water snakes, so be on the lookout for many interesting reptiles.

I was incapable of paddling Smith Creek in a straight line. As soon as I had settled into paddling along the southern shoreline, something even more beguiling would beckon from the northern edge, causing me to zig across the water. Then as soon as I would arrive, something would enchant me on the southern side, and back I would zag. When the creek branches, take the right fork because the left quickly dead-ends in the midst of a farm field. After you pass a house with a green lawn and a little dock, the creek narrows, with shallow depths and tight meanders. This section of the river would not be navigable at low water. At the next fork, take a right and reach the Baum Road Small Boat Put-In. It is a 1⅓-mile journey upstream on Smith Creek and a little over 3 miles from the landing on Indian Creek. This is the only real dry land on the creek, and it is a good place to stretch your legs—I was joined by a pileated woodpecker during my rest. There is a house across the road from the landing, with farm fields and silos behind that. By land, this landing is accessible from Indian Creek Road.

While the creek continues to flow upstream above the landing, it ends at the road, where it is blocked by culverts. From Smith Creek, head back toward Indian Creek, remembering to stop at the Northwest River Park for lunch or a rest break—there are no additional good break spots for the rest of the trip description. Paddling across the mouth of Indian Creek, head up the inside of Barron Island. At the top of the island, across from a duck blind on its northern shore, there is

Northwest River, a trip on the edge of Virginia

an entrance to a tiny gut. It is the very sort of gut that is easy to bypass because the map so obviously shows that it does not lead anywhere. However, it is these very side trips to nowhere that uncover the gems of a trip. I stalked a blue heron, slowly allowing the gentle breeze to push me near the bird so that I could sit still and watch it hunt. As I watched the heron, my attention was drawn to the water next to my kayak, where less than a paddle-length away, I witnessed two snapping turtles mating. Drifting farther up into the creek, I paused to watch a damselfly alight on my kayak, where it sat for several minutes, oblivious to my intent gaze. I spent 20 minutes in less than 50 yards of water—this is the blessing of sea kayaking. It is a sport that encourages athletic laziness, an activity of both paddling and drifting.

Leaving the peaceful seclusion of the cove, continue your westward journey upriver for about ½ mile, until you pass alongside the next small island. For paddlers looking to cover a lot of distance, many more scenic miles lie upriver of this island. However, for an easy day-long journey of 10 miles, round the top of this island and cross over to the southern shoreline of the river to begin to paddle eastward, back downriver. There is a red-and-white stick marking a submerged log in the river, and on the inland side of that is the entrance for the final side creek exploration of the day. It is a little over ½-mile up this small creek, which after the first bend to the left is primarily a straight stretch of water, with a familiar rippling shoreline. At the end of the straight section on the northern bank, there is a duck blind, which, when I passed it in the spring, was empty of hunters but surrounded by waterfowl. The creek rapidly narrows after this and then branches, with both options blocked by fallen trees.

Like all the trips in this book, I urge you to vary from the described route as much as you desire. A day's paddle on the river should be modeled upon the spirit of the water's gentle tidal cooperation with the elements. Follow the edges, chase butterflies, and linger in shallow coves. Be the smart kind of lazy and paddle against the wind first, so that you can ride its escorting force home. Travel slowly, so as to experience the river richly. When I finished my final side journey, I paddled homeward, around the southern side of Barron's Island and into Indian Creek. I shortened and lessened the power of every pull of the blade; and if you are at all like me, your pace may slow considerably in that final mile back to the landing, in the struggle to stall the sad and inevitable end to a day spent on the Northwest River.

Alternative Trips

Launch at Bob's Fishing Hole, which is accessible via VA 168, a little south of Indian Creek Road. Paddle westward and upriver, staying on the southern/left branch when the river splits. The river is much narrower in this section, with considerably fewer bass fishermen. It is about a 6-mile journey to some old railroad trestles, which serves as a good marker for a turnaround point. The farm field that comes down to the river here would make a fine lunch spot. Both Tidewater Adventures and Wild River Outfitters guide groups along this route.

Part IV — Eastern Shore

24.

Virginia Coast Reserve — Mockhorn Island

Features: Wild barrier islands, primitive camping, excellent birding, unlimited route possibilities.

Length: It is a 7-mile round-trip to the Cushman farm, and a 10-mile round-trip to the towers; however, the route and mileage possibilities are unlimited.

Put-in site: Eastern Shore of Virginia National Wildlife Refuge, 5003 Hallett Circle, Cape Charles, VA 23310, 757-331-2760. The put-in location for this trip is the Eastern Shore of Virginia National Wildlife Refuge, which protects the southern tip of the peninsula. Like many refuges, the land here was originally occupied by the military, first as Fort John Custis, and then as the Cape Charles Air Force Station. That station closed in 1981, and the management of the land transferred to the U.S. Fish and Wildlife Service in 1984.

The refuge is open from sunrise to sunset, and the landing is primarily for carry-in boats, although some small, trailered johnboats can also use the dirt ramp. There are no facilities at the landing, but there are bathrooms in the visitors center, which you pass on the way into the park. The visitors center is open from 9 to 4 from April through November, and from 10 to 2 from December through March (and is only open weekdays during January and February).

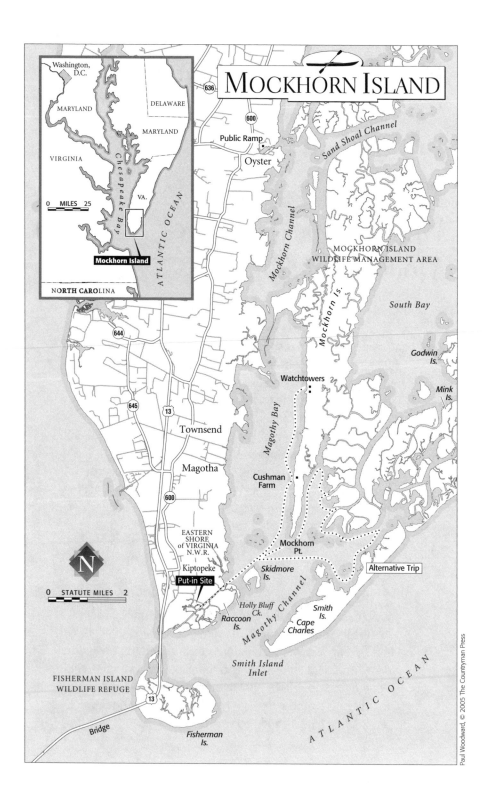

MOCKHORN ISLAND

Map labels

Inset map:
Washington, D.C.
MARYLAND
DELAWARE
MARYLAND
VIRGINIA
Chesapeake Bay
VA.
ATLANTIC OCEAN
0 MILES 25
Mockhorn Island
NORTH CAROLINA

Main map:
636
600
Public Ramp
Oyster
Sand Shoal Channel
Mockhorn Channel
MOCKHORN ISLAND WILDLIFE MANAGEMENT AREA
South Bay
Mockhorn Is.
Godwin Is.
Watchtowers
Mink Is.
Magothy Bay
644
645
13
Townsend
Magotha
Cushman Farm
600
EASTERN SHORE of VIRGINIA N.W.R.
Kiptopeke
Put-in Site
N
0 STATUTE MILES 2
Mockhorn Pt.
Alternative Trip
Skidmore Is.
Holly Bluff Ck.
Raccoon Is.
Smith Is.
Cape Charles
Magothy Channel
Smith Island Inlet
FISHERMAN ISLAND WILDLIFE REFUGE
13
Bridge
Fisherman Is.
ATLANTIC OCEAN

Paul Woodward, © 2005 The Countryman Press

There is primitive camping on Mockhorn Island, or you can find excellent tent and RV camping nearby at Kiptopeke State Park. Also, there are bed & breakfasts in Cape Charles, and there are several area hotels, including the Days Inn, which is just across from the refuge entrance. Southeast Expeditions' kayak shop is across the road from the park. It is an excellent company that offers both rentals and tours of the area.

Directions: From the western shore, follow US 13 North across the Chesapeake Bay Bridge Tunnel. In 2004 the bridge/tunnel toll was $12 each way, although there is a substantial discount if you complete a round-trip within 24 hours. Take a right into the Eastern Shore of Virginia National Wildlife Refuge about 1 mile north of the bridge, opposite the Days Inn and Southeast Expeditions' kayak shop. The entrance to the visitors center is the first right 0.1 mile.

To reach the landing, follow the main road for 0.3 mile from US 13 (past the turnoff to the visitors center), and take a right at the T-intersection. Take the second left in 0.5 mile, and then take a right onto a dirt road in 0.4 mile. The dirt landing is 0.1 mile on your right.

If you are traveling to the refuge from the north, use the same directions, but take a left off US 13 South, about 1 mile before reaching the Bay Bridge Tunnel.

AN ENTIRE BOOK could be written about paddling the barrier islands of Virginia. There are 18 different islands that make up this archipelago, which stretches 60 miles from the Maryland/Virginia line to the Chesapeake Bay. The Virginia Department of Game and Inland Fisheries owns Mockhorn Island, and the Nature Conservancy protects 14 of the other islands, having purchased over 38,000 acres in order to prevent a developer from turning the islands into an ocean resort community. Metomkin, Cedar, Parramore, Hog, Cobb, Little Cobb, Ship Shoal, Myrtle, Smith, Godwin, Rouge, Sandy, Revels, and Mink islands now make up the Virginia Coast Reserve. Parramore, Ship Shoal, Little Cobb, and Revels are closed to any access, and portions of other islands, like Smith and Hog, are also clearly posted with NO TRESPASSING signs during the spring and summer nesting seasons. However, the rest of the islands of the reserve are open for minimal-impact day use, like sea kayaking.

The following route description covers just the southern end of Mockhorn Island and is not meant to be an exhaustive reporting of the island chain's kayaking opportunities. Rather, my intention is to show you the way to begin your journey and then leave the details up to you. This is a place for exploration, pure and simple.

Trip Description

The landing places you on a small inlet in the salt marsh. Trees frame the western and southern sides of the marsh, with nothing but salt marsh to the east of inlet. The water is a clear, slate blue, and periwinkles dot the cordgrass like berries. Bear left when you reach the wider water. Pay attention to the red-and-white antenna tower to your left—this is a useful landmark for finding your way back home as the inlet to the landing lines up directly with the tower. You will pass a little gut on your left, which you can follow as a side detour, or you can continue straight—both options will bring you to the main channel. It is wide and unmistakable, and you can see the Bay Bridge Tunnel to your right/south. Bear left to paddle north toward the barrier islands.

You will pass a watermen's landing on the left, just above where the side gut detour enters into the main channel. This collection of pilings and docks will give you a good landmark for finding the gut entrance on your return trip. In about ½ mile you will pass a smaller dock on the left/western bank, and Holly Bluff Creek is opposite that, along with a couple houses on Raccoon Island. While the majority of the barrier islands are wild, there are some buildings and private property left scattered about. Cedar Island is partially private property, with numerous summer homes on one side of the island. Other islands have old watermen cottages, farmhouses and hunting lodges. Chincoteague Island is a fully settled summer resort community at the northern tip of the Virginia, and just south of that is Wallops, which supports NASA's Goddard Space Flight Center.

Once you pass Raccoon Island, you enter the wide waters of Magothy Bay and can paddle northeast to Skidmore Island, which is about ⅓ mile away. You can see the Cape Charles Lighthouse to your east, on Smith Islands, with three smaller World War II army towers around its base. This 192-foot-tall lighthouse that marks the entrance to the Chesapeake Bay is the second tallest on the East Coast and the brightest in the Bay. It is the third lighthouse to stand here. The first, constructed in 1827, was too short and too dim to effectively mark the Chesapeake's entrance. Its replacement was finished in 1864 after almost seven years of construction, which was greatly hampered by the Confederacy's sabotage of the project. Less than 20 years after this second lighthouse was built, the natural erosion of the island endangered it. Despite jetties and bulkheads, it had to be replaced by the lighthouse that currently stands on the island, which was completed in 1894. It is an iron tower, reinforced by an octagonal steel cage. It was automated in 1963, and the vacant light keeper's house burned down in July 2000. It is not the most attractive lighthouse I have ever seen, but it is tall and bright and does its job.

Beaches rim Skidmore Island, and this is a good place to take a break before making the open-water crossing to Mockhorn or Smith Island. I used a beach on the western side, by the old foundation of a house, and the sand was littered with conch shells. A bald eagle joined my friend and me on the island and calmly sat in a nearby tree while we munched on our granola bars. Magothy Bay is big water, and Mockhorn and Smith Islands are both a little over 1 mile away from Skidmore. The bay is mostly shallow, and with no land forms to break up the force of the wind, waves can quickly build up in here, making for rough, difficult paddling during any wind higher than 7 to 8 knots. Because of this, like all open-water paddling, the barrier islands are not well suited for novice paddlers, and beginners would do well to paddle with more experienced friends, or with an organized group like Southeast Expeditions.

Paddle north, toward Mockhorn Island, paralleling the east side of the channel. With an area of 7,000 acres and a length of 8 miles, this island is one of the largest in the archipelago. The tip of Mockhorn Point is all low marsh, with a good sandy beach on the interior of this point. A grove of trees begins about ¾ mile up the point, and you should paddle toward the long roofline in the middle of that grove of trees. It is almost a 2-mile crossing from Skidmore to the trees of Mockhorn.

As you approach the trees, you will notice a cement retaining wall and old cement wharves. Larimore Cushman, a New Yorker who had dreams of farming, constructed these in 1925. We ate lunch on his beach, using his walls as our picnic tables and benches. Beside fortifying the front of his property, he also built a dyke and moat to surround the sides and back of his land. The entrance to this waterway is hidden, and the moat barely shows up on highly detailed topographic charts, but it does exist. Just paddle along the edge of the marsh, south of the brick farmhouse, and you will find the small south-facing entrance to the creek. It is almost blocked by marsh grasses, but just push over these and into Cushman's world.

The passage wraps around the back of the Cushman property, with flat wetland to the left side of the moat, and marsh elder and cedar on the higher land of the dyke walls to your right. The brick farmhouse is deep within the marsh on your left and has almost entirely been overtaken by a dense growth of trees. Then the moat passes through a narrow wooded tunnel. Dozens of egrets and herons rose from their perches, sounding a noisy protest as we passed under their roosts, and we also startled a great horned owl into silent flight. Once past the trees, you will see the long barn to your left, and you can land on the marsh in order to explore the barn and stable building by foot. Just be careful where you walk because the ground is littered with rusty nails and old farm implements.

As you may be able to tell from the feed yard and stables, this was primarily a cattle farm, with some of the marsh put under cultivation for alfalfa. Larimore Cushman was not the first to see the islands as naturally water-fenced pastures for raising livestock. People had tried ventures such as this since the Colonial days, and entire towns were built on some of the larger islands, like Hog Island to the north, which once had a population of 250. Chincoteague Island was settled as a farming town, although its residents soon turned to the sea for their sustenance.

Marshlands of the Virginia Coast Reserve

Ranching is tough, even in easier, inland environments, and while Cushman and others fought a constant battle against the elements, their cattle were driven into the water, standing immersed up to their necks in an effort to escape the biting flies and mosquitoes. His enterprise eventually failed, and the state purchased Mockhorn as a wildlife management area in 1959, ending the last attempt to farm the islands.

Three grasses dominate the majority of the marsh: saltwater cordgrass, salt meadow hay, and black needle rush. However, paddling in the moat gives you a closer look at some of the smaller, diverse species that make up this harsh, salty environment. There are two common succulent plants in the salt marsh, the saltwort and the prickly pear cactus. Saltwort is a round, jointed plant that lives on the water's edge, grows to be between 8 and 20 inches tall, and is the brilliant color of jade. The prickly pear cactus grows slightly higher up on the dyke and naturally occurs on sand dunes. Like the saltwort, the cactus is filled with water, which allows it to regulate and retain its fresh water in this salty maritime environment. Neither plant is particularly nutritious for animals, but humans eat both. The saltwort is commonly pickled (and is even

(continued on page 218)

Ancient Mating Rituals—Horseshoe Crabs

Horseshoe crabs have evolved little in the last three-hundred million years and have simply gone about their business of living, mating, eating, and dying. They were named after their resemblance to a horse's hoof print, and while they look fearsome with their hard black shell, spiked rear edge, and dagger-sharp tail, they are harmless. Their shell and spiked rear edge are to keep other creatures from eating them, and their tail is used like a rudder while swimming, or as a lever to right themselves with if they are flipped onto their back. They do not belong to the crab family but are a class unto themselves, their only distant living relative being the common spider. Their feathery claws cannot pinch you, and their jaws are used only for grinding their preferred food—clams. In fact, kissing the underside of a horseshoe crab has served as a rite of passage for many environmental education students, and I can vouch that holding the wiggling legs of the crab to your face is a strange but harmless experience.

Horseshoe crabs find their food by burrowing into the mud and sand. They are blind to anything that is more than 3 feet away and literally only have eyes for other horseshoe crabs, using their sight to find one another for mating. Usually content to swim the deeper waters of the Chesapeake and coastal bays, every spring the solitary creatures begin to gather in shallow water. They make their landward march during the high tides of the new and full moons, usually reaching peak activity during the first full moon of May and using the high water of the nocturnal tide to help them swim high up onto the beaches. The female is larger, so the male attaches himself to her tail with the small pincer claws that only males have. Often one male will attach behind another, thus forming a train of males behind the one female. She then drags the male (or males) up the beach and digs a shallow hole in the sand with her rear legs. She deposits up to 20,000 pea-sized green eggs in the nest, and after pulling the male(s) over the hole so that he/they can fertilize them, the crabs return to the water and wait for the next high tide. She repeats this cycle over and over, laying up to 100,000 eggs in a single mating season.

Of all of these eggs, only 10 horseshoe crabs will survive out of every 100,000. This abysmal ratio is because thousands of shorebirds depend on horseshoe crabs for their survival. Every spring, as sand-pipers and plovers return north from their winter homes, they feast upon the protein-rich eggs to gain back most of the weight and strength lost during their long flight north. Watching these rituals of survival is overwhelming. I have watched hundreds of crabs cover a beach, going about their business with single-minded devotion. They pay no mind to observers and will bump against you as they feel their way up the beach. The sheer volume of crabs and eggs seems impossible to comprehend. In the morning, the crabs are gone and the birds descend, filling the beach with an undulating mass of feathers, gorging themselves on the feast of horseshoe crab caviar.

The mating ritual of crabs happens all around the salty waters of the lower Chesapeake and in the coastal bays of the barrier islands. After a beach bonfire on Great Fox Island, Virginia (opposite the Saxis trip), I waded through high tide with a group of inner-city high school students toward our canoes, which were pulled up high on the marsh. Kids began to holler and scream, and all flashlights were turned to the water, revealing hundreds of crabs swarming around us in search of the beach. The hollering soon ended, to be replaced by the calm voices of students as they helped one another avoid stepping on the defenseless crabs. It was a night that none of us will ever forget.

It is easy to plan your own night of crab-watching, paired with a morning paddle off the same beach to watch the thousands of shorebirds. Many refuges and state parks even have scheduled watching parties, with naturalists on hand to answer questions about these odd creatures.

While cockroaches are often heralded as the only species that will survive until the end of the world, I have my money on the horseshoe crabs. One barrier to this may be the discovery that their blood serves as a useful clotting agent and as a test for the purity of medicines. However, as long as the harvesting of these animals stays at sustainable levels, there is no reason they should not continue for another three-hundred million years, oblivious to everything but other horseshoe crabs.

referred to as pickleweed), and the cactus and its flower can be cooked and prepared in a variety of ways.

If you paddle farther up the west side of Mockhorn, you will reach the old World-War-II–era watchtowers, which were built in association with Fort John Custis as submarine watchtowers, and used to monitor artillery practice. There is a long beach at the base of these towers, along with higher ground salt meadow hay in the area. Mockhorn is a Virginia Wildlife Management Area, so unlike the 14 islands owned by the Nature Conservancy, it is permissible to camp anywhere you want on the island for up to 14 days at a time. With no reservation or permit system, it is truly primitive camping where you find your own site, bring your own water, and pack out all of your trash. The best camping is on the upper part of the beach by these towers, and on the high ground of the Cushman property. Due to the massive swarms of summer mosquitoes, the optimum time for camping is from October to April. Be sure to secure your boats and pitch your tent well above high tide.

There are dozens of different routes to paddle just by leaving from the wildlife refuge or by base camping on Mockhorn Island. The whole east side of Mockhorn is filled with guts, sloughs, and channels, all of which lead you through a marshland of unmatched beauty. Smith Island, named by (and after) Captain John Smith, is an exterior barrier island, so it has salt marsh on its interior and wide sand beaches on its Atlantic side. You can enjoy the beaches by landing on the protected east side of Smith and walking over the marsh and dunes to the ocean side of the island. There is a plethora of inlets to explore on the interior of the island, with guts intersecting with one another to form marsh islands. Edward Teach, better known as Blackbeard the Pirate, once sought refuge in these hidden coves, using their shelter to repair his ship for more plundering on the open seas.

Experienced kayakers can also paddle out to the ocean from here, entering either to the south of the island, through the Magothy Channel below the Cape Charles Lighthouse, or through the little inlet, between Smith and Myrtle Islands. Both inlets can have strong currents, and landing on the Atlantic side of the island requires surfing skills. Because of this, only experienced paddlers should paddle into the open waters of the ocean. You need to have solid braces and should be able to roll your kayak. However, if you do kayak out here, you will be traveling along the longest stretch of wild Atlantic beach left in the United States.

You can also paddle through the guts and inlets northeast along Smith to explore the shores of Mink, Ship Shoal, Myrtle, and Godwin islands. There is a hundred-year-old cabin in the marsh by Myrtle Island. Be sure not to land on Ship Shoal; it used to be a bombing range and is closed to public access for safety reasons.

This area is interesting to paddle during all seasons, and hundreds of species of birds pass through and live here during different times of the year. During the spring and summer, osprey, gulls, terns, and eagles rule the sky, while sea ducks, loons, geese, and other waterfowl pass through the area in the winter, as well as winter here. Muskrat, raccoons, and river otters live in the marshes, and the waters are teeming with fish life. The Virginia Coast Reserve's importance as a natural resource cannot be overestimated, and it provides coastal bay paddling opportunities that are unparalleled, whether you spend a week camping on Mockhorn or just head out for the day.

Alternative Trips

For a one-way version of the Mockhorn paddle, you can launch at the small waterman community of Oyster and paddle south along Mockhorn Island. This is an excellent full-day, 13-mile paddle. You can reverse this route if the wind is blowing from the south; but regardless of your direction of paddle, you will need to leave a shuttle vehicle at one end. If you are paddling solo, or traveling with one car, you may be able to arrange a drop-off with Southeast Expeditions. Oyster is accessible off US Business 13, near the end of County Route 639 (CR 639)—just follow the signs for the turnoff to the public landing. Oyster also provides excellent access to the middle islands of the reserve, including Wreck and Cobb Islands, both of which are exterior islands. See the Machipongo trip description for access to the more northern islands of the chain.

You can leave from the landing at the wildlife refuge in order to paddle alongside Fisherman's Island, which is the southernmost island in the chain. The federal government has owned this island since 1886 and operated it as an immigrant quarantine station capable of housing a thousand people. Then, during World Wars I and II, large guns were placed on the island and used to protect the mouth of Chesapeake Bay. You can paddle under the spans of the Chesapeake Bay Bridge Tunnel, which crosses the island. It is the largest bridge-tunnel complex in the world and was opened in 1964 to replace the ferry service between Cape Charles and Norfolk, Virginia. A second span was added in 1998. The rest of the island is preserved as bird habitat, and in order to protect nesting habitat, you cannot land anywhere on the island, but you can paddle into the guts that crease the marsh. Such paddles will unveil a world of birds, and you will be surrounded by species such as sandpipers, oystercatchers, brown pelicans, arctic terns, and glossy ibises. Southeast Expeditions runs excellent half-day paddles here, and their informative guides are well versed in the birds and history of the island. The wildlife refuge also leads a 4-mile walking tour of the island during the non-nesting season, on Saturdays from October through March.

25.

Old Plantation Creek

Features: Cape Charles, open Bay and tidal creek, the tomb of John Custis II, pelicans, herons, egrets, and kingfishers.

Length: 9 to 12 miles (depending on number of side creeks paddled).

Put-in site: The launch location for this trip is Cape Charles, which is a late 1800s town that is now a popular summer destination with a swimming beach and several bed & breakfasts. Southeast Kayaks is a few miles down US 13 from here, and they run a day trip that is similar to this trip description. Camping is available a few miles to the south at Kiptopeke State Park, and you can do a variation of this trip by paddling north from Kiptopeke to Old Plantation Creek.

There are two places to launch in Cape Charles: the public boat landing and the beach. The landing is geared toward trailered boats and has two wide concrete ramps. There is a port-a-john in the nearby small marina. While the landing can be busy, particularly on weekends, there is room on either side of the ramps to unload your kayak without getting in the way of the trailered boats, making this an easy launch site. The swimming beach does not have any trailered boat traffic but requires you to carry your equipment from the street, over the dune, to the beach. The best place to carry across is at the southern end of the beach, by the pier and the bathrooms. If you are paddling with a group of people, the beach may be the better option for staging your trip because you will have people to help carry boats and you will not fill up the boat ramp. However, since I was paddling solo, I chose to leave

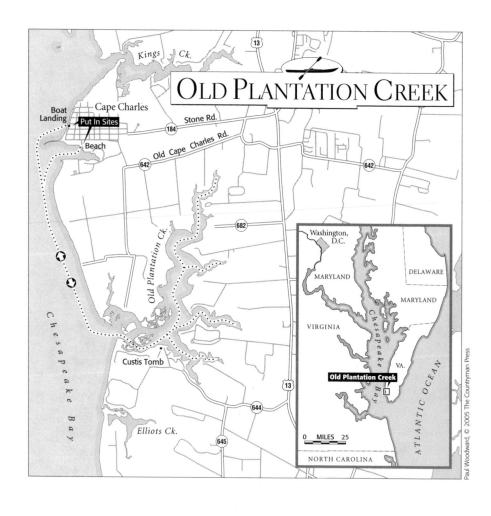

OLD PLANTATION CREEK

Kings Ck.

13

Boat Landing
Cape Charles
Put In Sites
Beach
Stone Rd.
184
Old Cape Charles Rd.
642
642

Old Plantation Ck.
682

Custis Tomb

Chesapeake Bay

Elliots Ck.
644
645
13

Washington, D.C.
MARYLAND
DELAWARE
MARYLAND
VIRGINIA
Chesapeake Bay
VA.
Old Plantation Creek
ATLANTIC OCEAN
0 MILES 25
NORTH CAROLINA

Paul Woodward, © 2005 The Countryman Press

from the public boat landing because I would rather exert my energy paddling than carrying my boat over sand.

Directions: *For the boat landing:* Take VA 184 West/Stone Road, which is off US 13, south of Cheriton at a traffic light (take a left if you are traveling from the south, or a right if you are traveling from the north). Follow for 2 miles to Cape Charles. Take a left onto Fig Street. This bends to the right in 0.1 mile and becomes Mason Avenue. Follow Mason Avenue for 0.1 mile, and then take a hairpin left onto Old Cape Charles Road/CR 642. Drive over the overpass and in 0.3 mile take the first right onto Bayshore Drive/VA 1108. There is a brown public landing sign at this turn. Follow for 0.2 mile and then take a right onto Marina Road. Drive across the railroad tracks, past the coast guard station and the marina. It is 0.3 mile to the landing on the other side of the marina. *For the beach:* Follow the same directions from US 13, but when you reach the junction with Fig Street, continue straight, following signs to the beach. The road becomes Randolph Avenue. Follow for 0.7 mile until it ends at the beach. Take a left and park at the end of the road (parking is also available on Mason Avenue to the left).

ALTHOUGH IT APPEARS as flat and unassuming as the rest of the Eastern Shore, Cape Charles was formed by a great impact. A 2-mile-wide comet or meteor slammed into the ground here about thirty-five million years ago, splashing up a mile-high plume of melted rock, forming the peak of land that Cape Charles sits on today. The object was apparently traveling about 21 miles per second when it hit, causing an explosion greater than what would be generated by detonating all of the world's nuclear weapons. That image of natural destruction is hard to imagine on the peaceful paddle from Cape Charles to Old Plantation Creek. This trip provides a little bit of every kind of paddling. Beginning along the small town industrial waterfront, you paddle onto the open Bay, along low bluffs and beaches. Brown pelicans roost on pound nets and fish the open water, their wings almost brushing the water as they glide past. After a couple miles on the Chesapeake, the paddle leads you into Old Plantation Creek, which is rich in natural and human history and provides miles of quiet, wind-protected water to explore. It is the best of all worlds.

Trip Description

Cape Charles is built on the northern bank of a small, nameless working creek. A coast guard station and a watermen marina occupy the top (eastern) end of the creek, and the public boat landing is just below the marina, on the north side of the creek. From the landing, bear right to head out toward the Chesapeake, and travel on one side or the other to avoid colliding with powerboats. Cape Charles is the headquarters of Eastern Shore Railroad, and their trains and tracks fill the northern shore in the space between the creek and the Victorian-era waterfront of Mason Avenue. Old cars from the Southern Comfort and Philadelphia Star serve as a backdrop for rust-streaked working containers filled with grain, coal, and concrete products.

Cape Charles was founded as the southern terminus of the New York, Pennsylvania, and Norfolk Railroad in 1884. Barges known as car floats, invented in 1885, enabled the line to extend 26 miles across the Bay to Norfolk. Passengers would travel this leg of the journey by steamboat until 1953, when the last passenger steamboat left Cape Charles. Consequently, passenger trains ceased coming to town in 1958. Hopefully the passengers found some other way to get to their final destination during the five intervening years.

The railroad's dock is just below the landing. With the exception of the lack of passengers, the only major difference between today's system and a hundred years ago is that diesel has replaced steam in powering the tugboats. The Eastern Shore Railroad is still bustling, and their car float operates six days a week during the May-to-August grain season, taking 12 hours to complete the round-trip transfer of cars.

One of the benefactors of this railroad shipping port is Bayshore Concrete Products, which dominates the southern shore of the creek. The plant builds concrete conduits and other structural forms, many of which you can see being loaded onto barges, trucks, and railcars with large cranes and container movers. The basic sand and gravel ingredients of concrete are stored in large waterside bays, and the southern shoreline is fittingly bulk-headed with concrete. While I love paddling in wilderness creeks, I also enjoy these sojourns alongside industry and find it fascinating to see people and companies working at their various occupations.

A long pier and riprapped breakwater extend out from the northern end of the mouth of the creek. The Bayside beaches are on the opposite side of this obstacle. Bear left around the point to paddle south on the open Bay. Bayshore Concrete extends for quite a way along the shoreline, and here the natural waterfront and dunes have been re-placed by industrial-strength riprap, comprised of discarded conduits, tunnels, and concrete slabs. It isn't pretty, but it gets the job done.

In rather dramatic fashion, the concrete stops and the wilder shore-line begins. The next 100 yards or so of shoreline is owned by the Cape Charles Sustainable Technology Park. While it is a large office park, it was built with energy-saving and sustainable environmental technolo-gies. This included keeping a forest buffer between the park and the Bay, and thus a wooden observation platform is the only evidence of all the white-collar workers busy at their jobs. The densely wooded shore-line quickly ends, thinning into the manicured and groomed woods of a golf course, which is part of a 1,700-acre luxury residential golf com-munity called Bay Creek.

To avoid running aground, you should paddle at least 100 feet or so away from the shoreline, increasing this distance during low tides. Wind- and boat-generated waves will also be calmer the farther away you are from the sandy shoals near the shore. However, do not venture too far into the open water because the main commercial channel is about ½ mile out from land. The channel is clearly marked with buoys. There is a pound net about ¼ to ½ mile out from the observation plat-form; and about 1 mile south of that, there is a second pound net, slightly closer to shore. While most pound nets have their long net wall staked out with poles, this 100-yard-long net is strung between small buoys and weighed down with anchors. Because of the lack of poles, it is safe for kayakers to paddle over any section of the net that they want. However, you may want to paddle around the outside of the pound net to get a closer look at the community of birds that uses the poles and nets of the funnel and pound as a resting place. Cormorants, gulls, and terns perch comfortably on the impossibly small ends of the poles, and pelicans sit on the rope ends of the exposed net, like children on a large playground swing. Fishing pelicans are funny to watch; although I suspect the watermen who own these nets would not find them quite so entertaining. There is a three-piling structure here, with a red-and-white range bolted to its side. A corresponding range stands on the shoreline, and ship captains use these visual cues to line up their approach to the channel.

The entrance to Old Plantation Creek is about 2½ miles from the boat landing. As you wrap around the shoreline to enter the creek, you may notice two things about it. One is that it resembles a white-quilled porcupine. The other is that it appears to only be a shallow bay, with a long and wide salt marsh as its terminus. The quills are actually PVC pipes, which are used to mark the boundaries of Cherrystone Aqua-Farm's leased clam beds. There are over 26 million clams growing in Old Plantation Creek, and every one has been planted by Cherrystone. You will likely see workers wading in the creek, accompanied by flat-bottomed, flat-decked work skiffs. They seed the beds by grabbing handfuls of fingernail-length clams from the buckets, which float beside them in inner tubes, and then tossing them into the water. They next lay thick netting over the beds to keep out predators like cownose rays, staking down the edges of these nets with the PVC pipes and iron bar anchors. The clams take two years to grow to maturity and are harvested by the same workers who work the clam beds with hand rakes. Cherry-stone has beds in all stages of maturity, and their littlenecks are sold all over the country, often advertised by name as Old Plantation Creek clams. Along with being an economically sustainable business, aquaculture may also be environmentally beneficial because clams filter the water as they feed. The clear green-blue water and thick beds of submerged aquatic vegetation throughout the creek seem to be proof of this hypothesis, although scientists are still working on a definitive study.

The northern shoreline has a long strip of beach that is actually separated from the private lands of the golf course by a small inlet that flows west to south between the sandbar peninsula and the mainland. There is a duck blind on the inside of the point, and the beach is an excellent place to stretch your legs. The nontidal portion of the highest part of the sandbar may be technically owned by the golf course, but anything below mean high tide is public property. Just be respectful of the golf course and its property, and do not interfere with the duck blind.

The impenetrable looking salt marsh that seems to turn the creek into a shallow bay is actually an archipelago of cordgrass islands. The main channels into the creek are in the center and southern ends of the creek, but it is also possible to pass through the dense northern section of marsh and into its heart. This is the route I chose, and I followed the northern edge of the marsh, passing between the salt marsh and the loblolly wooded shoreline. Herons and egrets filled the marsh, and periwinkles coated the cordgrass. The gut wrapped back into the marsh and connected with another small channel, and I chose to bear left again. I did this one more time, before finally bearing right to head out of the marsh into the open water of the inner creek. There is no wrong way to travel through the marsh. Paddling this labyrinth of salt marsh and

Some of the marsh islands of Old Plantation Creek as seen from Custis' Tomb

water is all about the journey and not about the destination. It does not matter how many dead-ends you chase down or how many circles you paddle. In fact, the more side trips you take in the marsh, the better, so the right way to paddle here is by following "wrong" passages.

Bear left when you reach the open water of the creek. The creek mostly flows from north to south, so your travel upstream will parallel your southern journey down the Bay to the creek's mouth. The water is still rather wide here, so it is best to pick a shoreline to travel down to maximize your wildlife viewing. I kept along the left/western shore on my paddle upcreek and then came back down on the eastern shore.

Most of the western shore is owned by the Bay Creek Golf Course. However, they have left a buffer of loblolly trees, and you can spot osprey and kingfishers all along this shoreline. The creek bends back and forth and narrows considerably about ½ mile from the salt-marsh island. Yellow-and-black signs mark the remainder of the creek as illegal for shellfish harvesting, so the PVC pipes completely disappear. There is one house on the western shore at the inside of the final bend back to the left/north, and then the creek ends below the power lines.

While the eastern shoreline is more populated with houses, it is also richer in salt marsh and woodlands. There are three ½-mile-deep creeks that leave from the eastern shore, each a microcosm of Old Plantation Creek worthy of exploring. Like the main creek, their shores are a combination of woods, marsh, and houses. While the shoreline is primarily marsh and woods, there are numerous small, brown sand beaches hidden between marshes and below overhanging trees. Look carefully, and you should be able to find a suitable place to get out for a break.

On the way out, across from the beginning of salt-marsh islands, you will see a board-lined oyster shell slip on the eastern shoreline. It is just south of the southernmost creek and north of a collection of houses and docks. The rules about this slip are unclear, but while it is not permissible to launch your boat here, it does appear to be fine to land here, which will allow you to visit the former plantation site of John Custis II. Custis farmed a 5,000-acre plantation here, which is where the creek got its name, and in 1670 he built a large, three-story mansion. He named it Arlington, after his father's home near Gloucestershire, England. When his great-grandson built a home on the southern shore of the Potomac River in the late 1800s, he took the name with him (see the Georgetown trip description for more about Northern Virginia's Arlington). The tombs of John Custis II and John Custis IV are on-site, and the rest of the grounds are mostly an open field with stakes marking the foundation of the old mansion.

The southern passage back to the Bay through the islands is broad, and the islands here are smaller. One of the perks of there-and-back paddling is that it gives you two chances to see the same area on a single trip, thus doubling your exposure to beauty and your chances of seeing wildlife. I encourage you to break free from the wide passage and dive back into the marsh for more exploration. In fact, if you are not paddling alone, this salt labyrinth is perfect for resurrecting the childhood game of hide-and-seek. Just leave someone out in the open, counting with their eyes closed (preferably out of the boat channel), and then lose yourself among the guts. Open your ears and prepare to sneak away from them if you hear their approach, keeping your paddles low in order to keep your location secret. Or, if paddling solo, declare yourself "it" and see how close you can sneak up to an egret. Kayaking is not serious business, so have fun, be silly, and leave working to the watermen, and the concrete, office park, and railroad employees.

Alternative Trips

There is a general lack of bayside boat landings between Cape Charles and Onancock. The one exception to this rule is the public landing in Harborton, which provides access to Pungoteague Creek, a deep, three-pronged waterway with plenty of interesting shoreline to explore.

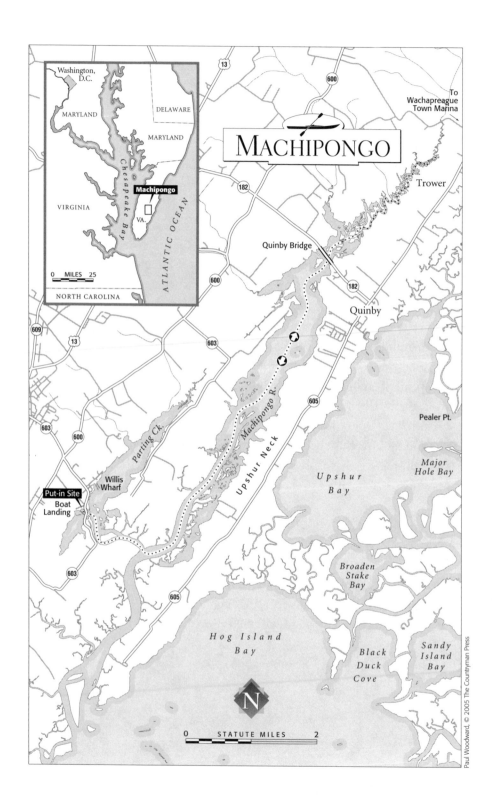

26.
Machipongo River

Features: A watermen town, a coastal salt-marsh river, egrets, herons, ibises, eagles, sea turtles, and sharks.

Length: 15 miles (but can easily be made shorter).

Put-in site: The trip leaves from the public boat landing in Willis Wharf. This small town has at least one bed & breakfast and is home to the E. L. Willis Store, an excellent down-home eatery. The town of Exmore is also nearby, with a railcar diner off US Business 13 that serves up great pre-paddle breakfasts. Both have a devoted local following, and listening to the fishing lies is some great, cheap entertainment. The public landing's boat ramps are extremely long and are framed in by wooden docks. There is plenty of room to the right of the ramps to unload without holding up trailered boat traffic, and there is a port-a-john here.

Directions: US 13 to US Business 13 to Exmore. Exit onto County Route 603/Willis Wharf Road (left if traveling south, or take a right if traveling north). Once you reach Willis Wharf, bear right, over the bridge, and then left into the boat landing.

THIS TRIP LEAVES from the watermen hamlet of Willis Wharf and leads the kayaker into the expansive salt marsh of the Virginia Coast Reserve. Unlike many of the paddles on the east side of the eastern shore, navigation of the Machipongo is straightforward, and there is no danger of becoming marooned behind an expanse of mudflats. A popular fishing spot, the river is closely tied to the Atlantic, which lies about a dozen miles downriver from Willis Wharf. It is truly a coastal river, and although you will find many familiar species like egrets, herons, and eagles, its warm river water also coaxes in many of the wide-roaming creatures of the deep, from sharks to sea turtles.

Trip Description

This trip begins in a small working harbor that is filled with seafood houses and workboats. Bear right out of here, onto Parting Creek. If the tide is up, you may want to explore the waters to your left/north. The creek flows past the small town waterfront of Willis Wharf and will bring you by many more seafood houses and workboats. (At low tide, though, this upriver section of creek is nearly emptied of water.) For the main body of this paddle, bear right to head south on Parting Creek toward the Machipongo River.

You will pass two more seafood houses with accompanying long docks on the left/northern side of the river. Willis Wharf is known as Clam Town and is where the booming clam aquaculture business got its start, thanks to Tom and Wade Walker. The brothers started farming clams over 20 years ago, using ideas they had gained from a Virginia Institute of Marine Science seminar. Clam aquaculture had proven to be a risky undertaking in Virginia; the last aquaculture venture, in Chincoteague in the mid-50s, had failed miserably. The Walkers' risk paid off though, as they are now one of the two largest aquaculture companies in Virginia. Their clam hatcheries are housed in some of these buildings; and using the clean water of Parting Creek and the Machipongo, they grow much of the clam "seed" for the other aquaculture businesses in the town and in the state.

Commercial and recreational fishermen travel this creek as fast as their boats will take them to the Machipongo and the Atlantic Ocean, so stay near the edges of the marsh and out of their way. There are numerous side guts into the salt marsh on the left, and after about the third gut, there is a cove with some houses on the right/southern shoreline. Artificial banks of oyster shells have been created along the northern shoreline as a natural riprap; and in about ½ mile from the landing, you can pass to the right or left of a marsh island. It is about

1 mile to the mouth of Parting Creek, which is marked with day marker number 13. Bear left to head north on the Machipongo.

The Machipongo River is relatively short, flowing for less than 20 miles through salt marsh and mudflats before merging with the Atlantic Ocean between Cobb and Hog Islands. Most powerboaters turn to the south, following the river to the ocean, leaving the upper part of the river as a sea kayaker's domain. This half of the river's journey is nestled between the higher loblolly-filled lands of Bell Neck and Upshur Neck, and the wide river is engulfed in salt marsh. Due to this low marshland, there is almost no development along the western shore of the river, leaving the shore wild and the water clean. Because the tidal current is fairly noticeable, you may want to time this paddle to catch the second half of the flood current upriver on the Machipongo and the first half of the ebb flow back home. This makes the trip easier, but it is not absolutely necessary.

There are many excellent side guts to explore along this river, and in about 1 mile from Parting Creek, some of the western guts will bring you deep into the marsh, alongside a grove of dead trees. At high tide it is possible to follow these interconnecting guts for about 1 mile northward, all the way to a farm that is on the western side of the river. These side passages are accessible only at high tide, so explore them whenever the water will be highest, on either your way up or down the river. I paddled the main passage on my way upstream and the back guts on the way back downriver, thus allowing for different scenery during both legs of my journey. While I was on the broader passage in the morning, a loggerhead turtle rose out of the water a mere 10 feet away, eyeballing me before disappearing back into the river's depths.

The farm on the western shore is a collection of rundown buildings and barns that are slowly decaying back into the land. Two old docks stick out into the water and are little more than a collection of rotting pilings that serve as perches for cormorants and gulls. Just past the farm, the river begins to narrow and become shallower, and the main passage splits between salt-marsh islands. As the river narrows, so do the wetlands, bringing the woods much closer to the water, and shoring up the grass with firmer sand. This encroachment provides easy access to break

The gull, a coastal kayaker's constant companion

spots on dry land, and I stopped for lunch just south of a small duck blind, about 4 miles from Willis Wharf. To reach firm land, build up to full ramming speed and paddle your boat as high into the marsh as possible. Be sure to wear shoes because, while the marsh is firm, it is filled with sharp mussels, fiddler crabs, and periwinkles. There is a thin strip of beach between the marsh and the woods, allowing for a comfortable spot to stretch out for a post-lunch nap.

Although I was only on the beach for ½ hour, when I was ready to leave I could not find my kayak. It was only after I crunched back through the marsh toward the water that I finally stumbled upon my boat, which was hidden in plain sight in the middle of the salt marsh. My concealed boat reminded me of a game that I used to play when I was an environmental educator with the Chesapeake Bay Foundation. It was a version of hide-and-seek, where the person who was *it* had to stand in one place in the high marsh, and everyone else had to hide in the marsh around them. The person who was "it" would call out who they could see and then turn their back while everyone else crept even closer before re-concealing themselves in the marsh. This would be repeated until the last person was left hiding, sometimes only 2 feet away in the marsh. Just as my boat reminded me, the purpose of the game was to make students aware that although the marsh looks like nothing but a sea of uninhabited grass, it is in fact a shelter for a wealth of animals, easily concealed from our prying eyes. That, and it was a good excuse to get really, really dirty.

You will reach the Quinby Bridge in about 5½ miles from Willis Wharf. It is a low bridge, with a string of seafood warehouses along its western side. After this, the river narrows considerably. While the water is only navigable for about 2 miles north of the bridge, you can paddle for almost 3 miles (there-and-back)by circling the little islands. The world was peaceful and quiet. I never actually pursued the river to its ultimate end because I kept being seduced into following egrets and herons and spent many serene minutes silently watching a snowy egret stalk its prey, spearing minnows with a serpentine stabbing of its head. When I finally drifted back downstream, lazy with the calmness of the day, I paused to chat with the old man who was fishing from the side of the bridge. While I had been upstream playing, he had caught and released a 3-foot-long sand shark.

It turns out that sharks are quite common in this river, drawn in by the relatively deep water, following the fish that thrive in the river's clean, warm environment. Known by the common name of sand sharks, there are actually three species of shark that favor the inland waters: the spiny dogfish, the smooth dogfish, and the bull shark. The man I met probably caught one of the varieties of dogfish, both of which average between 2 to 4 feet long. However, other fishermen that I later met at the landing told of catching sharks almost as long as my 16½-foot kayak. Even allowing for the natural exaggeration of the recreational fisherman, these sharks were most likely the beefier bull shark that can grow to be about 12 feet long.

As is true with all there-and-back paddles, because I was freed up from navigating I saw even more eagles, herons, egrets, and ibises on my return journey. In addition, remembering the lesson of my hidden boat, I drifted close to the edges, studied the sea of grass intently, and was rewarded with a glimpse of an elusive rail. Altogether, it was a beautiful and relaxing day on a warm, peaceful river. That is until something nibbled at my toes while I was cooling off in the river, sending me leaping clear out of the water, landing in a hard belly flop on my boat with irrational thoughts of shark attacks playing through my mind.

Damn you Steven Spielberg—your animatronic shark has ruined me forever.

Alternative Trips

Instead of paddling there and back, you could do a shuttle trip by dropping your boat over at the Quinby Bridge and paddling downstream to Willis Wharf. Or, you could launch south of Willis Wharf and paddle upstream from the boat landing at the end of CR 617. Also, a trip quite similar to the Machipongo can be found a few miles to the north, leaving from the town of Wachapreague. This is another watermen town, but slightly bigger than Willis Wharf, with a couple of good restaurants. The paddle leads you out on the Wachapreague Channel, where you can explore the labyrinth of guts and waterways including the Bradford Channel, Bradford Bay, and Millstone Creek. You can even paddle all the way out to Parramore Island, which is closed to public access but is beautiful to paddle near. If the waterway combinations look too confusing, you can easily sign up with Southeast Kayaks and allow one of their guides to lead you into the salt marsh. You can also launch in the town of Quinby and paddle out on the Great Gap Channel toward Revel and Hog Islands. Revel Island is closed to access, and the water here is shallow, with expansive mudflats that are impassable at low tide, so plan your trip here accordingly. For both Wachapreague and Great Gap, you should have a compass and be a competent navigator.

27.

Onancock

Features: Historic small town, marshland circumnavigation, wild beaches, a lot of birdlife.

Length: 10 to 14 miles.

Put-in site: The public boat landing is at the town dock of Onancock, a Colonial town founded in 1680. Originally called Port Scarborough, it later took the name of its waterway, which means a foggy place. It is a small town with many historic buildings, bed & breakfasts, antiques shops, and restaurants. The protected deep-water harbor of Onancock Creek makes this a popular destination for Chesapeake sailors and commercial boats, and the two disparate populations seem to blend easily. Onancock is also an increasingly popular destination among kayakers, and the creek's population swells every autumn for the annual Onancock kayak race, which is partially sponsored by Southeast Kayaks.

The boat slip is small, and there is plenty of parking in the harbor parking lot. The Hopkins and Brothers General Store, established in 1842, is across from the landing. A Chesapeake Bay Gateways water trail map of this paddle will be available in 2005, and a new kayak dock will be built at the White/Ingleside Park.

Directions: From US 13, turn onto VA 179 West toward Onancock. Follow it for about 2 miles, all the way into town. The road becomes Market Street and ends at the small harbor parking lot, by the marina office and Hopkins and Brothers General Store.

ON A GORGEOUS SATURDAY in the middle of the summer I sat with my back against my kayak at the tip of a mile-long beach, and was alone in

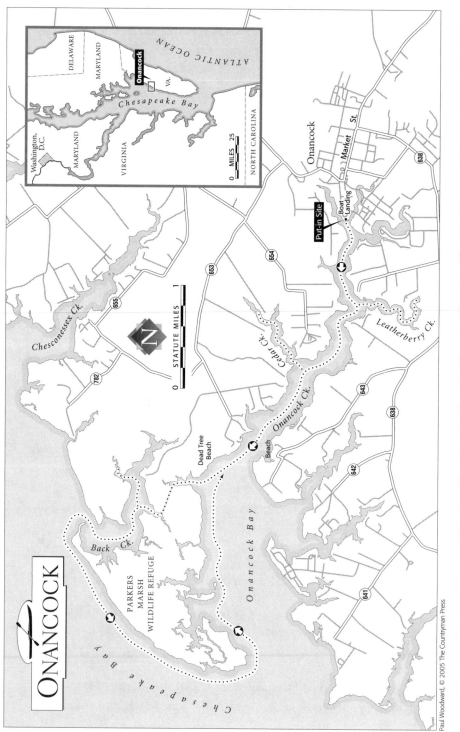

ONANCOCK

Onancock

Market St.

Put-in Site

Boat Landing

Chesconessex Ck.

Leatherberry Ck.

Cedar Ck.

Onancock Ck.

Dead Tree Beach

Beach

Back Ck.

PARKERS MARSH WILDLIFE REFUGE

Onancock Bay

Chesapeake Bay

655

782

653

654

643

638

642

641

638

N

STATUTE MILES

0   1

DELAWARE

MARYLAND

MARYLAND

Washington, D.C.

VIRGINIA

MARYLAND

Chesapeake Bay

Onancock

VA.

ATLANTIC OCEAN

NORTH CAROLINA

0   MILES   25

the world. Not a single boat crossed the horizon, and all I could see for miles was sand, marsh, woods, and blue water. This was the culmination of a trip I had originally not wanted to paddle. I had kayaked Onancock a couple of times when I was filling in as an instructor for a Wallops Island summer science program, and while I found the town charming, I was less than impressed with the creek, which seemed over-populated with houses. However, after some thought, I decided to give the place another try, because the town provided a strong counterbalance to what I thought was a less-than-thrilling waterway. That was one of my better decisions. What I discovered were salt marshes without equal, passages that should not have existed, and wild beaches that stretched for miles. This unwanted paddle transformed into the perfect trip, close to the comforts of bed & breakfasts, and restaurants, but far removed from the everyday pace of life. The key to this wetland paradise was to open my mind and paddle just a little bit farther to find it.

Trip Description

The landing places you at the junction of three inland finger creeks. All three lead back up into the town, and are an interesting way to see the historic homes and graceful yachts of Onancock. However, save this for the end of the trip. For now, head away from town, and make haste in your search for the wild marshes to the west.

This is a popular waterway, with a fair number of sail, power, and workboats traveling up and down the deepwater channel. However, while this creek is popular, it is remote, so the boat traffic is not too overwhelming even during a summer weekend. The creek is relatively narrow at the beginning, so you should feel free to cross back and forth across the well-marked channel to view whatever house piques your fancy. Just do not linger in the center. In a little less than 1 mile you will pass Leatherberry Creek on the left/southern shore, opposite channel marker number 34, and in another ½ mile you will pass Cedar Creek on the right/northern shore, opposite channel marker number 27. When I paddled through these creeks with the Wallops Island students, I saw some interesting waterfront homes and some thin marshland with herons and egrets. However, I would recommend saving these diversions for the end of your paddle. Your trip will not be defined by what you see in these populated creeks.

There are several thin beaches along the shore, their number and width increasing as the tide drops. About ½ mile west of Cedar Creek there is a wide, long white sand beach on the southern shore, between channel markers 22 and 20. This was the ending point for my Wallops Island group, and covering this distance was not a bad accomplishment for a group of 11-year-old novice paddlers. However, now I wish I had been more than a substitute teacher for that trip, and had seen more of the water beforehand. Had I known then what I know now, I would have driven them onward, tired muscles be damned.

The creek widens dramatically, and if you are not already there, you must now cross over to the right/northern shoreline. I try not to be too demanding or particular about routes, but this is the best and only way to do this paddle. You will come up to a piece of wooded property, with broken concrete riprap and one final house. Then that last gasp of civilization gives way to woods, then a beach and a forest of dead, salt-poisoned trees. The monotony of green manicured lawns is replaced by cordgrass, black needle rush, dead trees, salt meadow hay, tree stumps, some phragmites, driftwood, and a sandy creek bottom with scrubby sea grass. From this point westward, as far as the eye can see, the northern shore is wild. This is Parkers Marsh. This is the reason for the trip.

The deadwood beach is about 2½ miles from the boat landing, and is a good place to stretch your legs so that you are fresh for exploring the marsh interior. Enter the gut that is just west of the dead trees. The sign on the west side of the gut's mouth indicates that you are entering a Virginia natural resource area. There is one house present in this wilderness, and it is the red house that you can see straight north of you. Forget about it, you will see it later. Instead, follow the gut straight into the marsh, paddling with it as it makes a 90-degree bend to the left/west.

According to my chart, this gut went nowhere, as guts are wont to do. However, destination is not the point with gut travel. Rather, embrace your surroundings of periwinkles, cordgrass, and fiddler crabs.

The Dead Tree Beach, and the beginning of the wilderness on the Onancock trip

Follow the serpentine curves of the unnamed waterway, staying with it as it steadily grows narrower and shallower. At a T-intersection, take a right to stay with the main flow. The higher the water the better for gut traveling, but I was still able to pass through here at mid-low tide. Bear right again at the next T-intersection, staying with larger water and the main current. Take curves wide to avoid running aground on the sediment that is deposited on the inside of bends. After I passed through a straight section, with a pole planted in the center, I rounded a curve and caught my breath as about 30 egrets rose in the air from a large tree in the distance. Silent serenity and the call of a bobwhite were my only companions.

Then, just as I was sure that the gut was ending, at the next bend the gut defied all my expectations and experience and widened suddenly into a larger passageway. A smaller gut also flowed to the left/south, and I followed this road less taken to see where it would go, stamping down my yearning to follow the bigger water to learn if I had discovered a hidden passage through Parkers Marsh. The lesser gut brought me even closer to the egret tree, but it eventually petered out with the ever increasing smell of sulfur, which springs from the anaerobic decomposition of marsh vegetation. Laughing gulls sailed overhead, with dark gray wings, white bodies, and black heads.

I then followed the larger water to the north, which leads to the enormous cove of Back Creek, confirming that this gut passage had indeed led me to the other side of Parkers Marsh. The water here flows in four directions, including the gut that you enter from. The large egret rookery is visible to the left/west, and the water continues to broaden toward the northwest. The other main direction of the water's flow is to the right/east. The house that was just barely visible when entering the gut is now visible at its waterside location on this eastern passage. Then, up to the northeast, there is a fourth, smaller passage. Everything to the east is marsh with trees backing it. To the west there is salt marsh with the open sky of the Bay above. While the waterway that goes up past the house appeared to be a major one, I did not pursue it, for I did not wish to find any more houses, and wanted to save some mystery and discovery for the reader. Instead, I headed up the creek that is slightly to the northeast. It quickly becomes small and shallow, particularly where it broadens, and is almost impassable at low tide. It is necessary to imagine the current's path as you follow the winding route of the channel, bearing wide around bends, and paddling diagonally across the broad sections. The creek heads to the trees, kisses the shoreline and then twists away, wrapping in a serpentine fashion through the marsh. Then it again comes to the woods and shies away, before it finally shallows and narrows into nothingness. The sound of rails surrounded me and a bald eagle soared above.

Once back in the bigger water, head west toward the open-sky marsh. While there is a nice beach on the left/southern shoreline, keep your paddle blades moving for a few more minutes, because once you wrap around the creek's bend to the right, the Chesapeake will be unveiled. Its broad, blue water is visible through the mouth of Back Creek, which is framed in by a long sand spit beach that hooks inward from the northern side of the creek's mouth. You can land on the quiet waters on the interior of this sand beach, well protected from any waves that may be washing in from the open Bay. Make sure to pull your kayak well above the rising tide, and then explore, sleep, swim, eat, in whatever order you desire.

The beach wraps around the point, continuing around the outside of Parkers Marsh for 4 miles, all the way back to the original gut that brought you into this wonderland. It is a great walking beach, and allows a different perspective of the salt marsh. Instead of being enveloped by the green cordgrass and black needle rush, you can now look down into the sea of grass and see all of its contours, including the shallow pools of water called salt pans, and the slightly raised hills covered with wispy salt meadow hay. On a clear day you can see far out into the Bay, where Watts Island is visible about 5 miles to the northeast. On low-humidity days, the keenest sighted among us may even be able to see as far as Tangier Island, which is beyond Watts, in the center of the Chesapeake.

When you are done strolling the beach, you can then paddle alongside the same shoreline as you enter the open Chesapeake Bay and paddle back south toward Onancock Creek. Pelicans cruised past me with their wing tips barely touching the water. In about 1 mile, what appears to be the southern point is actually a shallow gut that bisects the beach. It is about 2 miles to Ware Point at the southern tip of the marsh, and as you turn back into Onancock Creek, you might notice the islands to the south of the creek. Save these in the back of your mind for another day. While I missed it, there is supposed to be a gut that cuts to the inside of Ware Point before rejoining with the Onancock in about ½ mile.

Heading back east into the creek, the shoreline remains wild beach, backed by salt marsh. The river is huge, and you will likely want to stay somewhat near to shore, both to avoid the bigger boats and to remain closer to the wildlife. There is a healthy growth of widgeon grass waving beneath the clear green-blue water, and there are several large osprey towers built along the marsh.

I returned to the deadwood trees about 4½ hours after I left them. I beached my boat and waded out into the gently sloping creek, getting just deep enough so that I could lie down on the creek bottom, my head supported by my PFD pillow. This immersion cooling beats the best air conditioner. My friends kid me because I always want to paddle just a little bit farther on a creek. I am always sure that the water is even prettier around the next bend. Well, that was exactly the case with the Onancock. Sometimes the grass really is greener on the other side.

Alternative Trips

There is a landing just north of Onancock off VA 782 that will provide you access to Parker's Marsh to the south, and to the aptly named Big Marsh to the north. Big Marsh is about twice the size of Parkers, and is another salt-marsh wonderland.

For an overnight trip, you should look toward the open Bay to Tangier Island. You can take a ferry from Onancock to the small island town of 800 people. The *Captain Eulice* ferry leaves daily at 10 and returns at 3:30, from May through October (Tangier-Onancock Cruises, 757-891-2240). I visited Tangier often when I worked for the Chesapeake Bay Foundation, and it is a truly unique place. Isolated from the rest of the Bay, the residents of this island are mostly descendants of the Crocketts who settled here in the late 1600s and early 1700s, and the islanders' accents still retain traces of Elizabethan English. While Tangier is primarily a watermen community, the residents are as adaptable as the blue crab that they catch, and have welcomed tourism to their isolated outpost. While most tourists usually travel out to the island for a day, there are several bed & breakfasts, and restaurants in town, so bring your kayak and stay for at least one night, if not more. You can circumnavigate the island and paddle its guts and sloughs. The Chesapeake Bay Foundation has an education center just south of the main island, with several buildings in its complex. Similar ferry services also leave for Tangier from Crisfield, Maryland, or from across the Bay from Reedville, Virginia.

28.
Saxis

Features: Marsh island circumnavigation, small, watermen community, salt marsh, good winter birding.

Length: The entire trip can range between 8½ to 12½ miles, depending on how many side guts you explore.

Put-in site: Hammock Landing is a small, quiet public landing that is mostly used by the watermen who own the crab shanties and long peeler float piers that surround the ramp. The landing is concrete but is covered with a thick layer of soft sand. The community dumpster is here, and there are also two port-a-johns.

The landing is located between the two watermen communities of Saxis and Sanford and is a few miles away from the campgrounds of Tall Pines Harbor (757-824-0777, www.tallpines campground.com), which Chesapeake Paddlers Association members highly recommend. They accommodate both tent campers and RVs, and their group tent sites (for 10 or more people) are on the water, providing easy beach access to this trip (just adapt the paddle for approaching Saxis from the north, rather than from the south). A Chesapeake Bay Gateways water trail map of this route will be available in September 2005.

Directions: From US 13 southbound, turn left, or from US 13 northbound, turn right, onto County Road 695 (CR 695) West. Follow for 8.8 miles and then take a left onto Hammock Landing Road/VA 788. There is a public landing sign marking this turn. Follow Hammock Landing Road for 0.9 mile until it ends at the water.

SAXIS IS A LITTLE WATERMEN TOWN at the edge of the world. Kids ride four-wheelers around the quiet streets, everyone knows everyone else's

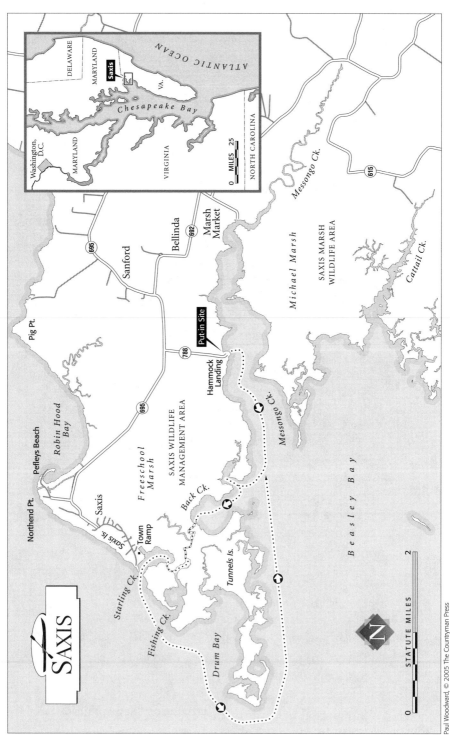

SAXIS

Paul Woodward, © 2005 The Countryman Press

business, and the docks and wharves bustle with the commerce of commercial fishing. The protected salt marsh of the Saxis Wildlife Management Area covers the land to the south of town, with sweeping acres of cordgrass and miles of wild, white sand beaches. West of Saxis is Tunnels Island, and the water surrounding all of this land is clean and full of life: miles of eelgrass wave beneath the surface, and the majority of the Bay's soft-shell crabs are harvested from these waters. Saxis is a place for all seasons. Pelicans, gulls, terns, herons and osprey fill the area during the summer months, and in the fall and spring, migratory waterfowl rest here, sustaining themselves with a diet of marsh vegetation and submerged grasses. The coves and creeks are filled all winter with sea ducks that thrive on the ample fish that the Chesapeake provides, and the southern marsh is specifically managed as a black duck breeding ground.

Trip Description

Head out between the peeler floats, and then take a right from the landing on Messongo Creek to head west toward the open Chesapeake. The lands to the north and south of the creek are protected as a 5,500-acre wildlife management area, and are thus left as natural expanses of salt marsh. The southern marsh is called Michael Marsh, and the northern area is the Freeschool Marsh. Osprey have built a nest on the channel marker near the landing, and there are wooden habitat boxes throughout the marsh for ducks. About 1 mile from the landing you will pass a small wooden dock next to the marsh, and this dock is always covered with gulls, cormorants, and occasionally with pelicans and terns. Additionally, while this is a wildlife management area, the watermen of the area enjoy a working relationship with the marsh managers, and they store their crab pots throughout the marsh from spring through fall. This way the pots are near where they set them, making it easy to pick them up and drop them in the water wherever they think the crabs are running particularly thick.

So the south Michael Marsh drops away, tapering into two small islands. In about 1½ miles from the landing, you will bear right to head north around a point of land to enter the large, ¼-mile-wide cove opening of Back Creek. There is a 100-foot strip of beach just inside the point; take advantage of this break spot. While there will be a lot of beaches later on along the route, this is the last piece of sand you will see for about another 1½ to 2½ miles. However, if you do need a break between here and the next spot of sand, all you need to do is look to the marsh for a rest-stop alternative. The wetland is a firm mixture of cordgrass, with *Spartina alterniflora* (saltwater cordgrass) melding with *Spartina patens* (salt meadow hay). You can see the root masses of these species during low tide, and they are so densely interwoven that they provide solid platforms for disembarking from your kayak. The soft, higher ground species of salt meadow hay provides particularly good grounds for napping.

While this route describes the circumnavigation of the marshland, there is also a plethora of byways. Major and minor guts spring off the main waterways and all can yield great beauty and hours of exploration. Just north of the entrance beach of Back Creek is a small cove with a little gut that runs off its back, northeastern bank. I spent nearly an hour in the miniature wilderness of the waterway. First I followed the major flow of the gut, wrapping with it as it bent to the left and right and left and right. It progressively narrowed, and then split around a large marsh island that bisected the flow into even narrower channels. When I came to a T-intersection, I took a left, and then when I came to the next T-intersection, I took a left again, and then again, following passages through high walls of cordgrass and black needle rush. I repeatedly startled herons and ducks into flight, and I watched fiddler crabs patrol the marsh for food, scrambling over the Atlantic ribbed mussels that fill any available space between the thickly growing blades of grass. Herons and egrets feast upon these small crabs and the mussels filter the water for algae and plankton, making both small species pivotal pieces of the Chesapeake ecosystem.

Paddle up into the broad cove of Back Creek in order to begin your counterclockwise circumnavigation of the Tunnels Island. By paddling counterclockwise, you can take advantage of the predominant wind of the area, and will have the western wind at your back for the final 4-mile return journey to the landing. Additionally, it allows you to arrive at the

Saxis**249**

village of Saxis through the marsh, which simply seems like the more natural and preferred way to approach the little town. You will see the white buildings of Saxis clearly throughout your paddle. While paddling northward into Back Creek, you need to paddle straight toward these buildings in order to find the opening of Fishing Creek, which is on the northern shore of Back Creek, just beyond a minuscule island of marsh.

Fishing Creek bends to the left/west, around a little clump island, and then, when it bends back to the right, the creek splits, with the main creek continuing to the left/west, and Mantrap Gut branching off to the right/east. Mantrap will bring you close to the backside of Saxis, leading you through a long, wandering exploration of the marsh. It will ultimately end before reaching the town, so you will need to backtrack to follow the main creek toward town. Opposite of Mantrap gut, there is a little stand of phragmites on the left bank growing tall above the natural salt marsh that surrounds this invasive species of grass. While it had been thought for years that this was an exotic species, phragmites may in fact simply be an opportunistic local species. In much the same way that loblolly pine springs up to replace clear-cut hardwoods, phragmites appears on any disturbed patch of marsh, and quickly establishes dominance over the original species of vegetation.

The ebbing tidal current can be strong in here, but it lessens considerably once you are past the mouth of the side creek. The main channel narrows and shallows, and the firm marsh mixture of salt meadow hay and cordgrass shifts to lower marsh clumps of cordgrass, with thick mud in and around the green vegetation. After paddling alongside a wooded hummock on the left/west that rises well above the surrounding marsh, you will pass a PVC pole that marks the creek's center channel. The waterway splits shortly after this pole, and the main flow of Fishing Creek bears to the left, and empties into the open water of the Pocomoke Sound in about 1 mile. It is a scenic channel, with oyster floats suspended in its clean water column. Each rectangular mesh box is connected to a floating frame of PVC, and the piles of empty oyster shells in the bottoms of these bins provide a platform for oyster spat (young oysters) to set and grow, safe from the sedimentation and predation dangers of growing on a natural oyster reef.

However, rather than following the main creek toward open water, bear right, past the second PVC pipe, into the mouth of Starling Creek. This is a short thoroughfare, and in about 100 yards you will enter a broad cove, with the town of Saxis to your right at the cove's mouth. There are two boat graveyards on either side of the cove, where old wooden workboats are decomposing in the grass. This is a typical feature of Chesapeake wetlands, and you will rarely find a marsh near a watermen village that does not have at least one boat that has been set out to pasture to die after being stripped of everything useful or restorable, like engines or hardware. While as an environmentalist I must say that it is wrong to dump in the marsh; my inner poet finds symmetry and beauty in allowing workboats to decompose in the very waters that sustained their owners for so long. A Chesapeake marsh just would not be the same without these relics.

Paddle along the eastern shore of the creek in order to get a closer look at the business of crabbing. On the wharf is a mixture of white, red, and blue buildings, which bristle with piers of peeler floats. Water pumps whir, circulating oxygenated water through the white rectangular boxes filled with peeling crabs, and a flotilla of workboats fills the slips in the small harbor that cuts into the right bank, without a single sail or pleasure boat in sight. The first slip on the northern bank of the

Crab-shedding floats

harbor is a boat ramp, and you can pull ashore here to gain a closer look at the busy pier.

This landing is broader and harder than the sand slip at Hammock Landing, and it can be busy with trailered boats, so be sure to pull your kayak all the way up the slip and set it off to the side. Then head up the road in order to walk around the broad wharf. The area bustles with life as recreational fishermen wet their lines from the new fishing pier, and commercial watermen unload their catches, stack crab pots, mend nets, and go about their daily work. While you are here, you can buy cold drinks and snacks at the bait shop or get a sandwich at Marsh Tump Café (757-824-0065).

From Saxis, enter the broad water of the Pocomoke Sound and bear left to paddle to the west, along the shoreline of Tunnels Island. There is a grove of trees at the point, and then continuing beyond these isolated trees is the vast plain of marsh grass. There was a beach across Starling Creek from Saxis, and those beaches continue along the northern shoreline of the marsh. In about ½ mile you will pass the opening for Fishing Creek, and there is a pound net out in the water, opposite the creek's mouth. Then the broad, mile-wide opening of Drum Bay begins, and you can either cut across the bay's mouth, or add distance and beauty to your journey by following the contours of the bay inland, alongside 2 miles of marsh and beach. Following the contours will provide you access to the gut that flows inland from the bay's eastern shore, and exploring the wanderings of that waterway will add an additional mile to your trip, allowing you to spend several hours just within the confines of Drum Bay.

The sandy point of Tunnels Island is about ½ mile west of Drum Bay. The beach here is wide and long, and save for an inlet on the northern shore that flows with water at high tide, the sand wraps around the point almost uninterrupted for over 1 mile. There is an abandoned fishing shanty on the eastern end of the north-facing beach, with only a rusting cot remaining inside this marsh hideaway, and washed-up crab pots are embedded in the beach. The high and low tide marks on the shore are defined by strips of small pebbles, and treasures are intermixed with these pretty stones, in the form of centuries-old

(continued on page 254)

The Commerce of Crabbing

More than any other species, the blue crab defines the Bay, and the commerce of crabbing makes up the most productive and profitable fisheries on the Chesapeake. Crabs are the centerpiece of summer feasts and sought after by recreational and commercial fishermen alike. Crabs, and the men who catch them, are fascinating subjects, and much has been written about them over the years. Possibly the best book on the subject is the Pulitzer Prize winning *Beautiful Swimmers* by William Warner—a fine addition to any kayaker's library.

Like us, crabs are omnivores and eat whatever crosses their paths, from clams and worms to fish and other crabs. They in turn are eaten by a host of other animals, including rockfish, sea turtles, and herons. Unlike most other crabs, the blue crab has an extra set of legs that are flat swimmer fins, allowing them to move gracefully both on the bottom of the Bay and throughout the water column and earning their scientific name *Callinectes sapidus,* which translates as beautiful swimmer.

Wherever crabs roam, watermen try to catch them. They use crab pots, trot lines, bank traps: and in the winter they dredge the bottom for hibernating crustaceans. Crab pots are the most visible method of crabbing, and these small, wire cubes, with heavy steel-rimmed bottoms, are as ingenious as they are simple. Crabs are lured through the funnels on the bottom of the pot by the oily menhaden bait and work their way upward through a second funnel to the upper chamber, which surrounds the bait held in its own wire cylinder. Once the crabs are in the upper chamber, they are confounded as to how to exit. A long line is attached to the top of the pot, with a buoy on the other end that both marks the pot's location and identifies the pot's owner, and the Bay and tributaries are filled with colorful lines of these bobbing markers all summer. These pots are private property and the watermen's livelihood, so do not be tempted to haul up a pot for a closer look.

Watermen tend their pots once a day, culling through to separate the legal 5-inch crabs and mature females (which can be any size as long as they do not have a sponge of eggs on their underside apron) from the undersized and immature crabs. Its apron easily identifies the crab's sex; males (jimmies) have the Washington Monument, immature females (she-crabs) have a pattern that resembles an Egyptian pyramid, and mature females (sooks) have the U.S. Capitol. Watermen can set up to 500 pots at any given time, and most of them tend these lines alone, day after day, from April to November, rising well before sunrise and working their lines until early afternoon.

While hard-shell crabs drive the industry, soft-shell crabs are even more lucrative. Blue crabs must shed their hard shells to grow. Their shell is their skeleton, and in the 24 hours that it takes for their new shell to fully harden, they are defenseless—unable to move, swim, or use their claws. Thus, they retreat to the grass beds in preparation for shedding, seeking shelter by hiding among a dense forest of eelgrass. These soft-shell crabs are caught in two primary ways, through peeler pots and through scraping. The pots take advantage of the crabs' reproductive instincts. Females can only mate once in their lives, immediately after their final molt, when they are still soft but have transformed from immature to mature. Male crabs cradle the females while they await their final molt, mate while she is still soft, and then protect her as her shell re-hardens. Watermen use this knowledge and bait pots with live male crabs to lure ready females into the trap. You can distinguish peeler pot buoys from regular crab pots by the "P" that precedes the license number.

Watermen also plow the grass beds all summer, mowing the grass with their scrapes—rectangular iron frames with a soft net that catches the large rolls of cut grass. The scrapes are pulled aboard, and the grass roll is dumped onto the culling platform. What looks like just a roll of grass is actually teeming with life, which is revealed as the watermen pick apart the grass and sorts the catch. The delicate soft-shell crabs are gently placed on eelgrass in a wax-coated box, and the swimmer fins of hard-shell crabs are quickly inspected. The keen eye of the watermen can detect the new shell growing beneath the old and can accurately gauge when crabs are getting ready to peel. Rank crabs that are hours away from peeling are tossed in one basket, less ready crabs are tossed in another basket, and so on.

Small crab shanties, with corresponding rickety piers of peeler floats, line the edges of most watermen towns in the southern Bay, and it is here that the commerce of soft-shell crabs occurs. When the watermen return to the dock, they sort all of the peeler crabs that are near

(continued)

molting into white peeler floats and sends the soft-shell crabs and non-prime, hard-shell crabs off to market. The name "floats" is a holdover from pre-electricity days, before water pumps could circulate oxygen and fresh water through the boxes, and the boxes were actually floated in the water. Crabs ready to shed are placed into boxes separated from those that are still a day or two away from busting out of their shells. They are watched closely, and as soon as crabs begin to bust (molt), they are quarantined from the others because, if they shed in the vicinity of non-shedding crabs, they will be devoured the moment they are defenseless. Once a crab sheds, it needs to be immediately re-moved from the water or it will form a paper-thin shell about an hour after molting, becoming a buckram, and absolutely valueless as a soft shell. Just as watermen's wives often pick hard-shell crabs to supple-ment the family income, the entire family often tends the floats, so that they are watched 24 hours a day, ensuring that the family can survive the tough business of making a living from the water.

arrowheads. They are white, black, and brown, and it takes a keen eye to find these bits of shaped stone, which range in size from 1-inch arrow tips to 6-inch-long spearheads. I know a few watermen from Smith Island who can spot arrowheads within minutes of arriving on a beach, but I can spend a delightfully frustrating two hours without finding a single thing.

As you wrap around the point, the open Chesapeake is to your right/west. The water is a clear, olive green, and most of it is less than 6 feet deep. This shallow water is filled with one massive underwater meadow of eelgrass, and during the summer months you can watch the white workboats move slowly over them, scraping the grass for soft-shell crabs. These grass beds drive the economy of Saxis and other com-munities like it, and the health of these beds is partially assured by the salt marshes that filter and prevent the surrounding land's erosion, thus keeping the water clear so that photosynthesis can occur.

Once you wrap around the point, it is about 3½ miles back to Ham-mock Landing. The shoreline is pocked with coves and guts, and beaches continue along the marsh's edge for about another 1 mile. I first visited the Saxis marshes years ago, when I was working for the Chesapeake Bay

Following dead-end passages reveals an intimate and endless beauty

Foundation as a summer college intern, and we took a skiff over to roam its beaches on a day off. Even though I was living on Fox Island, which is a stunning, uninhabited marsh in the middle of the Chesapeake, I was still enchanted by Saxis. The combination of the grasslands with the fishing village reminded me of the remote island communities of Tangier and Smith Island to the west, and exploring the beaches occupied me all day. Years later I have seen hundreds of miles of marsh on the Chesapeake and beyond, but Saxis still bewitches me with its beauty. While you can find treasures of arrowheads hidden in the sand, the real treasures of this area are the town and marsh themselves.

Alternative Trips

There are many trips to be paddled just from Hammock Landing. You can paddle inland for about 4 miles, up to the headwaters of Messongo Creek. Or, you can paddle along the southern marsh of Saxis and into Cattail Creek. South of Saxis, you can paddle in the bayside waters of Muddy Creek and Guilford Creek, with landings off CR 684 and CR 682.

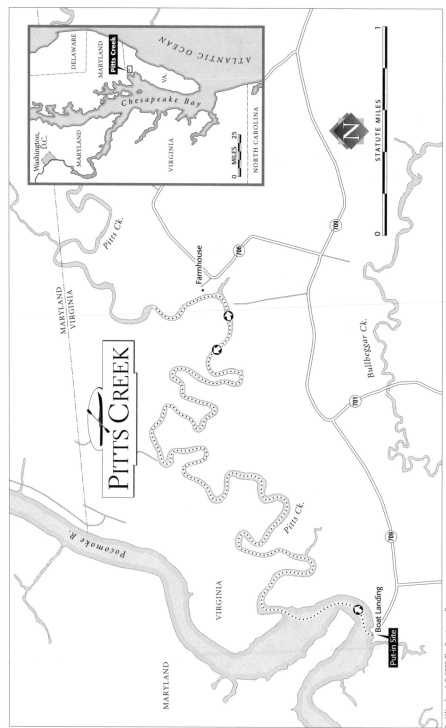

PITTS CREEK

MARYLAND
VIRGINIA

Pitts Ck.

Farmhouse

706

709

701

Bullbeggar Ck.

Pitts Ck.

Pocomoke R.

VIRGINIA

MARYLAND

709

Boat Landing

Put-in Site

STATUTE MILES

0   1

N

Chesapeake Bay

ATLANTIC OCEAN

DELAWARE

MARYLAND

MARYLAND

Pitts Creek

VA.

Washington, D.C.

VIRGINIA

NORTH CAROLINA

MILES   25

0   MILES

29.

Pitts Creek

Features: Pastoral countryside, expansive freshwater marshes, and forests of cedar and pine alongside a deep, black water river with a strong tidal current. Turtles, deer, bald eagles, and waterfowl all can be seen along this paddle.

Length: The route described is about 9 miles, but many more miles are available.

Put-in site: This is a small landing with limited parking and a concrete ramp. There are no bathrooms at this landing, so you might want to use the Virginia Welcome Center's rest room. The Welcome Center is on US 13, about 1 mile north of VA 709. No outfitters service this remote creek. Survival Products is in Salisbury, Maryland, about one hour north of the creek, and they offer car-top kayak rentals. Pocomoke River State Park is an excellent Maryland state park located upriver from the creek. Information and reservations can be made by visiting their web site at www.reservations.dnr.state.md.us or by calling 1-800-432-CAMP.

Directions: From US 13 Northbound, take a left onto VA 709/Farlow Road (about 1.5 miles south of the Maryland border). Take an immediate left at a T-intersection, and then a quick right, back onto VA 709. Cross over railroad tracks in 0.4 mile and then, in 0.7 miles from the tracks, take a left to remain on VA 709. In 1.5 miles, take a left at a T-intersection. Follow for about 0.7 mile and then take a right onto Pitts Creek Road (VA 709). Follow this for 3.3 miles and then take a right onto Bell Road (a farmhouse is straight ahead). Follow Bell Road for 0.2 mile to the landing.

I SCOUTED THIS PADDLE with my friend Jodie Clark and her boyfriend, Andrew Cox, who were visiting from England. While Jodie is originally from the Eastern Shore, Andrew had visited America only once; and because I wanted to show him the best of our region, we went kayaking. I chose the Pocomoke River because I have long enjoyed its beauty and have paddled often on the section of this black-water river that flows for 55 miles from the Great Cypress Swamp on the Maryland/Delaware border. However, I had never explored Virginia's side of the creek, and with the natural anxiety of playing host, I worried about paddling an unknown area. However, my fears dissipated with every pull of the paddle because I could not have invented a more perfect showcase for the subtle beauty of the Bay than Pitts Creek. Kayaking alongside pastoral countryside, sweeping marshlands, and cathedrallike groves of trees, we paddled from midafternoon to dusk, enjoying a sunset on the water before being accompanied home by the occasional lights of the last fireflies of the season. It was a day of peace and beauty—the very best the Bay has to offer.

Trip Description

From the landing, paddle to the right/northeast to head upstream on the Pocomoke River. You will only be on the broad waters of the Pocomoke for about ¼ mile, but hug the shoreline while you are on the main section of the river, especially as you round the first bend to the left. Although powerboat traffic is light in this area, it does exist. More important, this section of the Pocomoke is host to occasional commercial traffic in the form of tugboats pushing large barges, likely full of chicken manure or other agricultural products. They move deceptively fast and are not able to stop quickly or stray from the channel.

After the bend, you will see the entrance to Pitts Creek ahead on your right, with the far side of the entrance marked by a lone wooded hillock. After you bear right to head upstream on Pitts Creek, you will round bend after bend after bend for the remainder of the paddle. The turns of this creek are too many to count, with the waterway appearing like a child's scribble on a large-scale map. The sweeping pastoral countryside that borders the Pocomoke gives way to a more immediate landscape of woodland and marsh. Pocomoke is the Algonquin word for *black water,* and the same tannic black color is found on Pitts Creek, belying the existence of cypress on the upper sections of the creek. Like the Pocomoke River, which is the deepest river for its width in the United States, Pitts Creek is also deep, measuring around 12 feet deep (or more) for much of its length. The early section of marsh consists of primarily two species of grass: big cordgrass intermixed with stands of the invasive and opportunistic species phragmites. There are occasional groves of trees along the banks, which are primarily a mixture of cedar and loblolly pine, with marsh alder along the edges.

The tidal current is strong; and once you enter Pitts Creek, it is visually noticeable at the inside corners of the meanders. Here the water swirls into minor whirls and boils that will grab and push your kayak in contrary directions. While it is possible to paddle against the current, you should try to plan your paddle in order to take advantage of this strong tidal flow, paddling upstream during flood tide and downstream at ebb.

About ½ mile upstream on the creek, you will pass by a deep section of forest on the left. It is a mature forest of cedar and pine, with trees well spaced from one another, creating the effect of an open-air cathedral as you gaze into its depths. This place perfectly exemplifies the intimate scale of the Bay's beauty, best experienced at the slow pace of the paddler. The air is rich with the scent of pine, and as we floated by a bald eagle flew out of its center, weaving its way with ease among the trees. After talking our way up the creek, my friends and I were lulled into a silent and relaxed peace by the calm water, light breeze, intricate beauty, and fragrant air.

As you continue upstream on the creek, there are occasional large and small guts that crease the marsh. Some of the larger guts appear to slice entirely through the marsh, allowing for other ways to head back into the Pocomoke River, and thus opening up an almost unlimited number of route varieties. By contrast, the small guts, which are barely noticeable except as an indentation in the marsh grass, seem insignificant

Water Quality

The Chesapeake Bay is a struggling ecosystem, surrounded by densely populated states that are still growing rapidly. With growth comes a depletion of the natural buffers of forests and wetlands, which are replaced by nonpermeable roofs and roadways. Pollutants of all sorts are able to flow, unencumbered, into the Bay. Nonpoint source pollution from millions of lawns, driveways, roads, and farms fill the Bay with nutrient overloads, sediment, and toxic chemicals. Point source pollution sources like sewage treatment plants and factories also contribute about 20 percent of the nutrient pollution to the Bay.

In 1998 the conservation group American Rivers listed the Pocomoke River as the third most endangered river in the United States. It made the list due to an outbreak of *Pfiesteria*. This microbe causes large-scale fish kills and can lead to illness in humans, with resulting fatigue, lesions, respiratory irritation, and intestinal problems. The outbreaks appear to occur when an overload of nutrients enter an ecosystem, which ties *Pfiesteria* to the runoff from the manure of the chicken industry of the Eastern Shore. All of the boat landings on the Pocomoke were well posted with closed/warning signs during the 1998 outbreak. The majority of the river's watershed lies in Maryland, and that state responded aggressively to the problem by funding and encouraging *Pfiesteria* research and by setting tighter standards for the chicken industry.

The economy of Virginia was built on the back of the Bay's fisheries, but 400 years of human pressure has also affected the Bay's animals. A combination of overfishing, pollution, and disease has nearly killed off the native Chesapeake oyster. The harvest of these

and not worthy of mention. However, this is where small fish feed on the nutrient-rich swill that flows out of the marsh and the larger fish feed upon the smaller—an excellent place to throw a line over for some fishing. The day we paddled the creek, fishing of a different sort was being done in the form of wire traps, cylindrical in design with buoys in the interior that kept a portion of the trap above water. The traps are baited with fish, likely oily menhaden, and the intended quarries are the snapping turtles that prowl the gut's openings. Snapping turtles are a regional oysters is currently 8 percent of what it was in 1950. Blue crabs have replaced oysters as the spine of the Bay fishery, but they are under ever-increasing pressure, with the amount of effort that it takes to catch the same number of crabs increasing every year.

There are thousands of people working to improve the water quality of this well-loved ecosystem, including countless local, regional, and national coalitions of watermen and farmers, politicians and scientists. Submerged aquatic vegetation (SAV) has rebounded, almost doubling from 38,000 to 69,126 acres, after the record low acreage of 1984. SAV is vital to the health of the Bay. It serves as a nursery and breeding ground for crabs and fish, is a major food source for waterfowl, and grabs and traps free-floating sediment out of the water column, enabling the light to shine through and allowing more grass to grow. Bald eagles and osprey once again fill the skies over the Bay, and shad are returning to Virginia's rivers thanks to aggressive fishery programs, dam breaches, and fish ladders.

Better development and agriculture legislation has preserved buffers and regulated manure discharge. Six years after the Pocomoke was declared unsafe due to *Pfiesteria,* my friends and I swam in Pitts Creek. The same problems that affect the Bay also affect the rivers of southeastern Virginia and the coastal bays. However, for as many problems as there are on these waterways, there are as many solutions. I began guiding because I believe that more people paddling on the Bay will result in more people learning about its amazing qualities. Once people know the Bay and fall in love with its subtle beauty, it is hard not to work to protect it.

delicacy and most often found in a rich, spicy snapping turtle soup cooked with a healthy dose of sherry.

About 2 to 3 miles from the Pocomoke, the creek bends to the left, and the marsh dramatically changes from a monochromatic blend of two grasses to the rich overflowing diversity of a healthy freshwater marsh ecosystem. The creek becomes even more beautiful here with the addition of the deep green and vibrant colors of pickerelweed, arrow arum, and marsh mallow. Soon after the marsh changes, you will come

The author cooling off on Pitts Creek ANDREW COX

upon a wooded bank on the outside corner of a left-hand turn. This is a good spot for a break, and there is a small clearing in the trees large enough to accommodate three or four kayakers.

Rather than climbing back into our boats, we plunged in for a refreshing swim. It was impossible to swim against the strong flooding current, so we swam with our boats in tow. While we expended no effort, in very little time we were ¼ mile downstream at the next bend to the right. Water is generally deeper on the outside of bends, so if you do swim with your boat on this or any other creek, when you are ready to get into your kayak again, you should beach your boat on the inside of the bend, stepping easily from river to kayak. We tried to embark from the deeper water on an outside bend and had much flipping and hilarity for our troubles.

The creek gradually narrows in the journey upstream, the marsh vegetation continues to diversify, and the creek becomes more spectacular with every bend. About 4 miles upriver of the Pocomoke, the wilderness views of the creek are interrupted by houses in the distance.

The house on the right bank is overrun by vines and just barely visible as you pass by the remainders of a dock. Straight ahead, at the topside of the bend to the left, is a two-story white farmhouse with possibly the best waterfront location on the Bay.

We paddled for a little way past the house, coaxed into rounding bend after bend by the unremitting beauty of the paddle. Eventually we were forced to retreat due to the impending sunset. I would not be surprised to learn that there is another 4 miles of navigable creek above the 4 to 5 miles we paddled, with each turn more stunning than the next, but I leave that for you to discover. As for my party, we had to be content with the six hours we spent on the river. The sun set as we were still 1 mile above the Pocomoke—with dusk arriving just in time for us to paddle past the cathedral of trees that we had worshiped in the beginning of the paddle. Andrew reached the spot before Jodie and me because our chatter slowed our paddling rate. It was Andrew, then, who discovered another feature of the trees that we had missed in the silent awe of our journey upstream. Through some quality of their spacing and depth; the grove created a natural amphitheater, causing our echoing words to ring clearly in the night. "Here I am," Andrew said, "floating in what very well might be the most beautiful place in the world, when what do I hear but the words 'health insurance deductible' echoing all around me." High praise from a normally non-effusive Englishman, and I will have to agree that this certainly is one of the most beautiful places in the world.

Alternative Trips

There are many other trip alternatives on Pitts Creek, with loops possible by following some of the later side guts northward. Also, you can head up the Pocomoke into Maryland and paddle the river between Snow Hill and Pocomoke City, or around Jane's Island by Crisfield, Maryland. (See *Sea Kayaking Maryland's Chesapeake Bay* for more details about these trips.)

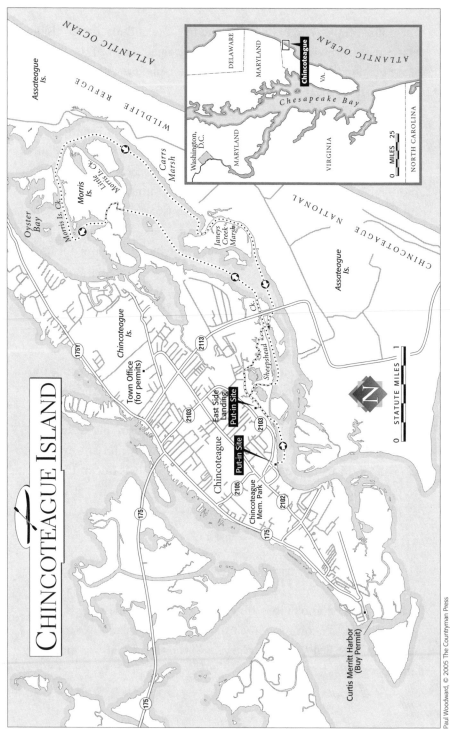

CHINCOTEAGUE ISLAND

30.

Chincoteague

Features: Summer resort town, wild ponies, salt marsh, excellent birding.

Length: 8 miles (with unlimited mileage combinations).

Put-in site: There are five boat landings on Chincoteague, with four of them on the east side of the island facing Assateague. Of these, the East Side ramp and the Memorial Park ramp work well for the route description, with Memorial Park allowing for more distance and providing better facilities. You have to purchase a permit to use any of the town's landings. A one-week permit is $5 and an annual permit is $20. You need one permit per car. You can purchase the permits from the police station and town office complex, or from the Curtis Merritt Harbor, which is the southernmost boat landing on the island and is not well suited for kayakers. The town office is open from 8 to 5, Monday to Friday (757-336-6519). When they are closed you can buy your permit from the police station, whose office is next door and is open 24 hours a day, seven days a week.

There are several kayak companies on the island, and the group at Oyster Bay Outfitters is particularly friendly and knowledgeable, offering tours and rentals. For accommodations, you can choose from hotels, house rentals, bed & breakfasts, and camping; and there are a plethora of restaurants to feed you, including the Creamery on Maddox, which serves up delicious homemade ice cream.

I stayed at Tall Pines Harbor (757-824-0777, www.tallpines harbor.com), which had good sites for tents, as well as for RVs, and there are several other good private campgrounds on the island. This trip travels along the edges of Chincoteague National Wildlife Refuge (757-336-6122).

Directions: To reach Chincoteague, turn onto VA 175 West from US 13. *To reach the town office from the VA 175 bridge:* Take a left onto North Main Street. Then, take a right onto Maddox and a left onto Deep Hole Road. The police station and town office complex is on the left, in about 1 mile. *To reach the boat ramps from the town office:* Drive back to Maddox, and take a left, toward the ocean. Take the next right onto Chicken City Road. Then, take a left onto Church Street. Follow the road as it bends to the right, southward along the water, and becomes East Side Road. The East Side landing is on your left, just after some condominiums. For the Memorial Park landing, keep on following the road past East Side landing, and after it bends back toward the west, the park will be on your left. It is well marked. *To reach the boat ramps from the VA 175 bridge:* Take a left onto North Main Street and then take your first right onto Church Street. Pass Chicken City Road and continue to follow the directions above.

CHINCOTEAGUE means "beautiful land across the water," and a more fitting description could not have been found for this small, 7-mile-long island. Chincoteague hides in the shelter of Assateague Island and is closely tied to its larger cousin. The island was settled in the 1670s, and although once primarily farmers, the settlers soon turned to the water to make a living as watermen. Life on these exposed coastal islands was a tough and tenuous existence, with inhabitants forever at the mercy of the elements. In 1821, everything was wiped out by a tidal wave, and hurricanes continue to wreak havoc on the barrier islands, shifting and reshaping the sands with every storm. People persevered, and a loose group of settlers came together by the 1850s to form the village of Chincoteague. The town remains tied to the water, but while there are still some commercial fishermen working the bays, most residents make their living from tourism, catering to the thousands of people who retreat to this quiet oceanside village every year. Sightseers come to Chincoteague for the beauty, the seafood, the ocean, and the wild ponies of Assateague. Despite the island's popularity, it remains a restful place to visit and an easy place from which to base a week of kayak exploration (trips as far south as Onancock are still less than one hour away from Chincoteague).

Trip Description

From Memorial Park, bear left and follow along the shoreline for about 1 mile. As you enter into a broad channel, you will come alongside the East Side boat landing. From here, the channel splits into two branches, and you have three options of how to continue. You can backtrack slightly and paddle south in the main waterway, which is Sheepshead Creek. This will turn to the east, toward the bridges. Or, you can paddle southeast from the East Side landing into the small channel, which flows through the marsh south to join with Sheepshead Creek. The water at this opening is shallow with mudflats, so try to follow crab pot buoys to the channel, or just bear slightly left of center. You should then turn left and follow Sheepshead Creek east. Or, from the East Side landing, you can follow the Chincoteague shoreline northeast into the narrow channel, which will lead you through the marsh in a serpentine southeastern direction, ending just shy of the smaller of the two bridges for Maddox Road. I like to paddle the wandering passage on my way out and one of the more direct passages back to the landing. This trip is all about options, so plot your own course and go. Once you are on Sheepshead Creek, paddle east toward the small bridge.

A major landmark of this paddle is the lighthouse on Assateague. Prior to the construction of a lighthouse in 1833, the islanders supplemented their fishing and farming with scavenging the frequent shipwrecks that occurred on the shoals just offshore. While this was a boon to the local economy, it was hardly beneficial for boat captains, and thus the lighthouse was constructed. Due to the sandbar geology of the islands, the shoreline grew in the years after 1833, expanding with the rolling sands and storms, until the lighthouse stood over 1 mile inland, rendering it useless. Consequently, the original tower was destroyed in 1866, and another lighthouse built in 1867. Painted with red-and-white horizontal stripes to increase its visibility, the current lighthouse was

Monarchs

Anyone who lives in the coastal region of Virginia is familiar with the sounds of honking geese and the sight of their flying-V migration through the autumn sky. However, every fall there is an entirely different migration, one that is as noiseless as it is colorful. It is the migration of the monarch butterfly.

The monarch butterfly is impossibly delicate. Its weight would not even register on the most sensitive of scales, and it seems erratic and unfocused in its bouncy, flapping flight. However, unlike most species of butterfly, the monarchs that are born late in the summer put off the normal insect business of mating and dying, and instead migrate south to avoid the cold winter, postponing their mating until they return in the spring. Because they are cold-blooded, they move fast, never lingering long because they are unable to fly if the temperature grows too cold. While they are usually solitary animals, they band together for the migration. They fly in conical swarms and gather together on trees and bushes at night, huddled in colorful mats for warmth.

This migration happens on both coasts. West Coast monarchs migrate to the southern California coast to wait out the winter before returning to their more northern and mountain homes. However, these butterflies are lazy when compared to the East Coast monarchs, who migrate up to 3,000 miles to central Mexico and southern Florida. They fly to the exact same trees every year, despite the fact that there

built on a 22-foot-tall hill, and the tower rises an additional 142 feet into the sky, allowing its light to be seen for 22 nautical miles. It is not permissible to land anywhere on the Chincoteague National Wildlife Refuge, except at the extreme southern end of the island in Tom's Cove, so you cannot walk up and take a closer look at the tower. However, if you drive onto the island, the lighthouse is open to visitors Friday through Sunday from Easter to Thanksgiving (cost $4 per person).

There is plenty of clearance under the small bridge at mid to low tide, but during high water you may need to bear right and pass beneath the tall bridge to your south. After crossing under the bridges, continue to paddle along Chincoteague until the waterway narrows and are no old butterflies to show the way. Each butterfly makes the round-trip only once, and when they return in the spring, they get on with the traditional butterfly life cycle, laying their eggs on milkweed and then dying.

No one knows exactly how the monarchs accomplish their amazing navigational feat. It was only recently, in 1975, that scientists even discovered where the butterflies go. It is possible that there are other wintering spots that are still unfound. Groups of enthusiasts gather each year to tag the delicate creatures in an effort to help the scientists learn more about these insects. Everyone from young schoolchildren to grandparents fasten thin plastic wafers on the wings. Anyone can register to help by contacting the research effort through the Chincoteague Natural History Association (www.assateague.org/plover).

The autumn migration is predictable, and every year the monarchs pass through Chincoteague from mid-September to mid-October. This is also one of the best seasons for kayaking the barrier islands. The biting insects have diminished, the crowds have gone, and the air temperature is cooler, but the water is still pleasantly warm. The monarchs serve as a wonderful bonus. I have returned to my campsite at night to find the sandy spot entirely redecorated in orange and black, with the marsh elder trees dripping with slightly quivering butterflies. It is as if Mother Nature is bragging a little, showing off her strange beauty for all who care to look.

houses begin to appear on the left side. Then, cross over to paddle alongside the grasses of Janeys Creek Marsh. This is where the true beauty is, and you will be able to avoid colliding with any powerboaters by staying along the edges. Janeys Creek Marsh ends about 1 mile from the bridge, and the water opens up into a large bay. Paddle north from here, past the little island in the center of the open water, straight toward Morris Island. Much of the water here is shallow, varying in depth from waist deep to ankle deep, and the small island is surrounded by tidal flats that are non-navigable during low tide. This is also apparently a bird nesting area because several terns attacked me as I paddled past. They actually pecked me on the head a couple of times, nearly stealing my lucky Green Bay Packers hat. My friends were too busy laughing, and I was too busy fleeing to identify the species of tern, but they were small and determined.

During the windy weather that is very common in this area, the shallow water can be quite rough, although if you capsize you can simply stand up. However, if it is blowing hard, you can bear left and seek shelter along the shore of Chincoteague. This will lead you to the very tip of Morris Island. Alternatively, by paddling the ⅔ mile straight across, you will arrive at the small thoroughfare that cuts through Morris. The island has a big clump of trees on the east side, then low grass, and then a smaller clump of trees on the west side. The thoroughfare falls in the middle, between two white NATIONAL WILDLIFE REFUGE signs, with a duck blind to the left/west. The water here is absolutely clear, so you can see the grasses and red-bearded, coral-coated bottom.

The thoroughfare through the island is serpentine and wraps between a cordgrass marsh that teems with life. Periwinkles coated the grass, birds flew all around, ribbed mussels grew along the edges, terrapins poked their heads out the water at every turn, and fiddler crabs scrambled over it all. When you reemerge into the open water of Oyster Bay, continue to follow the shoreline of Morris Island north. The water remains crystal clear, with waving prairies of grass beneath the water. While your paddling companions may chuckle a bit at your unorthodox departure from your boat, you might want to bring your snorkel and splash overboard. Oyster Bay is not aqua-blue water and you will not see the colorful fish of a tropical coral reef, but you may come face-to-face with rays, crabs, sea horses, horseshoe crabs, and any number and variety of fish. There is a whole world within the grass, and you can only find it by immersing yourself within it.

Morris Island is part of the Chincoteague National Wildlife Refuge, and so it falls under the same landing restrictions as the rest of the refuge. This prohibition may change in the future because there have been some discussions of transferring oversight of the island to the national park service and allowing primitive camping on the island, thus linking Virginia with the chain of primitive campsites in Maryland. Until that is put into effect, you will need to take all of your breaks in the water, or below mean high tide. This is not difficult due to the high number of shallow shoals and tidal flats of the bay. Some places are firm sand, while others are firm to semi-firm mud, so be sure your shoes are well secured, or you may loose them. However, do not be tempted to wade barefoot, because the sand and mud is filled with sharp mussel, clam, and oyster shells.

Bear right into Morris Island Creek when you reach the top of the island, and you can pass between Morris Island and the smaller sister island above it. Or you can extend your paddle by another mile and paddle up and around this second island. There is a duck blind with an osprey nest in the creek, along with an old, weathered lodge at the top of the island. From here you can turn to the south and paddle along the eastern shore of Morris Island, through the Little Morris Island Creek, beside a few more old hunting lodges and docks. However, I prefer to cross over to Assateague. Assateague is lined with thin beaches that spill into the water and create shallow sandy shoals, which extend about 100 feet and make this a good inter-tidal break spot. One particularly scenic beach is Bow Beach, which is a small, crescent-shaped sliver of white sand shaded by loblolly and marsh elder.

Once you are along Assateague's shore, you can either paddle northward to extend your journey, or return southward toward home. Northward, the mileage is almost limitless, as you can follow the island for another 5 miles or so, past Ragged Point into Maryland. The island then continues for about another 20 plus miles until you reach the Ocean City Inlet. Once in Maryland, the protection of the island transfers from the National Wildlife Refuge System to the National Park Service, and it is now permissible to land on shore. There are six primitive campsites spaced along the island, allowing for extended backcountry expeditions.

Once you head southward, keep the island and Carrs Marsh close to your left side in order to have the best chance of seeing wild ponies (one of our group spotted a couple by Bow Beach). The Assateague ponies are the only wild horses east of the Rockies, and their origin is a matter of some debate. The most popular legend is that they were survivors of a shipwreck of a Spanish galleon in the 1600s. However, it is more likely that some of the horses of the early settlers turned feral after being set free in the marsh to graze. Regardless of how they arrived on the island, they have become a unique breed, able to withstand the rigors of living within a salt marsh. They subsist primarily on cordgrass, and the high salt content of this food causes them to drink enormous amounts of fresh water, which causes their stomachs to look swollen.

The one day you are guaranteed to see ponies is during the annual pony penning. While some of the wild horses have been rounded up and domesticated since Colonial times, the modern roundup of ponies is a result of devastating fires that ravaged the community in the early 1920s. A volunteer fire department was created in response to the damage, but they needed a little more than the $4 that was originally collected to begin the organization. They held a carnival, which included a roundup and auctioning of some of the wild herd. The carnival and auction has taken place ever since drawing thousands of people. The pony penning is always held on the last Wednesday and Thursday in July, and the carnival runs all month. For more information, call 757-336-6161. Mustang and Arabian horses were introduced to the island in the 1930s and 1940s to genetically diversify the herd and keep them suitable for auction. While ponies live on the entire length of the island, they are managed by two different governmental agencies and have been divided into two herds by a fence that runs along the Maryland and Virginia border. The penning helps keep the Virginia herd to around 150 horses, which is a sustainable level for the island's ecology, and the Maryland herd is managed to about the same number by contraceptive darts. The children's book *Misty of Chincoteague* brought national fame to the island, and now the auctioned ponies live all around the United States, with many of the young foals reaching the size of a full-grown horse when they are removed from the harsh salt-marsh environment.

The flat shoreline of Carrs Marsh kicks out into a little point about 3 miles south of Bow Beach, and on the other side of this point, you can enter Janeys Creek to pass between Janeys Creek Marsh and Assateague. It is a beautiful, wandering alternative to the open water. Once you do reenter the open water of the Assateague Channel, continue near one

Chincoteague...beautiful land across the water

edge or the other to stay out of the way of powerboats. You can cross back over and follow Sheepshead Creek to one of the guts, or you can continue alongside Assateague for a while longer. If you choose the latter, you will lose sight of the lighthouse for a while, which had been visible ever since rounding Morris Island. When it reappears, you should start bearing to the right to head back to Chincoteague. At high tide, you can paddle straight across the mudflats toward the middle/ southeastern passage. However, during low tide you will need to swing wide around the mudflats. When in doubt, follow the crab pot buoys to find the main channel, or in the off-season just paddle slightly left of center once you are in the gut. The white PVC stakes throughout the flats mark out the boundaries of leased clam beds, which have been a successful form of aquaculture for the town's watermen.

It does not matter where or how far you paddle in Chincoteague, just paddle here. I once led a group of students for a sunset paddle from the East Side ramp. We paddled out through the southeastern slough, toward the lighthouse, and then back in through the wandering north-eastern passage, for a round-trip paddle of about 1 mile. We could see silhouettes of horses on the shore as we listened to their whinnying and also watched heat lightning illuminate the distant sky. A light breeze kept the mosquitoes away, and the group of chattering middle-school students was silent for the first time that week. We had paddled miles of beautiful rivers and bays over the course of the previous week, but that two-hour, nighttime paddle was the highlight for everyone.

Alternative Trips

On your way to Chincoteague, you can launch from the boat landing on the right side of VA 175, just after Cockle Creek, on Shelly Bay. From here you can paddle south for ½ mile and then take a right into a shallow inlet and onto Cockle Creek. By paddling south into Cockle, you can explore countless guts, many of which interconnect into a massive labyrinth of salt marsh. You can access the southern side of this labyrinth by launching from the mainland, at the end of CR 695, in the little town of Wishart.

There are several more remote islands just south of Chincoteague where you will be absolutely alone. You can explore Assawoman Island by launching on Assawoman Creek off County Route 679 (CR 679). You can explore Metomkin Island by launching off CR 680, or by launching on Parker Creek off CR 666, both of which are accessible from US 13. You can launch on Folly Creek, off CR 651, to gain access to Cedar Island. Part of this island is private and part is owned by the Nature Conservancy. Like all of these islands, Cedar Island is dense salt marsh interwoven with guts, and the exterior is wild, Atlantic beach. You must have good skills and be in an expedition sea kayak or a sit-on-top kayak to paddle the exterior of the islands.

Appendix A:
Safety Information

THE BEST WAY to access help in an emergency is to call 911 to activate the emergency response system. However, for non-life-threatening emergencies, you may wish to contact one of the agencies below:

United States Coast Guard

For Search and Rescue: 757-398-6390, or use VHF Channel 16

Virginia State Police

Administrative Headquarters (24 hours): 804-674-2000
Division 1 (Central Virginia): 1-800-552-9965
Division 2 (Culpeper): 1-800-572-2260
Division 3 (Appomattox): 1-800-552-0962
Division 4 (Wytheville): 1-800-542-8716
Division 5 (Hampton Roads): 1-800-582-8350
Division 6 (Salem-Roanoke): 1-800-542-5959
Division 7 (Northern Virginia): 1-800-572-4510

Marine Resources Commission
Law Enforcement Division

Northern Area: 804-580-2901 (Heathsville)
Middle Area: 804-642-2640 (Gloucester Point)
Southern Area: 757-247-2265 (Newport News)
Eastern Shore: 757-414-0713 (Belle Haven)

APPENDIX B:
Visitor Information

THE FOLLOWING is a catalog of visitor resources, beginning with statewide and national resources and kayaking organizations. Next, more specific visitor resources are loosely organized in the same order of the book but also grouped by their general areas: Northern Virginia/Northern Neck, Middle and Lower Peninsulas (including Richmond area), Southeastern Virginia, and the Eastern Shore. In general, specific bed & breakfasts, hotels, and private campgrounds are not listed because the local visitors centers can provide detailed information. However, I have included information about state and county campgrounds, as well as information about local outfitters.

Statewide and National Resources

Virginia State Parks, Virginia Department of Conservation and
    Recreation (DCR), 1-800-933-PARK (reservations), 804-786-
    1712 (main office), www.dcr.state.va.us.
    Virginia state parks are well maintained, affordable, and
    beautiful places to camp. The reservation system is simple
    and user-friendly. There is one reservation number for any of
    the state park campgrounds, and the web site is a clearing-
    house of information. In addition, to reserving campsites via
    their web site, you can read about natural areas and wildlife.

Virginia Department of Game and Inland Fisheries, 804-367-1000,
www.dgif.state.va.us.
> Runs the state's wildlife management areas, as well as regulates all hunting and fishing. Morris Creek and Saxis both fall underneath the stewardship of this agency.

U.S. Fish and Wildlife Service, 1-800-344-WILD, www.refuges.fws.gov.
> Manages the national wildlife refuge system, including the Great Dismal Swamp primitive campground and the Eastern Shore and the Chincoteague National Wildlife Refuges.

Virginia Tourism, 1-800-VISIT-VA, www.virginia.org.

Virginia Campground Association, 703-448-6863,
www.virginiacampgrounds.org.
> Web site and brochure list all of their member campgrounds.

All Campgrounds, 540-967-2431, www.allcampgrounds.com/va.
> Provides a relatively complete listing of Virginia's private campgrounds.

Bed & Breakfast Association of Virginia, 888-660-2228,
www.innvirginia.com.

Environmental, River, and Kayaking Organizations

Chesapeake Bay Foundation, 1-888-SAVEBAY, 804-780-1392
(Richmond), 757-622-1964 (Hampton Roads), www.cbf.org.
> The largest organization working to protect the Chesapeake Bay's environment. The agency spans the entire watershed with its work. There are education centers and programs throughout Virginia, as well as countless volunteer programs.

Chesapeake Bay Program, 1-800-YOUR-BAY, www.chesapeakebay.net.
> Oversees the US Environmental Protection Agency's alliance of Chesapeake Bay–oriented agencies and programs, including the Chesapeake Bay Gateways Network.

Chesapeake Bay Gateways Network, 1-800-YOUR-BAY,
www.baygateways.net.
> Catalogs 140 different locations in the Bay watershed and act
> as a clearinghouse of information about kayaking, the Bay's
> natural history, and area events. They also oversee the Chesa-
> peake Bay water trails program.

Chesapeake Paddlers Association, P.O. Box 341, Greenbelt, MD 20768,
www.cpakayaker.com.
> This sea kayakers club offers kayak workshops, day trips, and
> camping trips. They also have several groups that paddle in
> the evenings, once a week, throughout the summer. The Pi-
> rates of the Potomac meet in Alexandria every Tuesday, and
> the Pirates of Georgetown meet at Jack's Boathouse every
> Thursday.

Chincoteague Natural History Association, P.O. Box 917,
Chincoteague Island, VA 23336, www.assateauge.org/plover.
> This association partners with the U.S. Fish and Wildlife Ser-
> vice and provides interpretive natural history programs
> about Assateague.

Friends of Dragon Run, P.O. Box 882, Gloucester, VA 23061,
www.dragonrun.org.
> Owns and manages a 200-acre tract of land protecting the
> upper section of the Dragon Run and the Piankatank River.
> They run semi-annual paddles of the Run.

Friends of the Rappahannock, 540-373-3448,
www.for.communitypoint.org.

Mattaponi and Pamunkey Rivers Association, 804-769-0841,
www.mpra.org.

The Nature Conservancy, 434-29-6106, www.nature.org.
> This nationwide organization protects thousands of acres in
> Virginia, including much of the land alongside the paddling
> routes in this book.

Virginia Outdoors Foundation, 804-786-0801 (Northern Neck),
   804-225-2147 (Eastern Region),
   www.virginiaoutdoorsfoundation.org.
      Created by the General Assembly to preserve the open and
      wild spaces of Virginia.
American Canoe Association (ACA), 703-451-0141, www.acanet.org.
      Sets the standards for the United States paddlesports industry
      and offer a standardized curriculum for novice-to-instructor
      level courses. They also fight for waterway conservation and
      access rights.
British Canoe Union (BCU), www.bcu.org.uk.
      An English organization that also certifies instructors and
      kayakers in the United States with a two-tier ranking system
      of regular proficiency levels and coaching proficiency levels.

Northern Virginia/Northern Neck (Georgetown, Mason Creek, Fountainhead, Pope's Creek, Reedville, Wilmot Wharf, Belle Isle and Fleets Island)

Outfitters

Atlantic Kayak Company, 703-838-9072, www.atlantickayak.com.
      Judy Lathrop owns this company, which offers excellent half-
      day and full-day kayaking trips in Northern Virginia and
      D.C., and extended camping trips in other locations, in-
      cluding the Eastern Shore of Virginia. The company also
      teaches high-quality classes in Northern Virginia, and all of
      their instructors are ACA and/or BCU certified. They are
      based out of their store in Alexandria, Virginia.
Blu Gnu Kayak Company, 703-370-4442, www.glugnukayak.com.
      Tours on the Potomac and Occoquan.

Canoe and Kayak Paddle Company, 703-264-8911,
    www.canoeinstructor.net.
        ACA instruction and guided tours in Northern Virginia.
Jack's Boathouse, 202-337-9642, www.jacksboathouse.com.
        Kayaks and canoes are rented from this Georgetown location.
Hemlock Overlook Regional Park, 703-993-4354,
    www.hemlockoverlook.org.
        This George Mason University education center runs moon-
        light canoe paddles in the Bull Run and Fountainhead area.
Outdoor Excursions, 1-800-77-KAYAK, www.outdoorexcursions.com.
        Offers sea kayaking trips and classes, along with white-water
        programs.
Springriver, 1-800-882-5694, www.springriver.com.
        Offers rentals from two stores, in Rockville and Annapolis,
        both of which are relatively convenient to Northern Virginia.
        Their sales and rental staff have a wealth of knowledge.

Camping

Northern Virginia Regional Park Authority (NVRPA), 703-352-5900,
    www.nvrpa.org.
        Oversees campgrounds at Pohick Bay and Bull Run Regional
        Parks, as well as the boat landing for the Fountainhead trip.
Pohick Bay Regional Park, 703-339-6104.
        Camping, canoe and kayak rentals, and half-day tours.
Bull Run Regional Park, 703-631-0550.
        Camping, canoe rentals, and moonlight paddles
Westmoreland State Park, 804-493-8821 (Virginia State Park number
    for reservations).
        Camping, canoe and kayak rentals, and half-day tours.

Visitor Information

Washington, D.C. Tourism Corporation, 202-789-7000,
    www.washington.org.

National Cherry Blossom Festival Information,
  www.nationalcherryblossomfestival.com.
Mason Neck State Park, 703-550-0960.
Prince William County Visitors Center, 703-491-4045,
  www.occoquan.org/tourist.
Westmoreland County Visitors Center, 1-888-SEE-WCVA,
  www.westmoreland-county.org.
Reedville Fishermen's Museum and Visitors Center, 804-453-6529,
  www.rfmuseum.com.
Chesapeake Breeze, Tangier Island Ferry, 804-453-BOAT.
Lancaster County Chamber of Commerce, 804-435-6092,
  www.lancasterva.com.
Belle Isle State Park, 804-462-5030 (kayak and canoe rentals).

Middle and Lower Peninsula (Piscataway Creek, Urbanna, Winter Harbor, New Point Comfort Lighthouse, Pamunkey River, Poropotank River, Chickahominy Lake, Morris Creek, and Poquoson)

Outfitters

Mattaponi Canoe and Kayak, 1-800-769-3545 (Pamunkey River),
  www.mattaponi.com.
Porpoise Cove Kayak, 804-854-8227 (Northern Mathews County/
  Deltaville).
Bay Trails Outfitters, 888-725-7225, www.baytrails.com (Mathews
  County).
  Rentals, trips, and sales from their location near the Winter
  Harbor trip.
Adventure Challenge, 804-276-7600, www.adventurechallenge.com.
  Trips and classes in the Richmond area and statewide.

Blue Ridge Mountain Sports, 757-229-4584, www.brmsstore.com
(Williamsburg).

> Stores from Virginia to Tennessee, including stores in Richmond and Virginia Beach. However, only their Williamsburg location offers kayak rentals.

Camping

There are no county or state parks with camping in the Middle Peninsula. There is primitive camping on the Morris Creek Trip. There are plenty of private campgrounds, and you can get information about these from the statewide resources, in the individual trip descriptions, and from the visitors centers.

Visitor Information

Essex County, 804-442-4331, www.essex-virginia.org.
Middlesex County, 804-758-4330, www.co.middlesex.va.us.
Town of Urbanna, 804-758-2613, www.visiturbanna.com.
Urbanna Oyster Festival, 804-758-0368,
    www.urbannaoysterfestival.com.
Mathews County Visitor and Information Center, 804-725-4BAY,
    www.visitmathews.com.
Mattaponi and Pamunkey Rivers Association, 804-769-0841,
    www.mpra.org.
King William County, 804-769-4985, www.co.king-william.va.us.
Pamunkey Indian Reservation, 804-843-4792,
    www.baylink.org.pamunkey.
Gloucester County, 866-VISIT US, www.gloucesterva.info.
City of Richmond, 804-788-7450, www.richmond.com.
Williamsburg/Jamestown, 1-800-368-6511,
    www.visitwilliamsburg.com.
Poquoson City, 757-868-3000, www.ci.poquson.va.us.
Plum Tree Island National Wildlife Refuge, 804-829-9020.
Grandview Nature Preserve, 757-850-5134.
Hampton Visitors Center, 1-800-800-2202, www.hamptoncvb.com.

Southeastern Virginia (Blackwater River, North Bay Loop, Back Bay, West Neck Creek, Great Dismal Swamp, and Northwest River)

Outfitters

Back Bay Getaways, 757-721-4484, www.backbaygetaways.com.
Located just north of Little City Park in Sandbridge, they are the most convenient rental location for Back Bay. They offer guided tours and rentals.

Sandbridge EcoSports Ocean Rentals, 1-800-695-4212, www.ocean
rentalsltd.com.
Located off the North Bay Loop in Sandbridge, and are the most convenient rental location for that trip. They also offer on- and off-site kayak rentals and tours.

Tidewater Adventures, 888-669-8368, www.TidewaterAdventures.com.
The owner of the company, Randy Gore, keeps his company focus entirely on providing excellent trips and instruction throughout Southeastern Virginia and on the Eastern Shore.

Wild River Outfitters, 757-431-8566, www.wildriveroutfitters.com.
Wild River operates a kayak store in Virginia Beach, and they guide quality trips and classes throughout southeastern Virginia. The owner of the company, Lillie Gilbert, has authored several books about the area.

Camping

Chippokes Plantation State Park, 757-294-3625.
The closest state park camping to the Blackwater River (on the southern shore of the James River).

First Landing State Park, 757-412-2300.
The closest state park camping to West Neck Creek, Back Bay, North Bay, and Great Dismal Swamp (in Virginia Beach).

False Cape State Park, 757-426-7128.
Primitive camping only, for the Back Bay trip.

Great Dismal Swamp National Wildlife Refuge, 757-986-3705
   Kayak-access camping.
Northwest River Park, 757-421-7151, www.cityofchesapeake.net.
   Inexpensive car camping, convenient to Northwest River,
   West Neck Creek, and the Great Dismal Swamp. Canoe
   rentals for the interior pond; depending on experience, ca-
   noes may sometimes be rented for river exploration.

Visitor Information

Virginia Beach Convention and Visitors Bureau, 1-800-VA-BEACH,
   www.vbfun.com.
Newport News Tourism, 888-493-7386, www.newport-news.org.
Norfolk Visitors Center, 1-800-368-3097, www.norfolkcvb.com.
Back Bay National Wildlife Refuge, 757-721-0496.

Eastern Shore (Virginia Coast Reserve — Mockhorn Island, Old Plantation Creek, Machipongo, Onancock, Saxis, Pitts Creek, and Chincoteague)

Outfitters

Southeast Expeditions, 888-62-MARSH, www.SEKayak.com.
   The largest, most comprehensive company on Virginia's
   Eastern Shore, they offer half- and full-day trips all over the
   peninsula. Their kayak store and rental shop is 1 mile away
   from the Bay Bridge Tunnel, across for the Eastern Shore of
   Virginia National Wildlife Refuge.
Eastern Shore Canoe and Kayak, 757-302-1344,
   www.easternshorecanoeandkayak.com.
   A retail and rental store based in Olney, about midway up the
   shore; they rent canoes and kayaks and even deliver them to
   your location for an extra charge.

Broadwater Bay Ecotours, 757-442-4363,
www.broadwaterbayecotours.com.
> This is local watermen/naturalist Captain Rick Kellam's
> powerboat-based tour company, but he will shuttle paddlers
> out to remote kayaking spots.

Oyster Bay Outfitters, 888-732-7108, www.OysterBayOutfitters.com.
> A small retail store in Chincoteague, on the right side of
> Maddox Avenue (when entering town), and guide trips on
> the island. They also offer kayaking classes taught by ACA
> certified instructors.

Wildlife Expeditions, 866-C-KAYAKS, www.wildlifeexpeditions.com.
> Offers guided trips, rentals, sales, and instruction on Chin-
> coteague, and they are located on the left side of Maddox Av-
> enue (when entering town).

Camping

Kiptopeke State Park, 757-331-2267, (use Virginia State Park number
for reservations).
> Located between Cape Charles and the Bay Bridge Tunnel, on
> the Chesapeake Bay, this is a beautiful wooded state park for
> RVs and tents. They have a boat landing and beach.

Chincoteague private campgrounds
Pine Grove Campground, www.pinegrovecampground.com.
Tom's Cove, 757-336-6498, www.tomscovepark.com.
Maddox, 757-336-3111.
Inlet View, 757-336-5126.
Trail's End, 757-824-3428.

Other private campgrounds in the area
Tall Pines Harbor, 757-824-0777, www.tallpinesharbor.com
(near Saxis).

Visitor Information

Virginia's Eastern Shore Tourism Commission, 757-787-2460,
www.esvatourism.org.

Cape Charles-Northhampton County Chamber of Commerce, 757-331-2304, www.ccncchamber.com.

Cape Charles Museum and Welcome Center, 757-331-1008.

Eastern Shore of Virginia Barrier Islands Center, 757-678-5550, www.barrierislandcenter.com.

Town of Onancock, 757-787-3363, www.onancock.com.

Onancock-Tangier Ferry, 757-891-2240, www.chesapeakebaysampler.com/tangierisland.

Chincoteague National Wildlife Refuge, 757-336-6122.

Chincoteague Chamber of Commerce, 757-336-6161, www.chincoteaguechamber.com.

Chincoteague web site, www.chincoteague.com (a wealth of information and links).

APPENDIX C:
Resources

M ANY OF the following resources were consulted in the writing of this book. An asterisk (*) marks any book that is a portable and concise addition to your on-water natural history library. Magazines, maps, web sites, and water trails are also listed.

Field Guides and Natural History Resources

*Conant, Roger, and Joseph T. Collins. *The Peterson Field Guide to Reptiles and Amphibians: Eastern/Central North America.* 3rd ed. Boston, MA: Houghton Mifflin Company, 1991.

Horton, Tom. *Turning the Tide: Saving the Chesapeake Bay.* Washington, DC: Island Press, 1991.

Horton, Tom. *Bay Country: Reflections on the Chesapeake.* New York: Ticknor & Fields, 1987.

* Hurley, Linda M. *Field Guide to the Submerged Aquatic Vegetation of Chesapeake Bay.* Annapolis, MD: U.S. Fish and Wildlife Service, 1992.

* Little, Elbert L. *The Audubon Society Field Guide to North American Trees: Eastern Region.* New York: Alfred A. Knopf, 1980.

Lippson, Alice, and Robert Lippson. *Life in the Chesapeake Bay.* Baltimore, MD: John's Hopkins University Press, 1984.

Meanley, Brooke. *Birds and Marshes of Chesapeake Bay Country.* Centreville, MD: Tidewater Publishers, 1975.

Murdy, Edward, Ray Birdsong and John Musick. *Fishes of the Chesapeake Bay.* Washington, DC: Smithsonian Institution Press, 1997.

Ogilivie, Philip Woodworth. *Along the Potomac.* Charleston, SC: Arcadia Publishing, 2000.

*Peterson, Roger Tory. *A Field Guide to the Birds East of the Rockies.* 4th ed. Boston, MA: Houghton Mifflin Company, 1980.

Reshetiloff, Kathryn, editor. *Chesapeake Bay: Introduction to an Ecosystem.* Washington, DC: U.S. Environmental Protection Agency, 1995.

*Ruthven, John A., and William Zimmerman. *Top Flight: Speed Index to Waterfowl of North America.* 8th ed. Milwaukee, WI: Moebius Printing Company, 1979.

Tilp, Frederick, *Chesapeake: Fact, Fiction and Fun.* Bowie, MD: Heritage Books, 1988.

*Silberhorn, Gene M. *Common Plants of the Mid-Atlantic Coast: A Field Guide.* Baltimore, MD: John's Hopkins University Press, 1999.

Warner, William. *Beautiful Swimmers: Watermen, Crabs and The Chesapeake Bay.* New York: Penguin Books, 1976.

Waugman, Sandra F,. and Danielle Moretti-Langholtz, PhD. *We're Still Here: Contemporary Virginia Indians Tell Their Stories.* Richmond, VA: Palari Publishing, 2001.

Williams, John Page. *Chesapeake Almanac: Following the Bay through the Seasons.* Centreville, MD: Tidewater Publishers, 1993.

*White, Christopher. *Chesapeake Bay: A Field Guide.* Centreville, MD: Tidewater Publishers, 1989.

Virginia Guidebooks

Blake, Allison. *The Chesapeake Bay Book: A Complete Guide.* 6th ed. Woodstock, VT: The Countryman Press, 2005.

Gilbert, Lillie, and Vickie Shufer. *Wild River Guide to the North Landing River.* Virginia Beach, VA: Eco Images, 2001.

Grove, Ed. *Classic Virginia Rivers: A Paddler's Guide to Premier Whitewater and Scenic Float Trips in the Old Dominion.* 3rd ed. Arlington, VA: Eddy Out Press, 2001.

Rhodes, Rick. *Discovering the Tidal Potomac: A Cruising Guide and Boating Reference.* St. Petersburg, FL: Heron Island Guides, 2003.

Williams, John Paige. *Exploring the Chesapeake in Small Boats.* Centreville, MD: Tidewater Publishers, 1992.

Venn, Tamsin. *Sea Kayaking Along the Mid-Atlantic Coast: Coastal Paddling Adventures from New York to Chesapeake Bay.* Boston, MA: Appalachian Mountain Club, 1994.

Sea Kayaking

Broze, Matt, and George Gronseth. *Sea Kayaker's Deep Trouble: True Stories and Their Lessons from Sea Kayaker Magazine.* Camden, ME: Ragged Mountain Press, 1997.

Burch, David. *Fundamentals of Kayak Navigation.* 3rd ed. Guilford, CT: Globe Pequot, 1999.

Foster, Nigel. *Nigel Foster's Sea Kayaking.* 2nd ed. Old Saybrook, CT: Globe Pequot, 1997.

Hutchinson, Derek. *The Complete Book of Sea Kayaking.* 4th ed. Old Saybrook, CT: Globe Pequot, 1995.

Johnson, Shelley. *The Complete Sea Kayaker's Handbook.* Camden, ME: Ragged Mountain Press, 2002.

Lull, John. *Sea Kayaking Safety and Rescue.* Berkeley, CA: Wilderness Press, 2001.

Schumann, Roger, and Jan Shriner. *Sea Kayak Rescue: The Definitive Guide to Modern Reentry and Recovery Techniques.* Guilford, CT: Globe Pequot, 2001.

Sea Kayaking Magazines

Atlantic Coastal Kayaker, P.O. Box 520, Ipswich, MA 01938.

Canoe and Kayak, P.O. Box 3146, Kirkland, WA 98083, www.canoekayak.com.

Paddler, P.O. Box 775450, Steamboat Springs, CO 80477, www.paddlermagazine.com.

Sea Kayaker, P.O. Box 17029, Seattle WA 98107, www.seakayakermag.com.

Wilderness Medicine and Outdoor Ethics

Hampton, Bruce, and David Cole. *Soft Paths.* Harrisburg, PA: Stackpole Books, 1988.

Issac, Jeff, and Peter Goth. *The Outward Bound Wilderness First-Aid Handbook.* New York: Lyons & Burford, 1991.

The Wilderness Medical Associates, 1-888-WILDMED, www.wildmed.com.

Offers Wilderness First Aid, First Responder, and Wilderness EMT certifications and sell wilderness medical kits.

Weather and Tide

*Lehr, Paul, R. Will Burnett, and Zim S. Herbert, PhD, ScD. *The Golden Guide to Weather.* New York: Golden Press, 1987

*Ludlum, Dr. David M., Ronald L. Holle, and Dr. Richard A. Keen. *National Audubon Society Pocket Guide: Clouds and Storms.* New York: Alfred A. Knopf, 1995.

Web Sites (many excellent sites; also state park and visitors center pages have links)

www.noaa.gov (National Oceanic and Atmospheric Administration).

www.weather.gov (National Weather Service).
www.weather.com (The Weather Channel).
www.cbos.com (The Chesapeake Bay Observation System).

Water Trails

All of these water trails are a part of the Chesapeake Bay Gateways Network, and more information can be found at www.baygateways.net or by calling 1-800-YOUR-BAY. Many water trails have accompanying maps. Most of these maps are not detailed or accurate enough for navigation, but give a good idea of put-ins and some information about the local areas.

Potomac River Water Trail. Series of six maps from D.C. to the Chesapeake Bay. This trail is the result of a partnership between Virginia's Department of Conservation and Recreation (DCR) and Maryland's Department of Natural Resources (DNR). You can purchase the maps for $5 at any of Virginia's Potomac state parks or by contacting the DCR at 1-800-933-PARK.

Occoquan Water Trail. This trail begins in Bull Run and continues onto the Potomac River at Mason Neck, wrapping around to Pohick Bay. This trail is under development, and no maps currently exist. Contact the NVRPA at 703-352-5900 or visit www.nrvrpa .org.

Rappahannock River Water Trail. This trail covers both the whitewater and flatwater sections of the Rappahannock. Call 540-373-3448 or visit www.riverfriends.org for more information.

Mathews County Water Trail. Series of maps covering 90 miles of water. You can purchase the maps through the Mathews County Visitor and Information Center or from the Bay Trails Outfitters. Or, go to www.blueways.net.

Powhatan Creek Blueway. This water trail details the alternative trip to Jamestown Island. Call 757-259-3200 or visit www.james-city.va.us.

Lower James River Water Trail. A map of the Lower James, from Richmond to the mouth of the river.

Norfolk Water Trail System. Thirty-eight miles of Norfolk's waterfront. Contact the City of Norfolk Bureau of Parks and Forestry at 757-441-2435.

Eastern Branch Elizabeth River Trail. Currently the only launch site is at the Carolanne Farm Park, but more access points are under development (757-427-4621).

Onancock Creek Loop Trail. A map of the Parker's Creek Loop will be available in 2005.

Saxis Water Trail Loop.

Maps

"The Chesapeake Bay Chartbook: Maryland and Virginia" Alexandria, VA: Alexandria Drafting Company (ADC), 2001.

"The Chesapeake Bay, Susquehanna River and Tidal Tributaries: Public Access Guide" The Chesapeake Bay Program, 2000.

"Chickahominy Lake" Garrisonville, VA: GMCO, 1995.

"Fishing and Recreation Map of Chincoteague-Assateague, Virginia" Garrisonville, VA: GMCO, 2003.

"Occoquan Reservoir" 5th ed. Alexandria, VA: Alexandria Drafting Company (ADC).

"The Tidal Potomac River: From Georgetown to 301 Bridge (Waterproof)." Garrisonville, VA: GMCO, 2002.

"The Rappahannock River: From Fredericksburg to the Chesapeake Bay" Garrisonville, VA: GMCO, 2000.

"Topo!" San Francisco, CA: National Geographic Holdings, Inc., 2000 (Computer mapping software).

USGS Maps: Order at www.earthexplorer.usgs.gov, by calling 1-888-ASK-USGS, or by mailing a downloaded order form to USGS Information Service, Box 25286, Denver, CO 80225.

"The Virginia Atlas & Gazetteer" Yarmouth, ME: DeLorme, 2003.

"Virginia Barrier Islands: From Cape Charles to Chincoteague (Waterproof)" Garrisonville, VA: GMCO, 2002.

"York River, including the Mattaponi River and the Pamunkey River: From Route 360 to West Point" Garrisonville, VA: GMCO, 1998.

APPENDIX D: *Beaufort Wind Scale*

This scale was developed in the early 1800s for frigate ships.
The effects on the water can differ according to your paddling location.

Beaufort Number	Wind Speed (knots)	Wind Description	Water Description
No force	0 knots	calm	flat calm
1	1–3	light air	ripples
2	4–6	light breeze	small wavelets
3	7–10	gentle breeze	scattered whitecaps and large wavelets
4	11–16	moderate breeze	lots of whitecaps; small waves lengthen
5	17–21	fresh breeze	mostly whitecaps with spray: moderate waves Small Craft Advisory issued
6	22–27	strong breeze	whitecaps everywhere; more spray
7	28–33	near gale	foam from waves begins blowing in streaks; sea heaps up
8	34–40	gale	foam is blown in well-defined streaks; crests begin breaking Gale Warning issued
9	41–47	strong gale	dense streaking; spray reduces visibility
10	48–55	whole gale	sea begins to roll and look white Storm Warning issued
11	56–63	violent storm	sea covered with white foam patches; large waves
12	64+	hurricane	air filled with foam and spray; almost no visibility

Land
Description

nothing stirring

smoke drifts gently according to wind direction

air movement can be felt on your face

leaves and twigs in motion

loose paper blows around; small branches move

flags ripple: small trees begin to sway

large trees and branches move; whistling heard in sailboat rigging

whole tree sways

branches and twigs torn from trees, trouble making headway on foot

roof shingles peeled from houses

trees uprooted; structural damage to buildings

widespread damage

major, widespread damage

Index